1936

.y he kpp

CREATIVE WRITING

FOR ADVANCED
COLLEGE CLASSES

CREATIVE WRITING

For Advanced College Classes

By GEORGE G. WILLIAMS, M.A.

The Rice Institute

HARPER & BROTHERS PUBLISHERS

New York and London

1935

CREATIVE WRITING
For Advanced College Classes

DEDICATED TO

VIRGINIA M. WILLIAMS

PREFACE

ONE can think of a dozen helpful and beautifully written books on English style by masters of the English language; but unfortunately none of them is suitable in method or in purpose for use in the average college classroom. On the other hand, one can think of a hundred excellent and really indispensable handbooks of English grammar, English usage, and English rhetoric; but unfortunately none of them is of much value to people aspiring to literary levels higher than those of mere clarity and correctness. The first kind must always be the study and delight of mature writers; the second kind, the study if not the delight of immature writers. But one can hardly recall a textbook of composition written exclusively for people in the intermediate stage between immaturity and maturity.

This book is intended to supply the lack; it is written for people who know most of what is to be learned from the handbooks, but who do not yet know how to create literature.

The book consists of three parts. Part I is a discussion of certain principles which apply to creative writing of any sort. Part II is a discussion of principles which apply to exposition; and Part III, of principles which apply to fiction. This work is, therefore, both a generalized study of the methods of creative writing, and a particularized study of the most important types of creative writing.

It has been in the author's mind that Part I and the first three chapters of Part II should fill the needs of the first semester in a full year-course in advanced writing, and that the rest of the book should fill the needs of the second semester. Yet all the parts are so independent of one another that any part could serve as a text for a course lasting only one term; and at the same time, other parts could serve as private study for individuals interested in writing for other purposes than the attainment of a college credit.

All but two or three of the sets of Exercises in the volume are creative rather than critical. That is, they demand that the student produce something from his own mind or imagination, instead of merely examining and appreciating what others have written. Many more Exercises are included than can possibly be completed in a year. But it was thought that a superfluity which would allow both the instructor and the student wide liberty of choice would be preferable to a paucity which would force both the instructor and the student into deadening formalism.

And now about the point of view from which the book is written. Though the author believes that no important point discussed in the average correspondence course for professional fiction writers has been omitted from this book, the author's purpose has not been to discuss writing from the professional viewpoint. On the other hand, everything said in this book may be of real value to the student who intends to become a professional. The only difference, consequently, between this book and the books for professionals is in the spirit of approach.

Writing (the author believes) is valuable for its own sake. Every individual feels passing through him during every waking hour a thousand half-comprehended ideas, half-created characters, half-felt emotions, half-seen visions, half-heard melodies of language, half-constructed fabrics of fancy. The non-writing person allows all these to pass unheeded through the hazy background of his consciousness, and to be lost at last in a welter of immediate desires, common sensations, and material expediencies. But the writer clutches at them, halts their flight, and contemplates them until they materialize into the permanent actuality of words on paper. In doing this, the writer has transformed immateriality into materiality, the transitory into the enduring, the subconscious into the conscious, and the illusory into the real. And in doing this, the writer creates for himself the value of a stable, indubitable, and complete experience of mind and heart, where before there had existed only a drifting, dim, and embryonic vision.

Writing, then, is not to be regarded as a mere means of making a living, or even of transferring ideas from one person to another. Writing is a means by which the individual *grows*—by which he passes intellectually and spiritually from a realm of nebulous suggestion into a realm of valid experience. Accordingly, writing may be a direct instrument of education—where education is conceived as a means whereby the individual realizes his highest intellectual and spiritual potentialities. Every piece of original writing completed adds to the personality of the writer some intellectual or spiritual reality which was not there previously; and every piece done as well as it possibly can be done adds a still finer intellectual or spiritual reality.

Since writing can have for the student a very real educative value, an educational institution such as a college ought to look on writing as an instrument of education primarily, and as a contemplated profession for the college student only secondarily. At any rate, the author of this book looks upon writing in such a way, and has approached his task in the spirit of an educator rather than in the spirit of a professional literary adviser.

I should be more than ungrateful if I did not acknowledge my indebtedness for many ideas to such authors as Sir Walter Raleigh, Sir Arthur Quiller-Couch, President William Trufant Foster, Professor Brander Matthews, and Messrs. William Archer, Clayton Hamilton, and Joseph Wood Krutch. I am indebted also to many publishers through whose generosity I have been able to use copyrighted material in illustrative passages throughout this book. More specific acknowledgments to these publishers are made at proper places in the text itself.

GEORGE G. WILLIAMS,
The Rice Institute.

CONTENTS

xi

Part II: THE WRITING OF EXPOSITION

Part III: THE WRITING OF FICTION

Chapter I

FUNDAMENTAL PRINCIPLES

THIS chapter recapitulates as briefly as possible a few very old principles of composition. Doubtless the reader has heard of them time and time again. A thing worth saying once, however, is worth saying more than once. The constant reiteration of these principles in books about writing indicates how important they really are.

1. The first of these fundamental principles is that *the most important idea in a sentence, a paragraph, or a composition should come at the end.* In the sentence just written, the important words —"the end"—came last; and this chapter itself will work upward from the mechanical rule of position to more philosophical advice about interestingness in writing.

Because readers are always more than usually alert when they know that the conclusion approaches, a writer should make the most of his conclusions. Not only should he use his most vigorous and telling details last; but, in addition, he may give point to his entire composition, drive home his cardinal thought, reiterate his fundamental conviction in the last few sentences of his composition. He may do it (a) by saving to the last his most important and incontrovertible detail; (b) by rounding off his discussion with a renewed suggestion of the main idea; or (c) by a blunt summary of points brought out in the discussion. But however he chooses to end his composition, he should avoid letting it dwindle off into final insignificance.

2. *An important idea hinted at in the beginning, but reserved for the end, makes for suspense.* A writer may wish to catch the reader's interest, hold his attention, heighten his suspense during the course of a discussion, and finally gratify the reader with a breaking of the tension, a relief of the suspense. Shelley does this in the famous conclusion of *Prometheus Unbound*:

> To suffer woes which Hope thinks infinite;
> To forgive wrongs darker than death or night;
> To defy Power, which seems omnipotent;
> To love and bear; to hope till Hope creates
> From its own wreck the thing it contemplates;
> Neither to change, nor falter, nor repent;
> This, like thy glory, Titan, is to be
> Good, great and joyous, beautiful and free;
> This is alone Life, Joy, Empire, and Victory.

This principle of building up suspense by withholding an important idea is allied to the first principle discussed above. But the two principles differ slightly. A writer may place an important idea at the end of a structural unit, and yet have no thought of keeping the reader in suspense. For example, the following sentence builds up no suspense, though it places the important idea at the end: "The *Essay on Man* is Pope's most philosophic work; but *The Rape of the Lock* is his most poetic." The following sentence, however, does build up suspense: "Pope's greatest work is neither the philosophical *Essay on Man*, the descriptive *Windsor Forest*, nor the satirical *Dunciad*—but *The Rape of the Lock*."

Information given to the reader without warning, things happening to him of a sudden—these may surprise, but they create within him no suspense. Indeed, absolute surprise is the opposite of suspense. A reader can feel suspense only when he actually knows that he is waiting for something. The business of the writer, therefore, is to give the reader this bit of foreknowledge. It can be conveyed either directly or subtly.

a. The writer may convey it by a definite statement, like this: "In the following story I shall tell you how James Jones died, and then returned to life." Or, "At the end of this discussion I shall tell you the way out of our present plight." Such advance notices make the reader know for sure that he is waiting for something; accordingly, he will read on to find out about the thing he has been waiting for.

b. Sometimes a mere statement by a writer that he intends to discuss a certain number of points of a proposition will put the reader in a state of suspense while reading through the first few points and waiting to reach the last.

c. Sometimes, too, a series of negatives (as in the sentence about Pope given above) imply to the reader that a positive is to appear shortly. The reader will instinctively read on to find out about this implied positive.

d. And sometimes a lengthy suspended grammatical structure (as in the lines from Shelley quoted above) leads a reader on, almost by force, until he arrives at the completion of the structure.

These are some of the common methods by which a writer may create suspense. Many other similar devices might be mentioned; and some will be discussed at length later on. The examples given above are enough to show, however, the fundamental nature of all devices for creating suspense: The reader is given a suggestion; then he waits; and finally, he comes to a clarification of the suggestion. All suspense is built up in such a manner.

3. A third principle is that *ideas should be arranged in the order of climax*—that is, in the order of their increasing importance. This principle applies to a series of related ideas rather than to the expansion of one idea. It applies to situations where the writer wishes to give three or more incidents, three or more details, three

6   CREATIVE WRITING

or more examples, three or more causes, three or more effects. It
demands that the least important incident, detail, example, cause,
or effect shall be presented first; the next most important, next;
and the most important, last. As in the old family portrait, the
order of presentation in a composition should be the stair-step
order—beginning with unimportant two-year-old William and
ascending head over head to the supreme head of William, Senior.
The old ballads invariably proceeded in this manner, from the
least important to the most important idea:

> "Why dois your brand sae drap wi bluid,
>   Edward, Edward,
> Why dois your brand sae drap wi bluid,
>   And why sae sad gang yee O?"
> "O I hae killed my hauke sae guid,
>   Mither, mither,
> O I hae killed my hauke sae guid,
>   And I had nae mair bot hee O."
>
> "Your haukis bluid was nevir sae reid,
>   Edward, Edward,
> Your haukis bluid was nevir sae reid,
>   My dear son I tell thee O."
> "O I hae killed my reid-roan steid,
>   Mither, mither,
> O I hae killed my reid-roan steid,
>   That erst was sae fair and frie O."
>
> "Your steid was auld, and ye hae gat mair,
>   Edward, Edward,
> Your steid was auld, and ye hae gat mair,
>   Sum other dule ye drie O."
> "O I hae killed my fadir deir,
>   Mither, mither,
> O I hae killed my fadir deir,
> Alas, and wae is mee O!"

"First in war, first in peace, first in the hearts of his countrymen." This famous sentiment of Lee's, proceeding from point to point in the order of climax, is a skillful expression of a fine thought. But read it in the reverse order, and it becomes merely tawdry. Such is the power of climax.

4. To be considered with the principle just discussed is the other principle, that *ideas should occupy space in direct proportion to their importance*. Whether by accident or not, the most important phrase in Lee's eulogy of Washington quoted above not only occurs at the summit of the climax, but also takes up more space than the other two phrases. The whole expression was purposely designed, one could almost believe, to be immortal.

The principle of proportion should be considered both as an injunction and as a command. Unimportant ideas must not be treated at length, and important ideas must be treated at length. The elaboration of unimportant ideas leads to wordiness, triviality, and tiresomeness; the slighting of important ideas leads to disappointment of the reader, apparent pointlessness, and seeming lack of discrimination on the part of the writer. Ordinarily, the important part of a discussion should be developed with special amplitude; the important character in a story should be introduced with special privileges of space; the important action of a narrative should be recounted with special elaborateness of detail. Even when the temptation is to be brief, the writer should deliberately proceed with his amplifying. Brevity has its virtues, but also its vices.

The only time when the rule may be suspended is when a writer wishes to avail himself of the device of contrast, and so expresses an important idea with notable terseness. "Jesus wept." The simple statement, so noticeably short, contrasts so powerfully with the magnitude of the sentiment that the verse is effective. Such effective brevity, however, can be employed only on special occasions.

When it is used too often as a rhetorical device, it looks affected. Furthermore, it can never be effective unless it has the added advantages of position, climax, or isolation.

In general, therefore, we may say that the most important ideas require the most space. If we combine this principle with the principle of climax, we may express the result diagrammatically as follows:

The average composition should look like this. *The least important ideas come first, and require the least amount of space; the more important ideas come later, and require a greater amount of space.*

5. Not only must the important idea have the prominent position and the chief amount of space, but, in addition, *the important idea must have an important structure.* Importance of structure is relative. A paragraph is more important than a sentence; a sen-

tence is more important than an independent clause; an independent clause is more important than a dependent clause; a dependent clause is more important than a phrase; and a phrase is more important than a word. An idea expressed in any of the lesser structures may be made to assume a higher importance by being given a higher structure.

In each of the next two examples, a simple idea is important enough to be worthy of a structure so significant as a paragraph:

He who ever gives a thought to the life of man at large, to his miseries and disappointments, to the waste and cruelty of existence, will remember that if American or Briton fail in this climb, there can but be for us both, and for all other peoples, a hideous slip, a swift and fearful fall into an abyss, whence all shall be to begin over again.

We shall not fail—neither ourselves, nor each other. Our comradeship will endure.[1]

He had been melancholy the night before, and had talked of death. As we approached his house, we saw that a light was still burning in his room, though the sun had been shining for an hour. No one responded to our ringing. We opened the front door, which was unlocked, and entered the house. A sleepy cat rose from the sofa, stretched, and yawned in our faces. We called. There was no answer. We mounted the stairs to Warren's room, called again, and then pushed open his door. A glance at his form sprawled over a chair told us all.

He had shot himself.

If an idea is not worthy of a paragraph, it may yet be worthy of a sentence. Moreover, its worthiness may be apparent only when it is expressed as a sentence. In the first of the following examples, we lose sight of the really important idea because it has been given an unimportant structure:

[1] From John Galsworthy's lecture on *American and Briton.* Reprinted by permission of Charles Scribner's Sons.

Though we got fish for dinner, we had been anticipating something as substantial as a beefsteak all afternoon.

All afternoon we had been anticipating something as substantial as a beefsteak for dinner. We got fish instead.

Sometimes an idea not worthy of an entire sentence may yet be worthy of a clause instead of a phrase or a word. In the next examples, notice how ideas leap into unexpected importance by rising from the rank or words or phrases to that of clauses:

With the night's passing, the day is come forth.

The night is spent, and the day is come forth.

The much discussed civil war is less understood than any event in English history.

The civil war has been more discussed, and is less understood, than any event in English history.

This whole problem of the relation of sentence structure to idea will be discussed at greater length in a succeeding chapter.

6. *A fundamental idea placed at the beginning makes for clarity.*

Let us look at any convenient well-written book. Bernard Muddiman's *The Men of the Nineties* offers several good illustrations. The third chapter begins: "One endeavors to remember some one or two outstanding novels written by any one of the writers of this group. It must be at once admitted, one fails to recall a great novel." From these two sentences a reader obtains a clear conception of what the writer is going to talk about in the third chapter, and what he is going to say about it. His fourth chapter begins: "The poetry of the period is essentially an expression of moods and sentiments." His fifth chapter begins: "The Victorian literary era was fecund in essayists, and the last decade lived up to this reputation." His sixth and last chapter begins: "Here I propose to go through a litany of some of my omissions." Each sentence is a statement in brief of what the writer intends to say in the course of each chapter. Accordingly, each sentence does much to keep the reader's ideas clear, and to give the reader a firm grasp on a unifying thought in the midst of a detailed discussion.

Each paragraph of Mr. Muddiman's last chapter likewise begins with a clear statement of what is to be the author's chief concern in the paragraph. The first sentence of the first paragraph has already been quoted. The following are the first sentences in the three succeeding paragraphs:

Paragraph 2: "I have worried for some space over Aubrey Beardsley, but I have not spoken of men like Mr. S. H. Sime, whose work Beardsley so delighted in."

Paragraph 3: "Again, I have not alluded to Edgar Wilson's bizarre and fascinating decorations of submarine life and Japanesque figures."

Paragraph 4: "Once more, I have not spoken at all of Miss Althea Lyle's hectic visions, which, in her illustrations for Wilde's *Harlot's House*, probably reach the acme of the period's realisation of the weird."[2]

And so on. This method of beginning a discussion, and each portion of a discussion, with a statement of theme is the best and easiest of all structural devices by which a writer may gain clarity.

Sometimes, however, the device is varied. Instead of a statement of theme, an enumeration of points to be taken up comes at the beginning of a composition. Yet the clarifying effect is the same.

7. *Important ideas at the beginning of a composition serve the purpose not only of clarity, but also of interest, vividness, and strength.*

First, an important idea so placed may *attract attention or engage interest.* It may do so by means of appealing to the reader's self-interest, contradicting a statement usually accepted as true, stating a bold generalization or paradox, or making any other sort of startling observation. Lamb begins an essay, "I have no ear." A student begins an essay, "Life is never what it seems to be; it is

[2] All of Mr. Muddiman's sentences used here and in Section 8 below are quoted by permission of Mr. Muddiman's publishers, G. P. Putnam's Sons.

usually worse." Louise Spencer Portor begins an essay, "I have a definite, decided taste in taxi drivers." Will Durant begins an essay on Schopenhauer's philosophy, "Consider, first, the absurdity of the desire for material goods." *Time* begins an article on the expectant motherhood of the Empress of Japan, "The Imperial Household Ministry proclaimed throughout Japan last week that applications from wet nurses will again be entertained." All these beginnings are meant to startle the reader a bit, to catch his eye and tempt him to go on with the essay or article.

Another function of a beginning may be to *present in an arresting and compelling way a problem to be solved.* Huxley begins an essay, "What is education? Above all things, what is our ideal of a thoroughly liberal education?" Woodrow Wilson begins an essay, "What is liberty?" William James begins an essay, "Of what use is college training?" Alfred Russell Wallace begins an essay, "The majority of persons, if asked what were the uses of dust, would reply that they did not know it had any." Philip Gibbs begins a narrative, "When I read in the newspaper that the Turks had entered Smyrna and had celebrated their victory by burning the Christian quarters and massacring men, women, and children, according to the way of Islam, I thought of certain people whom I had met there the year before, and wondered what agony they had suffered before death, or what chance of escape had been theirs." All these beginnings set a problem before the reader in such a way that he is tempted to read further in order to find the solution of the problem.

A third kind of beginning involving an important idea may do one of two things: It may state the theme or principal idea of the composition which follows, or it may outline the points to be considered in the composition.

The statement of the theme or the outline of points does more than clarify: it gives the reader a vigorous intellectual jolt; it puts him at once on his intellectual mettle; it makes him feel that he is plunging directly into the heart of the subject; it gives him confidence in an author who expounds a doctrine or analyzes a situation so boldly.

As illustrations of beginnings which *state the theme*: Professor Alexander Meiklejohn begins an essay: "One of the greatest dangers of the American college is that it will be drawn into the common life, that it will conform to that life, will take the common standards as its own." Woodrow Wilson begins an address: "The equality of nations upon which peace must be founded if it is to be a lasting peace must be an equality of rights." Calvin Thomas begins an essay: "I contend that we have need of poetry, and the need is not diminishing with the lapse of time." W. D. Steele begins a story: "People have wondered . . . how I could ever have allowed myself to be let in for the East African adventure of Mrs. Diana in search of her husband."

Closely related to such beginnings are those which *outline the course to be followed in the body of the composition*. Lamb begins an essay: "The human species . . . is composed of two distinct races, *the men who borrow,* and *the men who lend.*" Arthur Twining Hadley begins an essay: "The three faults most commonly charged against our national character today are materialism, lawlessness, and unwarranted self-assertion." Louis Untermeyer begins an essay: "The poetry produced in America in the last decade has been distinguished by three outstanding features. These three dominating qualities are . . . its vigor, its vividness, and its variety." More examples need not be given. These will suffice to show how a writer may draw up a program at the beginning of a composition, and then proceed to carry out the program in the body of the discourse.

The psychological value of such beginnings has already been mentioned. They are clear, direct, vigorous, and bold. When they are combined with the first principle given above—that of putting an important idea at the end of a compositional structure—the result is a singularly clear and emphatic piece of writing, unified by enclosure between two important ideas, climactic in its arrangement, arresting in its beginning, and powerful in its conclusion. The Duke of Wellington long ago gave advice on writing: "Have something to say, and say it." We may justly amend the aphorism to make it read: "Have something to say; say that you are going to say it; say it; and say that you have said it." No plan is better adapted to give clarity and emphasis.

8. *Repetition serves many purposes of clarity, coherence, and all-round effectiveness.* Repetition is effective because no reader is wide-awake, alert, and critical at every instant. His attention may lapse for a moment; the words before him suggest ideas leading away from the subject in hand; he may have difficulty in making out the writer's main point hidden in a multitude of words; he may fail to see what bearing some portions of the discussion have on this main point. For any of a number of reasons, when the fundamental ideas of a piece of writing are mentioned only once, the reader may miss the entire significance of the writing. But if each important point is repeated again and again, the reader is certain to get it at one or another of the repetitions. Indeed, repetition makes it absolutely impossible for him to miss it. This, then, is the chief value of repetition—it makes the reader know the writer's principal thought and keep it in mind.

To give an example. Mr. Muddiman's main idea in Chapter III of the work quoted above is that no great novels were produced in England during the 1890's. This idea appears as the opening sentence of each of the first five paragraphs in the chapter. The sentences are: (a) "One endeavors to remember some one or two outstanding novels written by one of the writers of this group." (b) "None of the men of the nineties (as I have defined them) produced a great novel." (c) "But so far as English fiction alone is concerned, it cannot be said that the men of the nineties produced work of a very high order." (d) "Indeed, if the name of a good English novel by any one of them is demanded, it will be singularly difficult to suggest a satisfactory title." (e) "In the face of this strange dearth of novels in this school, one cannot help asking the reasons that engendered it." When a reader has thus faced this idea five times, he is pretty certain about Mr. Muddiman's opinion of the novels written by the men of the 'nineties, and about the main idea in Mr. Muddiman's chapter. The repetition both intensifies and clarifies.

a. Much repetition is for the sake of *intensification*. We often repeat ourselves in speech, as when we cry out, "Quick! Quick! Quick!" or "Stop! Stop! Stop!" Poetry is full of repetition of words and ideas:

> I will arise and go now, and go to Innisfree.

> Old King Cole was a merry old soul,
> And a merry old soul was he.

> Why weep ye by the tide, ladie?
> Why weep ye by the tide?

A large portion of the Bible, much of which was written in Hebrew as poetry, consists of repetitions for the purpose of intensification. The following five-fold repetition of idea is a good example:

The race is not to the swift, nor the battle to the strong, nor bread to the wise, nor riches to men of understanding, nor favor to men of skill; but time and chance happeneth to them all.

b. Often, however, repetition makes for greater *clarity* of writing. This greater clarity may involve two principles: First, the repetition may keep the reader constantly reminded of the subject under discussion, and so give *unity* to the reader's impressions.

And second, the repetition may show that parts of a composition seemingly unrelated are actually associated in content and purpose; that is to say, the repetition may make for *coherence*. In most of the remainder of this section, we shall discuss the relationship of repetition to unity and coherence in a composition. First it should be mentioned, however, that repetition may involve any of three compositional elements—idea, diction, or structure.

Unity.—(1) The sentences quoted above from Muddiman show how unity may be obtained by the *repetition of idea*. (2) The following paragraph from Matthew Arnold shows how unity may be obtained by *repetition of diction*; note the phrases in italics:

The need of *humane letters*, as they are truly called, because they serve the paramount desire in men that good should be ever present to them,—the need of *humane letters* to establish a relation between the new conceptions, and our instinct for beauty, our instinct for conduct, is only the more visible. The Middle Ages could do without *humane letters*, as it could do without the study of nature, because it supposed knowledge was made to *engage its emotions* so powerfully. Grant that the supposed knowledge disappears, its power of being made to *engage the emotions* will of course disappear along with it,—but the *emotions* themselves, and their claim to be *engaged* and satisfied, will remain. Now if we find by experience that *humane letters* have an undeniable power of *engaging the emotions*, the importance of *humane letters* in a man's training becomes not less, but greater, in proportion to the success of modern science in extirpating what it calls "medieval thinking."

This constant reiteration of the phrases "humane letters" and "engage the emotions" can leave no doubt in the reader's mind about Arnold's subject.

(3) Unity gained by *repetition of structure* is a commonplace device of rhetoric. In the following passage, half-a-dozen separate and actually independent ideas are molded into a unity by a mere repetition of structure:

We charge him with having broken his coronation oath; and we are told that he kept his marriage vow! We accuse him of having given up his people to the merciless inflictions of the most hot-headed and hard-hearted of prelates; and the defense is that he took his little son on his knee and kissed him! We censure him for having violated the articles of the Petition of Right, after having, for good and valuable consideration, promised to observe them; and we are informed that he was accustomed to hear prayers at six o'clock in the morning!

Coherence.—Not only does repetition of idea, of diction, and of structure assist a writer to obtain unity, but, in addition, it helps him to gain coherence. We say that a composition has coherence when its logical and structural elements have such a smooth continuity and such clear relationship to one another and to the purpose of the writer, that each element seems to grow out of the preceding element, to call forth the succeeding element, and to contribute clearly to the development of the main idea. To put it another way, a composition has coherence when each of its elements has an obvious relationship, first, to the other elements about it and, second, to the central idea of the composition.

(1) *Repetition of idea* can serve the ends of coherence by calling the reader's attention to the exact relationship certain elements in a composition have to the subject as a whole. In any discussion at all involved, a writer will do well to pause occasionally, repeat in brief what has been said at length, try to show what bearing his last point has on the principal theme of his discourse, and remind the reader what that theme is. For example, Rollo Brown in an essay on "The Creative Spirit of the Church" (*Harper's* for December, 1924) steps aside to follow up various ramifications of his thought, to investigate issues of minor importance, to propose remedies for observed conditions; but again and again he relates these side-branches of his argument to his central theme by repeating or implying that central theme over and over again throughout

the essay, as follows: "If men should ever come to appreciate how much of their freedom and self-respect is dependent upon their freedom to engage in creative enterprise . . . they would at once begin to inquire what attitude toward this spirit of pioneering is to be maintained by such a powerful organization as the church." "No one has preached more consistently [than Christ] the absolute need of the creative quest." The church "could avail itself of its unique opportunity to proclaim the salvation through inquiry and growth which its founder proclaimed." "To the proposal that the church proclaim a creative gospel," etc. The church should "depend on a program of giving high impetus to individual men and women." If the church "wishes to make its power unlimited and unending, it must bring its creative justification to each man."

This constantly recurring repetition of the main theme in the essay helps the reader to fuse into a coherent whole all the divergent elements of the essay. Without the repetitions, these elements would refuse to coalesce.

(2) An illustration will show how *repetition of diction* may knit together inchoate ideas. Ralph Barton Perry writes, "President Cleveland once remarked, as everyone knows, 'It is a condition, and not a theory, that confronts us.' I do not remember what condition it was that confronted us; but the practical man is always confronted by a condition. I shall suggest presently that every condition does in truth involve a theory; but if so, the practical man ignores it. His practicality lies in confining himself to finding an act which will meet the condition."

To see how valuable a part repetition of diction plays in this paragraph, we have only to rewrite the paragraph, omitting all repetition: "President Cleveland once remarked, as everyone knows, 'It is a condition, and not a theory, that confronts us.' I do not remember what circumstance it was that faced us; but the practical man always finds some situation before him. I shall suggest presently that every occasion does in truth involve a general principle; but if so, the man of action ignores it. His worldly wisdom lies in confining himself to finding out a deed which will meet the affair in hand." Whereas the original paragraph was a compact nexus of thoughts, the garbled paragraph is a straggling accumulation of unrelated abstractions.

(3) *Repetition of structure* may likewise give consistency to seemingly unrelated ideas. Macaulay's famous arraignment of Charles I, the passage from the Bible, and the lines from Shelley, all quoted above, not only make incongruous and divergent ideas seem to belong together through the authors' repetition of grammatical structure, but, in addition, each part of each passage is knit hard and fast to every other part because of that repetition of grammatical structure.

At this point, perhaps we should take the advice just given, and repeat what has been said in the present section. We have seen that repetition may *intensify a conception or clarify a thought* by expressing it in different words. Moreover, the repetition of idea, diction, or structure may *give unity* to apparently independent elements of a composition. The repetition of idea may *give coherence* to seemingly confused and unorganized data; repetition of diction weaves together sentences and clauses that would otherwise seem unrelated; and repetition of structure makes a coherent mass out of what would otherwise be a series of isolated facts.

To conclude this discussion of repetition: Let the writer who has something to say repeat it boldly and often; let him choose key-words and play them up again and again; let him voice the same idea time after time, now in the same words, now in different; let him weld together seeming incompatibles by forcing them into similar structures; let him at every opportunity avail himself of the impressiveness of new groupages, new masses, and new patterns of repetition.

It is almost possible to measure a writer's skill by the dexterity with which he repeats, and yet avoids monotony.

9. *Contrasts attract attention and make permanent impressions.* Contrasts may involve *mechanical tricks of printing*, like italics, capitals, or very small type in the midst of ordinary type, large spaces contrasted with a few words, paragraphs separated from the body of the writing, paragraphs consisting of very short sentences or phrases, and so on.

Or contrasts may involve *elements of structure*. A short sentence in the midst of long ones attracts attention to itself. "He was told to lead his men forward at any cost, to cut the barbed-wire entanglements, to capture the first line of trenches, and to prepare for the counter-attack. All this he did." This last short sentence stands out prominently because of the contrast between its shortness and the length of the preceding sentence.

Contrasts in lengths, however, constitute only the very simplest of contrasts. In addition, rhetorical questions occurring in the midst of declarative sentences; sudden learned words in the midst of familiar diction, or sudden words of doubtful respectability in the midst of formal diction; sudden inversions or unlooked-for twistings-about of sentence elements in the midst of plain straightforward writing; words which have certain almost invariable connotations, but which may be used in a literal and absolute sense— such are some of the devices of contrast.

Even more effective than these devices, however, may be *contrasts of subject matter, of mood, and (in fiction) of personalities.* Hamlet's scene with his mother, in which he demands that she "Look here, upon this picture, and on this," is so memorable because the two kings appear as such contrasting personalities. Byron's description of the night before Waterloo in *Childe Harold* is one of the great purple patches of literature because it presents a contrast between the warmth, gaiety, light, and love-making of the

Duchess of Richmond's ball, and the terror, darkness, and grief of war. Dickens uses the trick of contrast over and over again: the simultaneous deaths of Dora and Dora's lap dog; the death of Paul Dombey in the dark and desolate house on a lovely day when the outside world is full of sunshine and birds' songs—these are but two examples. Shakespeare uses contrast with unapproachable humor in the scene between the superstitious and verbose Glendower and the practical-minded, blunt Hotspur. Indeed, the technique of the Shakespearian play nearly always involves contrasting personalities for the principal characters. The hesitating Hamlet on the one hand, and the vigorous Laertes on the other; the traitorous Macbeth and the loyal Macduff; the passionate Antony and the level-headed Octavius; the strong-minded, manly Henry V and the weak, effeminate Dauphin; the etherealized Ariel and the beastly Caliban—and so on.

The student should deliberately examine his subject before he ever sets pen to paper, and ask himself wherein he can employ contrasts. Is he writing a paper on the present federal administration? Certain contrasts inevitably present themselves—social and economic conditions before and since the inauguration of this administration.

Is he writing an essay on cats? The contrast between the habits and the personalities of cats, and the habits and personalities of dogs will better characterize cats than will pages of description or analysis.

Is he writing a story with a naïve and gentle girl as the heroine? A contrasting character, worldly wise and hard, will bring out and intensify the character of the heroine.

Since few writers would hit upon such contrasts by instinct, *the student may well make it a rule never to do any piece of writing without first carefully examining the possibilities for contrast inherent in his subject.*

10. The laws already discussed and the devices already suggested may contribute to the unity of a composition, or to the coherence of its parts, or to the general vigor of its presentation. There yet remain to be mentioned, however, a few devices by which *the writer may deliberately heighten the interest of what he has to say*. Some of these devices may involve the actual structure of the composition and the development of the writer's ideas; others may be mere accretions cut out of whole cloth and inserted bodily into the composition after it is written.

Some of the general devices are quite obvious. One is the selection of perennially *interesting topics*—like sex, attacks on religion, murders, executions, disasters, evidences of rationality in animals, relics of past ages, cures for common diseases, methods of making money, morbid aspects of human nature, and similar subjects which we need not trouble to catalogue here.

Another obvious, but altogether different, means of giving interest is *humorous self-ridicule*—especially ridicule of one's own eccentricities.

Another is the *setting up of an opposing idea* to overthrow. Readers like a contest. That is, they had rather see something disproved than proved; something attacked rather than something created. A writer may cater to these combative instincts of his readers without descending to the level of cheap politicians ranting against their opponents. He can be vigorous, virile, and aggressive without being ignoble. He can prove even while he disproves; he can create even while he attacks. And he can succeed in being interesting where a more timid writer would be dull.

No writer can be interesting if he gives the impression of being exhausted at the end of his work. How to avoid finishing like a child's toy which has run down and is teetering feebly to a close is a problem that should exercise every writer. The solution of the problem differs with every composition. But the solution frequently lies in the application of principles discussed earlier in this chapter: arranging ideas in the order of climax, giving scant attention to unimportant ideas, and using a wealth of details to back up generalizations. An old but still effective trick is to say occasionally such things as, "This is not the place to dwell on that subject," or "Time and space will not allow me to deal with that question now," and so on. Remarks like these persuade the reader that the writer has depths beyond those exposed, and so tantalize the reader with the lure of the unknown.

A fifth very common way of giving interest is by means of *humor and a feeling of good humor* pervading much of the composition. Communists would be much more successful if more of them had a sense of humor, and socialism might be the reigning system if all socialists were good-natured. Intensity of passion, righteousness of cause, and intelligence of outlook all have their effect at times; but for persuasiveness and interestingness, they do not compare with humor. A writer may try to prove the soundness of an argument; but if he can create a laugh, he will not be asked to prove anything. He may try to show that what he has to say is so important that no one can afford to ignore it; but if he can create a laugh, he will have readers who will take the importance of his argument for granted. He may try to get others to take his words seriously; but before he can succeed, he must convince them by means of a smile that he does not take himself too seriously.

What has just been said is particularly true in America; it need not be true in other countries. But in any country, writing which shows good taste by being urbane and tolerant, but yet firm; which shows open-mindedness by being good-humored and dispassionate, but yet sincere; which shows consideration for others by avoiding violence and extremes, but yet remaining shrewd and witty—such writing is interesting anywhere in the world.

Other devices for gaining interest are not so obvious as those just mentioned. Some which may require special planning of structure or special methods of development are these: progression, the appeal to self-interest, analogy, and illustration.

To consider the first of these: We have all seen the lecturer who, as he reads his discourse to an audience and finishes each page, slips that page back under his manuscript. The audience perceives no diminution in the thickness of the manuscript; it feels that no progress is being made; and it despairs. Like an audience, *the reader must be made to feel that he is actually getting somewhere.* Nobody likes to read page after page of solid prose unbroken by mechanical devices indicating progression—paragraphs, divisions, chapters, parts. Everyone likes the feeling of accomplishment that comes with the end of one paragraph and the beginning of a new one—or of a division, or chapter, or part, or book. Everyone likes to feel that he is getting somewhere, not merely plowing on endlessly and pointlessly through page after page of writing.

In various ways (besides the mechanical devices of division just mentioned) can a reader be made to feel that he is progressing. The simplest way is for the writer to announce at the beginning what his objective is to be, in order that the reader may know the destination for which he and the writer are bound. A further elaboration of this method may consist in the writer's announcing at intervals, throughout the composition, just how much ground has been covered, and just how much yet remains to be explored. This sort of announcement may be made in so many words, like, "We have considered so-and-so; it remains for us to study such-and-such." Or it may be implied by numbers, as when, for example, a writer says, "In the first place," and "Next," and "Thirdly," and "A fourth point," and "Finally." With such an orderly system of announcement, the reader is certain to get a definite sense of progression, and to feel that the writer is covering ground toward the attainment of a definite end.

A second way to interest a reader is to *show how a subject may be of real and immediate concern* to him. For instance, people are ordinarily not much interested in talk about the gold standard and international finance until they discover that the country's abandoning the gold standard means higher prices for food, fuel, and housing; they are not much interested in local politics until they discover that their water bills have suddenly increased by about fifty per cent, and that the bad stretch of street in their block goes unrepaired; they are not much interested in plague epidemics until they discover a case of smallpox in the school which their children attend; and they are not much interested in anarchical plots until they discover that a bomb has been found under the railway track over which they commute every day. When a writer can make distinct contacts such as these between his abstract subject and his reader's self-interest, two-thirds of the work of being interesting is done.

A third source of interest involving the structure of a composition is the use of *analogy*. An analogy is a figure of speech chiefly differing from a simile in being an elaborate comparison between two things like each other in many respects instead of merely one. Besides being a variation from literal, straightforward statement, an analogy may be interesting for various reasons. (a) It may attract the reader's interest by drawing a parallel between conditions that concern the reader and conditions that do not concern him. For instance, a reader may not have the slightest interest in the economic problems of England following the Napoleonic Wars; but if the reader is made to see those problems of 1825 as analogous to the problems of 1935, he may become amazingly interested in the economic history of England.

(b) Moreover, analogies may serve to convert the abstract into the concrete. They show the play of the writer's imagination, and they demand of the reader a like image-making response. For reasons to be seen later, such imaginative activity is always more interesting than contemplation of abstract concepts. Let us take an example: "There is no doubt that contact with the things that they do not understand is to many minds distinctly disagreeable." This abstract statement is not particularly significant or memorable. But Frank Colby, the author, converts it into a strikingly concrete analogy by adding, "A dog not only prefers a customary and unpleasant odor; he hates a good one. A perfume pricks his nose, gives a wrench to his dog nature, perhaps tends to 'undermine those moral principles' without which dog 'society cannot exist.' " This concrete expression is obviously far more interesting than the abstraction.

(c) An analogy may be interesting because it clarifies or simplifies an intricate argument or an involved description. The complex tangle of knotted theological doctrines about the Roman Catholic purgatory may be cut through at once by the simple analogy, "Purgatory is a kind of waiting room or antechamber to hell." The complicated map of Greece can be presented clearly in a brief analogy: "Greece is shaped like a three-fingered hand with a great gash almost cutting the palm in two below the thumb." Such short cuts engage the reader's interest not only because they are imaginative, but also because they give the reader the triumphant feeling of having got along famously—of having mastered a difficult situation at a single stroke.

A fourth way in which a composition may be made interesting is by the use of *concrete examples* and *specific illustrations*. Nothing keeps a reader's interest quite so well as this development through particular details of an abstract generalization. Instead of the vague statement, "Jim began to associate with bad companions," how much more vigorous is the particularization, "Jim began to asso-

ciate with the boys who gathered at Fatty's Hamburger Joint—
young toughs like Butch Lewis, Red Mattson, and Pug Ham-
mond." Instead of the vague, "Women often imitate movie ac-
tresses," how much more effective is the particularization, "Everywhere one sees Greta Garbo jerseys and Jean Harlow hair, Mae
West vulgarity and Constance Bennett sophistication." And instead of the generalized, "All Americans are alike," how much
more interesting is the particularization made by a Frenchman,
"Americans are all alike: their meals are alike, their homes are
alike, their cars are alike, their tastes in magazines and moving
pictures are alike, their sentimentalities about dogs are alike, their
very habits of love-making are alike."

The development of a general idea by means of examples and
illustrations requires observation, memory of fact, and imagination.
It is not surprising, therefore, that the usual run of writers and
speakers employ in their compositions only abstract generalizations.
They have not observed life carefully enough to know it; instead
they know only the laws of their personal creed. They have not
been interested enough in life to remember what it is like; instead
they remember only that they believe a certain thing. They have
not imagination enough to create, or re-create, a vivid life in which
their reader or their listener can participate; instead they give out
only dry summaries of an intellectual system. A writer who wishes
to avoid both weakness and dullness cannot neglect to expand on
his generalizations by means of examples and illustrations. No
other device of composition is so convincing or so vivifying.

These four means of gaining interest—a sense of progression,
good humor, analogy, and examples and illustrations—involve the
elemental structure of a composition. In the following paragraphs
are to be discussed other means which require no fundamental
ordering of the composition, but may, indeed, be utilized after
the composition as a whole is finished. That is, they may take the

form of amendment, revision, and insertion before the completion of the final draft.

One of these means is *quotation*. When writers are very young, mistrusting their own judgment, they quote at length and with frequency; when they are a little older, they are so afraid of appearing unoriginal that they hesitate to quote anything. Both extremes are deplorable. Too much quotation sounds timid and immature, or (which is worse) pedantic; but no quotation at all may leave a composition with too little variety. Most readers tire of the same style extended through page after page, for no matter how various and rich a style it may be, it is bound to possess a certain inescapable sameness of tone which will at last weary the reader. Quotations inserted occasionally relieve this sameness and postpone the inevitable weariness. Sometimes quotations may come spontaneously to the writer while he is in the act of composing; but usually they come only after deliberate and laborious search when the act of composing is over. Accordingly, when he has made the first draft of almost any kind of writing except fiction, a writer might well make a practice of running through some of the published literature on similar subjects to find passages that express some of his own ideas, and then insert these passages into his own work or substitute them for his own words.[3] For example, a traveler describing scenes in Europe might go, to take the first authors that come to mind, to Stevenson's *Travels with a Donkey*, Byron's *Childe Harold*, or Mark Twain's *Innocents Abroad*; a student of socialism in America could hardly refrain from quoting from Norman Thomas, Henry George, or Eugene Debs; and an essayist writing on the social life of insects would certainly quote from Fabre, Maeterlinck, Wheeler, and even Virgil.

[3] This advice does not apply, of course, to writing which is a record of research done, or which is in any other way statistical, factual, or informative. It applies only to original creative writing which is imaginative or reflective.

While we are on this subject, we may pause to mention a few sources always good for quotations. There are, of course, the standard collections of selected quotations such as may be found in any good library. But possibly the most usable sources are the works of epigrammatists and maxim writers such as Oscar Wilde, Samuel Butler (of the *Notebooks*), Bernard Shaw, Carlyle, La Rochefoucauld, Pascal, La Bruyère, Poor Richard, Alexander Pope, Bacon, and Theophrastus. Likewise, most of the great classics contain lines suitable to almost any worthwhile thought. An hour's paging through Shakespeare, Tennyson, Milton, Virgil, or any good anthology of lyric poetry of any time or country will uncover a dozen lines seemingly penned for no other purpose than to be quoted. A special word should be said for the King James Bible. It is extraordinarily rich in quotable passages of all sorts—the straightforward earnestness of Paul, the bitter pessimism of Ecclesiastes, the sober business counsel of the Proverbs, the ecstatic imagery of the Psalms, the sensuous rapture of the Song of Songs, and the vivid epithets and flashing anger of Isaiah. No other book has had so profound an influence on English style and language; and no other book can give a writer more quotations, concrete and powerful, and filled with connotations that are rooted fast in the traditions and the spirit of the Anglo-Saxon race.

Quotations should not be used ostentatiously. In general, except for purely expository purposes, they should be short; that is, they should seldom be more than a couple of sentences in length, and they may often be incorporated as clauses or phrases within the writer's own sentences. The phrase, "As So-and-so says—or puts it —or remarks," should be avoided.

Even the lowest of us may have high ideals; or as Oscar Wilde says, "All of us are in the gutter, but some of us are looking at the stars."

This sounds formal and affected because the quotation is too ob-

viously inserted to impress the reader. It would sound better if it
went:

When Oscar Wilde said that "all of us are in the gutter, but some
of us are looking at the stars," he meant that even the lowest of us
may have high ideals.

When the language of a quotation is obviously Biblical, Shakespearian, Miltonic, or Burnsian, or when the quotation is familiar,
the source from which it is taken ought not to be mentioned. To
write, "As Shakespeare says, 'All the world's a stage' "; or, "As St.
Paul puts it, 'These three remain, faith, hope, and charity' "; or,
"As the old proverb has it, 'Honesty is the best policy' "; or, "In
the words of Burns, 'My heart is weary, fu' o' care' "—to write
thus is to insult the reader. The quotations themselves tell their
origins.

Quotations are like pebbles thrown into the glassy surface of the
lake; they make the surface less monotonous and more interesting.
Figures of speech, on the other hand, are like reflections in the
lake; they interest us, somehow, even more than realities themselves. It is a human characteristic to find pleasure in recognizing
similarities. We like to see imitations and miniatures; we like toys
and dolls and mannikins; we like to note how well the imitation
resembles the real. This trait it is which makes us think on looking
at a picture, "How like reality!" and on looking at a landscape,
"How like a picture!" It makes us think of a story, "How like real
life!" and of an incident in real life, "How like a story!" This
pleasure which we derive from the recognition of similarities makes
us always interested in figures of speech. For instance, we may
not be at all interested in an ordinary drop of water, or in a lamp
globe. But when someone says, "The lamp globe clung to the ceil-
ing like a heavy drop of water just ready to plump down to the
floor," we take notice. We may not be interested in either ladies'

veils or flies. But when someone says, "The veil over the woman's face was like a spider's web with black flies caught in it here and there," we take notice. And we may not be interested in either church choirs or dead boughs. But when someone writes, "Boughs that shake against the cold, Bare, ruined choirs where late the sweet birds sang," we take notice.

This demonstration of an essential unity in objects unlike in most respects stimulates the imagination, and gives the reader an opportunity to exercise the faculty for recognition already mentioned. The recognition may not involve mere pictorial images, as in the three examples just given. (a) It may involve the recognition in inanimate objects of attributes essentially human, as in, "No longer mourn for me than thou shalt hear The *surly sullen bell*"; or, "He carried a sort of suitcase made of imitation leather which had long since grown too tired to keep up the illusion."

(b) It may involve the recognition in abstract ideas of concrete processes, as in, "Cast thy bread upon the waters; for thou shalt find it after many days"; or, "Silence shall fall like dew"; or, "Goodness and mercy shall follow me."

(c) It may involve the recognition of an object or of a process from the mention of a word that suggests the object or the process, as in, "The scepter of Egypt shall pass away"; "Cold steel will solve the problem of most riots"; "The house of Judah shall perish"; "He keeps the finest stable in the county"; "He that lives by the sword shall die by the sword"; "The machine he drives is the handsomest in the city"; "The whole country was in arms." The difficulty with most of these last, however, is that one must be acquainted with them in order to understand them; yet if one is already acquainted with them, one finds them trite.

The use of figures of speech can be much abused. A writer, especially a writer of prose, may produce so many figures that his work sounds affected; or (a much more common fault) he may

make comparisons so far-fetched that his work seems strained.
An example of such strained figurative writing in verse is this by
John Davidson:

> The windows, Argus-eyed with knotted panes
> That under heavy brows of roses blink
> Blind guard, have never wept, with hailstones stung.
> No antique, gnarled, and wrinkled round wood porch
> Whiskered with hollyhocks in this old thorpe
> Has ever felt the razor of the east.

All these figures, fanciful as they may be, sound forced and unnatural, as if the poet were trying hard to be poetic, as if he were
going out of his way to be metaphoric.

A third abuse of figures is the over-elaboration of comparisons.
How much better would the following vivid metaphor of Davidson's have been if the last phrase had been omitted. The poet is
describing a battle scene between the Scotch and the English:

> Now they are hand to hand!
> How short a front! How close! They're sewn together
> With steel cross-stitches, halbert over sword,
> Spear across lance, *and death the purfled seam!*

Addison severely criticizes Cowley for similar over-elaborations
of metaphor. Poets, he says, have often "taken an advantage from
the doubtful meaning of the word fire, to make an infinite number
of witticisms":

Cowley observing the cold regard of his mistress's eyes, and at the
same time their power of producing love in him, considers them as
burning-glasses made of ice; and finding himself able to live in the
greatest extremities of love, concludes the torrid zone to be habitable.
When his mistress has read his letter written in juice of lemon,
by holding it to the fire, he desires her to read it over a second
time by love's flames. When she weeps, he wishes it were inward
heat that distilled those drops from the limbec. When she is absent,
he is beyond eighty, that is, thirty degrees nearer the pole than when

she is with him. His ambitious love is a fire that naturally mounts upwards; his happy love is the beams of heaven, and his unhappy love flames of hell. When it does not let him sleep, it is a flame that sends up no smoke; when it is opposed by counsel and advice, it is a fire that rages the more by the winds blowing upon it.

When the freshman wrote the following, he also was guilty of tiresome over-elaboration:

Life is a game of bridge in which luck is always trumps. [If he had left off here, he would have had an interesting metaphor, but he dragged out the comparison.] The suits are the different parts of our career, Spades being our profession, Diamonds being material fortunes, Hearts being our loves, and Clubs being our power to overcome opposition. The ace in each suit is our natural ability; the king is our education or training; the queen is the wife or mother who helps us; and the jack is our closest friend. The other cards are merely our acquaintances. In the game, we are matched against other people who have different gifts from those of ours, and who try to gain what we gain. Our business is to know our own strength and the strength of others, and to play our cards wisely. We try to get what we can by means of the small cards, and guard our more important cards closely to keep others from overcoming them with their superior gifts.

And so on. Much of this is ingenious, but it soon grows boresome.

A fourth kind of fault sometimes accompanying the use of figurative language is the mixed metaphor. Probably few people would say, as did the freshman, "I may be up a tree; but I will fight to the last ditch." Nor would few people correct the mixed metaphor, "He went drifting down the sands of time on flowery beds of ease," as did the freshman, who made it read, "He went drifting down the sands of time on an oasis." But Oscar Wilde can write:

> To think of that grand living after death
> In beast and bird and flower, when this cup,
> Being filled too full of spirit, bursts for breath.

We may possibly believe that a cup could be filled to the bursting point, instead of overflowing; but we cannot believe that it would burst for breath. Wilde writes elsewhere of the grave,

> Ah! sweet indeed to rest within the womb
> Of Earth, great mother of eternal sleep.

He forgets here that a womb has no relation to a tomb—except to rhyme with it in the next line.

To summarize all this advice about putting interest in a composition:

1. Select topics that are inherently interesting.
2. Do not give the appearance of being extraordinarily good and wise.
3. Put exposition in the form of argument.
4. Never appear to exhaust all the possibilities of a topic.
5. Be good-humored on most occasions.
6. Make the reader feel a sense of progression in the composition.
7. Show how the self-interest of the reader is concerned.
8. Use analogies.
9. Elaborate on most generalizations by means of concrete illustrations and specific examples.
10. Insert quotations from others into the composition; and resort often to figures of speech.

EXERCISES

1. The Ending.
    What would be the best way to end
        a. An explanation of the reasons why America should (or should not) have recognized Russia.
        b. An account of Spanish cruelties in the New World.

c. A campaign speech for a political candidate.

d. An essay on Schopenhauer's philosophy.

e. An article on the wild birds of your county.

2. Suspense.

Write a beginning which would create suspense in each of the following:

    a. A story about a man who deserted his wife.

    b. An account of some tour you have made.

    c. An account of a hunting trip.

    d. An account of the methods by which cancer may be cured.

    e. A series of paragraphs on the most important persons in your town.

    f. A character sketch of an absent-minded man.

Make each of the following groups of ideas into a sentence having good suspense:

    a. His daughter fell ill.
    She died.
    He was rich.

    b. Dante was melancholy.
    His melancholy came from within him.
    He did not want to be melancholy.
    His melancholy was not due to caprice.
    It was not a product of external circumstances.

    c. Unemployment is our outstanding problem.
    It troubles the workers.
    It agitates the government.
    It is the ruination of employers.

    d. Deliver us from fire.
    From sword.
    From sudden death.

    e. Knowledge got except by working is all hypothetical.
    It is a thing to be argued about.
    It is a thing floating in the clouds.

    f. Many young men left this country in 1918.
    They went to Europe.
    Thousands died in battle.

    g. It was always his deepest desire to go to college.
    But first he wanted to finish high school.

He wanted to pay his own way through college, too.
h. Dishonesty and crime are increasing.
The police are as competent as ever.
The public as a whole is worse.
i. He died in the spring.
It was at about the time the first swallow arrived.
j. The ideals of the American people have changed greatly in the last twenty years.
The cheap car is responsible.
Yet there has been little real cultural progress.

3. Climax.

a. In the sentences you have made above, have you kept in mind the principle of climax?

b. Arrange the sentences in the following paragraphs in climactic order, and study the climactic order within several of the individual sentences:

1. Man's breath is fatal to his fellows. 2. Men are devoured by our towns. 3. The more they are massed together, the more corrupt they become. 4. Of all creatures man is least fitted to live in herds. 5. Men are not made to be crowded together in ant-hills, but scattered over the earth to till it. 6. Disease and vice are the sure results of over-crowded cities. 7. Huddled together like sheep, men would very soon die.
—Jean Jacques Rousseau: A garbled paragraph from *Emile* (1762).

1. The minds of men were gradually reduced to the same level, the fire of genius was extinguished, and even the military spirit evaporated. 2. The natives of Europe were brave and robust. 3. The most aspiring spirits resorted to the court or standard of the emperors; and the deserted provinces, deprived of political strength or union, insensibly sunk into the languid indifference of public life. 4. The long peace, and the uniform government of the Romans, introduced a slow and secret poison into the vitals of the empire. 5. Spain, Gaul, Britain, and Illyricum supplied the legions with excellent soldiers, and constituted the real strength of the monarchy. 6. The posterity of their boldest leaders was contented with the rank of citizens and subjects. 7. They received laws and governors from the will of their sovereign, and trusted for their defense to a mercenary army. 8. Their personal valor remained, but they no longer possessed that public courage which

is nourished by the love of independence, the sense of national honor, the presence of danger, and the habit of command.

—Edward Gibbon: A garbled paragraph from *The Decline and Fall of the Roman Empire* (1776).

4. Proportion.

a. To what extent do the above sentences, as you have rearranged them, conform to the laws of proportion?

b. Revise the following sentences according to the laws of proportion so as to make the important idea in each really seem important:

After an absence of ten years, he returned to his native city, and found that his mother was dead.

The year moved on to an unusually warm March.

The many critics of our present age would have us believe that science threatens civilization.

She made a loving and devoted mother, though she was so nervous that she sometimes scolded the children when their faults should have been overlooked.

The roads are still very poor in country regions where horses are used, especially on hills.

c. Write one paragraph about three people who have influenced your life. Make one of the three seem more important than the others. Next, write two additional paragraphs, in each of which a different one of the trio is made to seem most important. As nearly as possible, use the same materials in all three paragraphs.

d. Suppose you were writing a story with this theme: "People who break social conventions always make themselves unhappy." Which parts of the story would you enlarge upon if you were writing for a serious magazine interested in real literature? If you were writing for a cheap newspaper-serial syndicate? If you were writing for a religious magazine?

5. Structure.

See the Exercises for Chapter II, Sections 2-3.

6. Beginning for Clarity.

Write an introductory sentence or paragraph for a somewhat recondite essay on each of the following topics:

a. Nationalism *vs.* Internationalism.

CREATIVE WRITING

b. Types of Citizens; or Biographies; or Novels; or Magazines.
c. Culture and the University.
d. An Ideal Program for Four Years of English.
e. My Philosophy.
f. Women in Politics.
g. The Business of Fatherhood.
h. The Development of my Religious Beliefs.
i. The Ideal University.
j. Politics as a Career.

7. Beginning for Effect.
   Using the above topics, write introductory sentences.
   a. To attract attention or engage interest.
   b. To set a problem squarely before the reader.
   c. To state a bold and striking thesis.
   d. To make classifications original and brilliant enough to attract prospective readers.

8. Repetition.
   a. Study the repetitions for intensification in some book of the Bible—say Ecclesiastes I, III, and IV; and then try to enlarge in a similar way on two or three of the Proverbs of Solomon—say those in Chapter XII.

   b. Rewrite the following paragraph, giving it a more obvious unity by reiterating its important ideas as often and as gracefully as possible.

   In our present economic order business and industry are the significant activities. They stand toward the social order of today where landholding stood toward the social order of the Middle Ages. Every one in business, great or small, is in a shareholder relation in which things are due him as shareholder, not because of any special undertaking. He is not freely competing. The great bulk of any urban community are upon salaries and owe service to corporations. . . . The individual businesses are more and more giving up and going into corporate form. These organizations themselves are more and more merging. Businesses which until now had been able to exist on the older basis have been given by the chain stores something like a feudal organization. If a new domain of business or industry is opened, those who have conquered it distribute stock as a great feudal lord distributed estates.

It has come to be the general course that individuals do not own businesses or enterprises or industries. They hold shares in them.
—Dean Roscoe Pound: A slightly modified paragraph from an address on "Some Analogies from History" (1932).

c. Rewrite it so as to have key-words appearing throughout.

d. Rewrite it so as to give as much unity of structure as you can to the sentences.

e. Show how repetitions of various words would make for greater coherence in the following paragraph:[4]

War books are in fact belligerent propaganda, no matter how ugly they make battle. There is such a thing as the fascination of things not lovely. Our eyes will come back again and again, not to the most beautiful, but the most overwhelmingly homely person in the room. And so with national hostilities and horrors. There was a time during the golden century of Spanish literature when the Picaresque Novel produced by Iberia was read and imitated by all Europe. The rascally heroes were the true antitheses of the great men of chivalry. This kind of work was written under the Inquisition as martial books come forth nowadays under a peace-philosophy. Volumes about conflict are to be deplored, because they fill up the place of better stimulants. It is true that more efficient excitants are, unfortunately, rare. Who will find them in the drabness of the photographic novel? Surfeited by reading about their own dullness, people seek to peruse extraordinary tales. And bloodshed is unusual enough to interest them.

9. Contrast.

a. Develop elements of contrast in the plot, character, and setting of the following suggested stories:

A young woman loves a man of whom her family disapproves, marries him, and then finds that her family was right.

A doting mother brings up a daughter with the ideal of denying her nothing. When the child grows up, and the mother cannot possibly satisfy all demands, the child begins to hate the mother.

A young college couple plan to elope after a dance. But during the course of the dance, the girl meets another interesting young man. She refuses to elope.

[4] Adapted from an article, "Do War Books Help Peace?" by Salvador de Madariaga in the New York *Herald Tribune*, January 19, 1930.

An artist wishes to paint a perfect madonna. But he finds that his idea of what she should be changes so fast that he can never paint her.

A rich man loses his money, is not contented to remain merely well-to-do, strives frantically to regain his wealth, and finally commits a crime for the sake of a fortune.

b. Write paragraphs defining the following by means of contrast:
Pleasant weather.
An interesting lecturer.
A career.
An old person.
The typical college student.

c. Study the contrasts in the following passage from Dr. Johnson's life of Addison. Write a criticism in Dr. Johnson's manner of the style of some other author. If you wish, rewrite your criticism, using other devices of contrast involving the length of sentences, rhetorical questions, inversions, unusual words, etc.

His prose is the model of the middle style; on grave subjects not formal, on light occasions not groveling; pure without scrupulosity, and exact without apparent elaboration; always equable, and always easy, without glowing words or pointed sentences. Addison never deviates from his track to snatch a grace; he seeks no ambitious ornaments, and tries no hazardous innovations. His page is always luminous, but never blazes in unexpected splendor.

It was apparently his principal endeavor to avoid all harshness and severity of diction; he is therefore sometimes verbose in his transitions and connections, and sometimes descends too much to the language of conversation; yet if his language had been less idiomatical it might have lost somewhat of its genuine Anglicism. What he attempted, he performed; he is never feeble, and he did not wish to be energetic; he is never rapid, and he never stagnates. His sentences have neither studied amplitude, nor affected brevity; his periods, though not diligently rounded, are voluble and easy. Whoever wishes to attain an English style, familiar but not coarse, and elegant but not ostentatious, must give his days and nights to the volumes of Addison.

10. Interest.

a. To find out what subjects are inherently interesting to people, let the members of the class keep a list of items in a week's reading (of newspapers, magazines, and books) which interest them individually. At the end of the week, the items may be read out, and classified on the blackboard by the instructor.

b. Write an account of some experience of yours in which you played a conspicuously excellent part; but in the account ridicule yourself so tactfully that the reader will not believe you egotistical.

c. How could you make essays on the following purely expository subjects have a somewhat belligerent tone:

Raising Corn (cotton, wheat, rice, zinnias, petunias, collie dogs, canaries, hogs, race horses, etc.).

On Persons One Would Wish to Have Seen.

My First Play (opera, circus, concert, etc.).

"It is not enough to do good; one must do it in the right way."

The Man of One Idea.

The Average Man.

National Politics in the 1920's.

The End of Victorianism in America.

The Radio and our National Culture.

The War to End War.

Types of Hotels.

The Small College or the Large University?

Humor.

Modern Biography.

Why Masefield Is (or Is Not) to Be Regarded as the Poet of the Common Man.

d. Review the work of the most important modern narrative-writers to determine how frequently they use the device of attacking something. Consider especially the work of Shaw, Wells, Galsworthy, Aldous Huxley, Anatole France, Sinclair Lewis, Theodore Dreiser, and Sherwood Anderson. To what extent does the season's most popular play or novel use the device? How could you use it in a story

About a college professor.

About a college girl.

About a far-western town.

About some foreign or distant locality you know.

About mothers of grown children.

About owners of small businesses.

e. In a very short essay on one of the subjects given under *c* above, try to convey the impression that you know more about the subject than you say.

f. Write short essays on two or three local, campus, or national abuses—first, in an earnest, serious style; then in a burlesque, satirical style like that of Will Rogers; then in a politely satirical style like that of Addison (e.g., *Tatler* No. 163; *Spectator* Nos. 13, 112, 275, 281) or of Pope (*Rape of the Lock*); then in a brutally ironical style like that of Swift (*Modest Proposal* and the later books of *Gulliver's Travels*). Which style do your friends and your instructor consider the most interesting?

g. Try to interest the reader in the subjects listed in *c* by engaging his self-interest.

h. Explain the following abstractions by means of concrete analogies:

> The evils (or benefits) of our tariffs.
>
> Our European debt problem.
>
> The failure of the League of Nations.
>
> The effect of the Great Depression on American life (morals, business, intellectual interests).
>
> Education and democracy.
>
> American poetry in the last twenty years.
>
> The place of the Negro in American life.

i. Clarify the following complexities by means of analogies:

> The way a camera (an autogiro, the piston of a gasoline engine, the valve of a tire, a dose of salts) works.
>
> The Federal Reserve System.
>
> The Gold Standard.
>
> Controlled currency.
>
> The respiratory system.
>
> The circulatory system.
>
> Bringing up a child.
>
> Preparing a dinner.

j. Write a paragraph giving examples and illustrations of the following:

> So-and-so is a typical college student.

Culture has no place in contemporary American life.
The dominant trait of my personality is ———.
I am disillusioned about college.
Kipling epitomizes British imperialism.

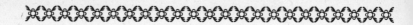

Chapter II

RATIONALITY IN STYLE

T HE word "style," like the words "religion," "goodness," and "patriotism," implies a vague, hazy sort of excellence which most of us would have a hard time accurately defining. But we are certain that no writing can be really good, or interesting, or worth-while writing without *style*. The cigarette advertisement has style (after its fashion); the classified advertisement has none. The newspaper account of the latest natural disaster has style; the schedule of radio programs has none. Gibbon's History of Rome has style; a mathematics textbook has none. Style, in a word, is that virtue in writing which makes it more than merely comprehensible.

I wanted to see a movie. John Barrymore was playing in it. It was being shown at the Rialto. So I went to town this morning and saw the show.

We can understand such writing easily enough. But it has no style. Between writing like that, and the writing of people like Conrad, Kipling, and Galsworthy are a thousand intermediate stages. The very uppermost of these stages are probably reserved for people who have a special talent and sensitivity beyond what mere training and advice can do for them. But training and advice can be a real help to any intelligent person trying to clamber from the lower stages of writing to the general region of the upper stages. This chapter and the four that follow are intended to give advice and foster training that will hasten the ascent.

44

The heading of this chapter is somewhat ambiguous. It means that the chapter will try to tell how meaning and structure should supplement each other—how a rational correspondence should exist between the thing said and the method in which it is said, to the end that it be said as clearly and as logically as possible, and that it convey the exact meaning and shade of meaning the writer desires.

1. Control.—The first requirement of all is that the writer have a rational understanding of what he wishes to say. That is, he cannot afford to write even a single sentence in a composition without first asking himself, What is the most important idea, emotion, or image I wish to convey in this sentence? He must pick out the one word he wishes to emphasize, the one phrase he wishes to plant in the mind of his reader, the one clause which he wishes to make linger and ferment. Probably more elementary faults of style are due to the failure of writers to weigh and properly evaluate their own ideas than to any other weakness. For if the writer himself has not decided which of his ideas is most worthy of the reader's attention, how can the reader decide? Rational, discriminating, judicious thinking is the first habit a writer should acquire. Without it, he is only a babbler.

A student writes:

There are types of students who go through college on the reputations which they received at the first of the year because they did extra-hard work then, though they do very little later on.

The writer has not evaluated his own thoughts here. One thought is that students go through college on reputations received early in the year; another thought is that these students worked hard for their reputations; and a third thought is that these same students do little work later on. Which of these ideas is most important? The writer had not decided, and the reader does not know. Accordingly, the sentence, though comprehensible, is flabby and styleless. Other examples follow:

Mrs. Rhymes had on an old pair of cotton gloves, and had evidently been puttering among the ferns and azalea bushes.

Surely you are not in sympathy with those people who raise one of their own kind to prominence and then hurl muck at their own creations, as we know some of our city politicians have been doing in the present campaign.

We had expected him to live, but he died.

I had been vaccinated and was immune to the smallpox which was sweeping through the city; so I had felt safe, and had come there on a business trip.

These sentences are all grammatically correct; they are not necessarily ununified; they are not incoherent. But in no sentence has the writer made a plain and definite choice of the most important idea in the sentence. In any one of them he might choose any one of several ideas as the most important, and construct a new and better sentence in any one of several ways. The choice never forces itself on the writer; but rather, the writer must always force his own choice on the sentence. This means that he shall have enough strength of intellect to make a decision, render judgment, and do execution on every idea that comes to him. He must decide that this one is important, and that one valueless—this one pertinent, and that one irrelevant—this one weighty, and that one light. If he fails to discriminate in this manner, he has failed in the very first step toward acquiring a rational style.

Having decided what is the most important idea in our sentence, we must let that idea control the sentence by appearing in a dominant structure. We must show the reader that this idea is dominant, and that we intended it to be dominant. Let us look at the last of the faulty sentences quoted above. As it now stands, no dominating idea controls it. We can use our own discretion, therefore, in deciding which of the four ideas is really the most important, and can frame four different sentences accordingly:

Though smallpox was sweeping through the city to which I had come on a business trip, I, having been vaccinated, felt immune.

I felt immune to the smallpox sweeping through the city to which I had come on a business trip, for I had been vaccinated.

Since I had been vaccinated and felt immune to the smallpox which was sweeping through the city, I had come there on a business trip.

Though I myself had been vaccinated and felt immune, an epidemic of smallpox was sweeping through the city to which I had come on a business trip.

Each of these sentences has a different meaning, a different implication from the others; each puts forward a different idea as the controlling and dominant element in the sentence. Which of the four sentences the writer shall use depends entirely on his own judgment as to which of the four ideas he desires to impress most strongly on his readers.

Whenever a writer is confronted by such a multiplicity of choices, he should cast his vote for one of them, make his decision for better or for worse, and then stick to his decision. If he cannot decide which of his ideas is most important, he should do one of three things: not write the sentence, or write two or three sentences instead of one, or use a balanced or parallel structure.

2. Structure.—A balanced or parallel structure is one in which the writer has considered two or more ideas to be of equal importance, has believed they supplement one another, and has expressed their equality and their supplementariness by placing them in similar structures within one sentence. The sentence just written was molded into three parallel structures because each of the three ideas expressed is of equal importance with the other two, and each forms only one portion of a complete idea. If they had not been

of equal value, they would not have had the same structure; and
if they had not been portions of the same idea, they would not
have been put in the same sentence.

We may call it a rule, therefore, that *ideas of equal thought-
value deserve structures of equal value, and ideas of unequal
thought-value deserve structures of unequal value.* The ascending
order of structure-value is this: word, phrase, clause, sentence, and
paragraph. The following sentences illustrate all these stages but
the last:

1. Word: I saw *armless* men and *legless* men.
2. Phrase: I saw men *without arms* and men *without legs.*
3. Clause: I saw men *who had no arms,* and men *who had no legs.*
4. Sentence: *I saw armless men. And I saw legless men.*

Since the ideas of "armlessness" and leglessness" are equal in
thought-value, the following sentences with unequal structure-
values would be absurd:

I saw armless men, and men who had no legs.
I saw men who had no arms, and men without legs.

In these last two sentences, equal ideas are given unequal structures. But a more common offense is that in which unequal ideas
are given equal structures. It is more common because so many
inexperienced writers have the habit of stringing together a hodge-
podge of ideas by means of "ands" and "buts." One of the sentences quoted in the preceding section illustrates this fault:

Mrs. Rhymes had on an old pair of cotton gloves, and had evidently
been puttering among the ferns and azalea bushes.

The two clauses are certainly not of equal thought-value; and
yet in this sentence they have the same kind of structure. Such
incongruity is an irrationality which thoughtful writers avoid.

The following sentences have the same weakness:

He stepped off the curb without looking, and was struck and killed by a passing car.

Here stepping off a curb, and being killed, are made to seem of equal importance.

The sun may shine tomorrow, and then we can go horseback riding.

Many people have no aim in life, and move in a circle which gets nowhere.

His mind was in a turmoil, so he decided to get drunk.

All these sentences can be improved by judicious subordination:

Mrs. Rhymes, with an old pair of cotton gloves on her hands, had evidently been puttering among the ferns and azalea bushes.

Stepping off the curb without looking, he was struck and killed by a passing car.

If the sun shines tomorrow, we can go horseback riding.

Many people, having no aim in life, move in a circle which gets nowhere.

Since his mind was in a turmoil, he decided to get drunk.

It will be noted that in each of these corrected sentences, the subordinate idea originally expressed in an independent clause has been re-expressed in a prepositional phrase, a participial phrase, or a dependent clause. That is, the structure-value has been reduced to correspond with the minor thought-values.

Sometimes, however, a writer finds it necessary to do the opposite—that is, to make an important idea really *seem* important. The writer accomplishes this feat by raising words to the rank of phrases, phrases to dependent clauses, dependent clauses to independent clauses, and independent clauses to sentences. An example follows:

Thompson was a *much-traveled* man.
Thompson was a man *of many travels.*
Thompson was a man *who had traveled much.*
Thompson, who was the man for us, *had traveled much.*
Thompson was the man. *He had traveled much.*

This deliberate heightening of an idea's importance requires more self-conscious artistry than does the proper subordination spoken of above. This heightening is a positive search for excellence; the other is merely a negative avoidance of error.

3. Position.—The most important positions in any element of composition are the beginning and the end. Reason requires, therefore, that (whenever clarity permits) we place our most important words, phrases, clauses, or ideas at the end of a sentence. The negative of this requirement, perhaps it is useless to say, is that we should avoid placing unimportant words, phrases, clauses, or ideas in the two important positions in the sentence.

a. *The Beginning.*—For example, sentences should seldom or never begin with words like "however," "also," "then too," and the like. The sentence just written almost violates the principle. If it were not that transition is made smooth and clear by the words "for example," the beginning of the sentence and of the paragraph would be a little weak. This one instance shows, however, that some laws supersede other laws. The law of clarity always comes first; other laws are secondary. Moreover, no rule should become a fetish. A certain fastidious student used to shudder at the very thought of beginning any sentence with "the" or "a." His instinct was right; but his practice was perverted.

b. *The End.*—Even more important than the beginning is the end of a sentence. If the reader will turn back a few pages to the sentence concerning smallpox, vaccination, and immunity, he will see that each of the corrected versions, except the last, ends with the principal clause and the principal idea in the sentence. In Section 2, likewise, each of the improved sentences ends with the principal clause and the principal idea. The practice illustrated in these sentences is, in general, safe. The important clause and the important idea should come at the end of the sentence. But like all other practices, it may be carried too far. It may become an obsession with the writer, and it may lead to monotony of style. Furthermore, it is not adapted to writing of a leisurely gait and a familiar tone. It is best adapted to exposition aiming at absolute clarity, and to argumentation aiming at conviction.

Yet no sentence should ever end with a tailing off into insignificant words and ideas:

Most of us would refuse to read more than a few sentences of it.

The gift of prophecy was also assigned to him.

The last two words in these sentences are flat and insipid.

Her voice failed, being broken by tears and sobs.

Here we have the common offense of a participial phrase dragged along at the end of a sentence.

He died yesterday, having been sick only a week.

He took to begging, being on the verge of starvation.

All these sentences end with a construction which should come at the beginning for the sake of both clarity and emphasis.

The dependent clauses in the following examples would likewise be better at the beginning of their sentences:

She raised her hands in prayer to Neptune as she stood by the seaside.

He would not answer, though I rang the bell several times.

He talked about the gold standard, of which I was glad to learn something.

These sentences are irrational because they indicate by means of subordinate structures that certain ideas are subordinate, and yet they place these subordinate ideas and structures in the prominent position in the sentences. A writer of such sentences is like a strawberry packer who would go to the trouble of culling out inferior stock, and would then pile this inferior stock at the top of the basket for prospective customers to see. The writer should be like a real berry-packer; he should carefully choose the best of his stock, and then pile it in the most conspicuous place—at the end of the sentence. If he has a word to emphasize, or a phrase, or a clause, or an idea, he should juggle the grammatical elements, manipulate the sentence-parts, rearrange the word-group, so as to make the important word, phrase, clause, or idea drop neatly into the prominent place. In a ballet dance, the chorus marches, wheels, converges, retreats, interlaces in a hundred gyrations; but always the star dancer appears in the prominent place. Good writing is like that. It coils, turns, pauses, retreats, converges—and always the important element appears magically at the supreme position.

Note how each member of the following pairs conveys a different feeling:

They found him drunk in the street.
They found him in the street, drunk.

Queen Victoria walked ahead of us.
Ahead of us walked Queen Victoria.

The tiger now had him by the throat.
The tiger had him by the throat now.

I went from the hotel to my train.
I went to the train from my hotel.

In these sentences, different end-words produce different effects because readers instinctively give to end-words their sharpest attention.

Perhaps the reader will be interested in the evolution of the sentence just written. As first constructed, its final clause went thus, ". . . readers instinctively pay more attention to end-words than to others in a sentence." But such a sentence, obviously trailing off into unimportant phrases, disregarded the very truth it expressed. Accordingly, the clause was revised, ". . . readers instinctively give their sharpest attention to end-words." But this version, though ending with an important word, ended with the wrong important word. The idea to be emphasized in that particular clause was not "end-words" but "sharpest attention." An easy transposition corrected the fault; and the clause assumed its present form, ". . . readers instinctively give to end-words their sharpest attention."

c. *Transposition.*—In the sentence just analyzed, a word was transposed from the important end-position so that the word might lose some of its importance. But, paradoxical as it may seem, words or phrases transposed from their normal place in a sentence usually gain in emphasis. This rule holds good except in sentences where transposition would take a word away from the end-position. Thus, in the sentence analyzed, the transposed word lost importance because its original place was at the end of the sentence.

Before continuing with this discussion, perhaps we had better see just what the normal sentence order is. The following sentence illustrates the elemental order:

The good man kindly gave the book to me.

   (a) Subject, preceded by adjective.
   (b) Verb, preceded by adverb.
   (c) Object.
   (d) Indirect object.

This elemental order has a few additional complexities which deserve mention:

The man in gray talked in a high voice.

(a) Subject, followed by adjective phrase.
(b) Verb, followed by adverbial phrase.

This order holds for adjective and adverbial clauses as well as phrases.

The man who lived down the street talked when he had the chance.

These examples show the fundamental orders. As for the order in more complicated sentences, the reader can more safely rely on his instinct for the language than on his memory of half-a-dozen special rules.

All this has been a digression. The main point is that *attention can be focused on a word in a sentence if that word is placed out of its natural order.* The italics in the following sentences indicate words out of their natural order:

Everywhere in the darkness, I saw men lying about, *dead.*

Patiently, he listened.

The sunshine, *cold and bright,* offered no sympathy.

Last of all these marching thousands *rode Napoleon.*

All day were the birds loud in my garden.

Among these visions wandered *my spirit.*

The last sentence is almost bad. So much distortion as is here looks artful and insincere. Indeed, a writer must use the device of transposition with the most discreet caution. He should reserve it for those occasions when he "would be very fine." There it is effective. But if he uses it every time he has the opportunity to do so, it soon tarnishes and looks cheap. How poor would be these verses from Ecclesiastes if they were distorted by transposition in the following way:

Of all the labor which under the sun he taketh, what hath a man the profit? Into the sea run the rivers all; and yet full is not the sea.

Yet on the other hand, how effective are these examples of transposition from the same book:

For in much wisdom is much grief.

In the day of prosperity, be joyful.

He by his wisdom delivered the city.

All things have I seen in the days of my vanity.

The reader should notice in passing that the transpositions in the first two of the examples given are designed to place important words in the important end-position, rather than to attract attention to themselves. In the last two examples, however, the transpositions are designed to emphasize the words transposed. Unless transposition can serve one of these two purposes, it is not worth while for its own sake. One other purpose, however, it may serve; and that is to make transitions from sentence to sentence more smooth.[1]

4. Continuity.— A piece of writing has continuity if the connections between its elements are tight and snug—if each part is locked hard and fast to its neighboring parts. Continuity is not always a virtue. It implies a strictly logical procedure on the part of an author, and it hints of an intellect controlled by rationality. Obviously, therefore, too strict continuity is out of place in writing which attempts to seem spontaneously emotional and unstudiedly sincere. It precludes a quick, nervous, energetic style. And often it gives writing clarity at the sacrifice of strength. Furthermore, the tendency of modern writing is analytic rather than synthetic; that is, modern writing is coming more and more to consist of an

---

[1] The last three sentences contain transposed elements. The reader may care to analyze their function and criticize their effectiveness.

accumulation of units rather than a nexus of parts. And finally, an unbroken continuity is likely to weary the reader.

On the other hand, even in our generation of hasty readers and impatient thinkers, some people demand logical writing instead of nervous writing, and some subjects require rational consideration instead of emotional contemplation. Moreover, writing in which no strong controlling intellect is apparent throughout never has been, and probably never will be, for a long time appealing. Even Shelley (to take the first example that comes to mind), who is the most purely lyric of the great English poets, felt the control of intellect. An analysis of such lyrics as the "Ode to the West Wind," "The Skylark," and "The Cloud" will reveal an amazingly solid and supple intellectual structure underlying the airiness of the poems. It is true, too, that the most powerful radicals and convincing innovators are those who know the ways of conservatism. Nearly every worth-while modernistic painter has had an early stage of conventionality, and nearly every modern stylist has had an early stage of imitation. It can probably do nobody any harm, therefore, to learn a little about the conservative style of writing—for writing with smoothness of continuity *is* conservative.

a. *Continuity of Ideas.*—Continuity depends, first of all, on the larger structure of the composition. In narration, it depends on a simple following of the time sequence. In description, it depends on the arrangement of details. In exposition, it depends on the arrangement of ideas. We shall discuss only the last of these three forms here.

It cannot be too often repeated that the easiest way to give smooth continuity to style is to have a clear and rational structure in the composition as a whole. When the parts of the composition are so thought out and arranged that each part leads logically and inevitably to the succeeding part, a writer will have little trouble in giving continuity to his style.

There are, however, a few devices which help the writer achieve this continuity. Some of these concern the continuity of ideas; some the continuity of paragraphs; and some the continuity of sentences.

As for the first of these, the adoption of a certain order of procedure—and adherence to it—is the simplest and most effective. For example, there may be an order of procedure altogether chronological; or the order may be from a general idea to particular illustrations of it; or it may be from the particular illustrations to the general idea governing them; or it may be from simple toward more and more complex ideas; or it may be from known or admitted facts toward unknown or disputed facts; or it may be from an enumeration of points that are to be considered to an elaboration of each of those points in turn. Which method the writer adopts will depend upon his subject. But once he has chosen his method, he ought to stick to it pretty closely throughout his work. If he does so, he will find the minor problems of continuity much easier to solve, and the reader will find the composition much pleasanter to follow.

b. *Continuity between Paragraphs.*—A more mechanical consideration is that of continuity between paragraphs. The device most commonly used to effect this continuity is the *transitional sentence*, that is, a sentence which points both forward and back— forward toward the new paragraph, and back toward the preceding paragraph. This paragraph begins with a transitional sentence. The words "a more" indicate that something has preceded; the rest of the sentence suggests the nature of the new paragraph. The second paragraph in this section also begins with a transitional sentence.[2]

A second device is the insertion of a short *transitional paragraph*

[2] Occasionally the transitional sentence comes at the *end* of a paragraph instead of at the beginning; but this type is uncommon, for it places an unimportant idea in the important end-position of the paragraph.

between two important paragraphs. Like the transitional sentences, the transitional paragraph hints at something that has gone before, and indicates the general outlines of what is to follow. The fifth paragraph in this section is a transitional paragraph; so is the paragraph beginning on the next line.

c. *Continuity within the Paragraph.*—More varied than the devices which make for continuity between paragraphs are those which make for continuity within the paragraph—that is, for continuity between sentences.

The first of these is the use of *transitional words*. In looking over the present section, one would find that the transitional words already used are "therefore," "furthermore," "that is," "finally," "on the other hand," "moreover," "too," "accordingly," and "however." This makes a sizable list, which may be supplemented from the following paragraph.

Somewhat akin to transitional words is the use of *pronoun references* in one sentence to nouns in a preceding sentence. The pronouns thus form a rational link between the two sentences. By way of illustration, the paragraph just above begins, "The first of *these*" —with *these* referring to a noun in the preceding sentence. And the first paragraph in this section contains several "its" referring to nouns in the preceding sentence. A better example follows:

The Pleiads were daughters of Atlas, and nymphs of Diana's train. One day Orion saw *them* and became enamored and pursued *them*. In *their* distress *they* prayed to the gods to change *their* form, and Jupiter turned them into pigeons, and then made *them* a constellation in the sky. Though their number was seven, only six stars are visible, for Electra, one of *them*, it is said, left her place.

The reader conceives these four sentences as a large unit, quite unconscious of the subtle device which cements them.

A little different is the trick of *repeating in one sentence impor-*

tant words of the preceding sentence. An example, also from Bulfinch, follows:

The story of the Iliad ends with *the death of Hector*, and it is from the Odyssey and other poems that we learn the fate of the other heroes. After *the death of Hector*, Troy did not immediately fall, but receiving aid from new *allies* still continued its resistance. One of these *allies* was Memnon, the Æthiopian prince, whose story we have already told. Another was *Penthesilea*, queen of the Amazons. . . . *Penthesilea* slew many of the bravest warriors, but was at last slain by Achilles. But when *the hero* bent over his fallen foe, and contemplated her beauty, youth, and valor, he bitterly regretted his victory. Thersites, an insolent brawler and demagogue, ridiculed his grief, and was in consequence slain by *the hero*.[3]

Such a weaving together of sentences becomes an even stronger union when the repeated words are brought close to each other by transposition. In the passage just quoted, for example, there would be a closer weave if the author had transposed his link-words in some such fashion as the following:

It is from the Odyssey and later poems that we learn the fate of the other heroes, for the story of the Iliad ends with *the death of Hector*. After *the death of Hector*, Troy did not immediately fall, but continued its resistance with aid received from new *allies*. One of these *allies* was Memnon . . . etc.

This revised version carries the thought swiftly from sentence to sentence with hardly a break. Bulfinch, however, had so simple a theme that he needed no such powerful coupler to fasten his sentences together, and so he dispensed with it. But in compositions where the idea is knotty and the coherence difficult, it is an extremely useful device.

The repetition of a word from sentence to sentence may couple together pairs of sentences. But it does not link together all the sentences in a paragraph. This latter feat is accomplished when

[3] The passages quoted are taken from chaps. xxvi and xxviii of Thomas Bulfinch's *The Age of Fable*, 1855.

one word is repeated from sentence to sentence throughout the paragraph. This repeated word (or phrase) becomes a distinctive brand burned on each sentence, and identifies that sentence as belonging to the particular herd of sentences which go together to make up a paragraph. We have spoken of this device in a preceding chapter, but it will bear further illustration here. The following paragraph from Matthew Arnold offers good examples not only of key-words but of other devices of continuity already mentioned; the key-words are capitalized, and the other transitional words are italicized:

This culture is more interesting and more far-reaching than that other, which is founded solely on the scientific ardor for knowing. But it needs times of faith and ardor, times when the *intellectual horizon* is opening and widening all around us to flourish in. And is not the close and bounded *intellectual horizon* within which we have long lived and moved now lifted up, and are not new lights finding free *passage* to shine *in upon us?* For a long time there was no *passage* for *them* to make their way *in upon us,* and then it was of no use to think of adapting the world's action to *them.* Where was the hope of making REASON AND THE WILL OF GOD prevail among people who had a *routine* which they had christened REASON AND THE WILL OF GOD, in which they were inextricably bound, and beyond which they had no power of looking? But now the *iron force* of adhesion to the old *routine*—social, political, religious—has *wonderfully yielded*; the *iron force* of *exclusion of all which is new* has *wonderfully yielded.* The danger now is, not that people should obstinately refuse to allow anything but their old *routine* to pass for REASON AND THE WILL OF GOD, but either that they should allow some novelty or other to pass for these too easily, or else that they should underrate the importance of them altogether, and think it enough to follow action for its own sake, without troubling themselves to make REASON AND THE WILL OF GOD prevail therein. Now, then, is the moment for culture to be of service, culture which believes in making REASON AND THE WILL OF GOD prevail, believes in perfection, is the study and pursuit of perfection, and is no longer debarred by a rigid invincible *exclusion of whatever is new*, from getting acceptance for its ideas, simply because they are new.

One final device by which continuity may be obtained, though it too has already been mentioned, will be discussed here. It is *parallel structure*—the expression of diverse ideas in so similar a form that they have a seeming relation. The grammatical structure here is to the ideas what a uniform is to a group of men. Each individual man is quite unlike his companions, and yet the whole group seems to be of a oneness because their dress is a oneness. In the following passage from Macaulay, note the number and variety of ideas presented, and the continuity which the grammatical structure gives to these ideas:

If these reasonings be just, no poet has ever triumphed over greater difficulties than Milton. He received a learned education: he was a profound and elegant classical scholar; he had studied all the mysteries of Rabbinical literature; he was intimately acquainted with every language of modern Europe from which either pleasure or information was then to be derived. He was perhaps the only great poet of later times who has been distinguished by the excellence of his Latin verse. The genius of Petrarch was scarcely of the first order; and his poems in the ancient language, though much praised by those who have never read them, are wretched compositions. Cowley, with all his admirable wit and ingenuity, had little imagination; nor indeed do we think his classical diction comparable to that of Milton. The authority of Johnson is against us on this point; but Johnson had studied the bad writers of the Middle Ages till he had become utterly insensible to the Augustan elegance, and was as ill qualified to judge between two Latin styles as a habitual drunkard to set up for a wine-taster.

With this we may leave the discussion of Rationality in Style. The whole subject demands only a clear understanding of just what one wishes to say, a clear knowledge of a few mechanical principles, and a little care in applying the principles.

EXERCISES

1. **Control.**

Organize each of the following groups of ideas into several
sentences with different controlling elements in each:

    a. William of Orange molded a commonwealth and united
hearts.

In doing this, he exhibited great contempt for danger.

Don John was no more courageous in scenes of carnage.

    b. Cubs of bears readily discover their natural inclination.

Men conform themselves to particular laws and customs.

Thus they alter or disguise their true natures.

    c. The painter chooses the fairest place.

It is usually the middle of a wall.

Here he sketches a picture.

Then he proceeds to finish it with his utmost care.

    d. They sheared in the great barn.

It was called for the nonce the Shearing-barn.

The ground-plan of the barn resembled a church with
transepts.

    e. We choose traits from many imperfect individuals.

These we put together.

And thus we form an ideal.

It is as if we were painters or sculptors.

2. **Structure.** See the following exercise.

3. **Position.**

Recast the following sentences so as to make thought-value
and structure-value consistent. Where clarity permits, put the
important idea in the end-position.

    a. All the student's financial affairs are handled by his parents;
therefore, the student is relieved of all financial respon-
bility.

    b. Virtually cast into a new world and thrown on his own
resources, the student overdraws his allowance at the
bank once or twice, thus learning the virtues of economy.

    c. These are vivid principles such as are remembered and ap-
plied throughout the life of the student.

d. When a horse is in the process of jumping over a fence, he brings his hind feet forward.

e. He is a man who is endowed with abilities of an extraordinary nature.

f. He was a good rider, but he could not stay on that horse.

g. Very often when I was a child I would slip into the bathroom, where I would occuy myself watching my father perform the morning ritual of shaving.

h. Dr. Pinkham is not really tall; but he is thin, and his thinness causes him to look taller than he is.

i. I finished college having a grossly exaggerated sense of my own importance.

j. The sandwiches were ordered, and they were soon placed before us by the waiter.

k. On our way to town we paused in the city park, which was glowing with dahlias, chrysanthemums, and purple gayfeathers.

l. Uncle Ned appears to be heart-broken, but he gives that impression at every funeral, and so no one pays any attention to him.

m. He looked over the side of the plane, only to see people scattering in all directions, or looking anxiously up, as if they feared the worst.

n. My brother is a wearer of a fraternity emblem, and I myself hope to be, like him, a member of a fraternity; yet I must admit that I am not entirely in favor of fraternities.

o. As yet his belief in himself has not proved to be a confidence which has been misplaced.

Experiment with transpositions in the following sentences, and study the different effects you obtain:

a. Her small, bare, and silvery feet gleamed in the black mirror of marble beneath her.

b. A prevalent feature of these compositions was a nursed and petted melancholy.

c. The noise and tumult was so great that conversation was impossible.

    d. The first rule for a good style is that the author should have something valuable to say.

    e. The ceremony over, they saw the small figure rise and, with the same consummate grace, the same amazing dignity, pass out from among them, as she had come in, alone.

4. Continuity.

    a. What arrangement of ideas would you adopt to gain continuity of idea in compositions on the following subjects:

The importance of Negro life in modern literature and art.

The American Punitive Expedition into Mexico in 1916.

How to play football.

The Yellow Peril.

The meaning of recent economic developments in America.

Types of sailing vessels.

Types of students.

    b. Write transitional sentences or paragraphs to connect the paragraphs suggested by each of the topic sentences in the following groups:

(1) Murillo studied under Velasquez.

Murillo's "Immaculate Conception" represents the Virgin as a beautiful vision of womanhood.

"The Adoration of the Shepherds" portrays the familiar story of the first Christmas night.

(2) Worn-out, second-hand books are often inefficient as texts.

They may be a means of spreading disease.

(3) In moments of reverie, we may idealize the simple bucolic state in which our ancestors lived.

Such a highly complex civilization as ours requires highly trained intelligences.

(4) A fundamental characteristic of child-life is that it struggles to move things.

Until recent times the schools taught by means of textbooks alone.

Laboratories now play a large part in the teaching of science.

(5) The layman should know the causes of tuberculosis.

Among the indirect causes may be listed anything that
tends to lower the resistance of a normal body.
The direct cause is the tubercle bacillus.

c. Give continuity to the sentences in the following paragraph by
using as many transitional devices as you can. Combine sentences
if you wish:

A few weeks ago I was reading *Mexico and its Heritage*, and
I came across two pictures of two Mexican huts which were very
different from each other. On one side of the page was pictured
a substantial house of native stone. The other picture showed a
ramshackle dwelling of reeds, corrugated iron, and rocks, all put
together in a slipshod fashion. The caption read: "The effect of
civilization." I paused to count again the blessings of Nordic culture. I felt very smug indeed until the other day when I came
across a replica of that Mexican hut on a farm near my own American city. This one was not intended for use as a dwelling; but
even so, it was a disreputable structure. Of course this shed was
built in such a slipshod fashion because of economic pressure. One
might use the American farm building as evidence that farm culture is declining. That would not be altogether justifiable. The
shed set me to thinking about farm-houses in general, and comparing them to their predecessors of a few years ago.

d. Write a paragraph on some subject suggested in the Exercises at the end of Chapter I. Use a key-word throughout your
paragraph.

Chapter III

VIGOR IN STYLE

SMOOTHNESS, beauty, and vigor are all terms of approval. But they are not the same thing, for a piece of writing may have any one of the three without having the others. Indeed, the presence of the last may often exclude the others. In the following delightful passage, Stevenson has adopted the smooth and easy style of the familiar essayist which, though not languid, would certainly never be described as essentially vigorous and forceful:

And what would it be to grow old? For, after a certain distance, every step we take in life we find the ice growing thinner below our feet, and all around us and behind us we see our contemporaries going through. By the time a man gets well into the seventies, his continued existence is a mere miracle; and when he lays his old bones in bed for the night, there is an overwhelming probability that he will never see the day. Do the old men mind it, as a matter of fact? Why, no. They were never the merrier; they have their grog at night, and tell the raciest stories; they hear of the death of people about their own age, or even younger, not as if it was a grisly warning, but with a simple childlike pleasure at having outlived someone else; and when a draught might puff them out like a guttering candle, or a bit of a stumble shatter them like so much glass, their old hearts keep sound and unaffrighted, and they go on, bubbling with laughter, through years of man's age compared to which the valley at Balaclava was as safe and peaceful as a village cricket-green on Sunday. It may fairly be questioned (if we look to the peril only) whether it was a much more daring feat for Curtius to plunge into the gulf, than for any old gentleman of ninety to doff his clothes and clamber into bed.[1]

[1] From "Æs Triplex," in the volume *Virginibus Puerisque*. Reprinted by permission of Charles Scribner's Sons.

Compare this graceful passage with a paragraph from Carlyle:

All true Work is sacred; in all true Work, were it but true hand-labor, there is something of divineness. Labor, wide as the Earth, has its summit in Heaven. Sweat of the brow; and up from that to sweat of the brain, sweat of the heart; which includes all Kepler calculations, Newton meditations, all Sciences, all spoken Epics, all acted Heroisms, Martyrdoms,—up to that "Agony of blood sweat," which all men have called divine! O brother, if this is not "worship," then I say, the more pity for worship; for this is the noblest thing yet discovered under God's sky. Who art thou that complainest of thy life of toil? Complain not. Look up, my wearied brother; see thy fellow Workmen there, in God's Eternity; surviving there, they alone surviving: sacred Band of the Immortals, Celestial Bodyguard of the Empire of Mankind. Even in the weak Human Memory they survive so long, as saints, as heroes, as gods; they alone surviving; peopling, they alone, the unmeasured solitudes of Time! To thee Heaven, though severe, is *not* unkind; Heaven is kind,—as a noble Mother; as that Spartan Mother, saying while she gave her son his shield, "With it, my son, or upon it!" Thou too shall return *home* in honor, doubt it not,—if in the battle thou keep thy shield!

How vigorous, how energetic it is! Rude, uncouth, and inelegant, yet it thrills with its strength and its vehemence. But Carlyle did not always write thus, as a study of some of his letters and of his earlier work will show.

Many a time, likewise, every writer must choose between two types of style. Patrick Henry did not invariably use the Give-me-liberty-or-give-me-death style; and Theodore Roosevelt could pen quaint little epistles to his children. The style to be used depends, of course, on the subject. A description of a tropical hurricane would require one sort of style; a description of Lake Placid in the moonlight would require another. A speech demanding war would require one sort of style; a funeral oration on a sweet old lady would require another. An argument in favor of scientific as opposed to liberal education would require one sort of style; an essay on the pleasures of fishing would require another.

Indeed, there are almost as many styles as there are kinds of subjects. To catalogue them would be difficult; to discuss them would be both impossible and useless. Yet we can quite profitably study the elements of writing which contribute toward making, on the one hand, for vigor of style, and, on the other, for beauty of style. We shall begin with the first.

1. Intellectual Vigor.—In a way, the two words just written look absurd in a book of advice about writing. For advice, however good, cannot create intellectual vigor in anybody. A cynic would say, as a matter of fact, that a writer who has any intellectual vigor needs no advice. Perhaps the cynic would be right. We have all seen beautiful girls who would be beautiful under any conditions, and need no artificial make-up or professional advice to help them. Nevertheless, even these beauties look their *best* under certain favorable (and frequently quite artificial) conditions. Moreover, we have seen girls who are not beautiful unless they have certain advantages of dress, light, or make-up, but who are undeniably beautiful when they have these advantages. Advice about intellectual vigor is like advice about beauty. A few writers do not need it; most writers can profit by it; and some writers would be nothing without it.

a. *Labored Intellectuality.*—As a first hint about creating a style with the appearance of intellectual vigor: It is paradoxical and unjust—but laboriousness of style often conveys a stronger impression of intellectual vigor than does ease of style. Laboriousness consisting of inversions, transpositions, difficult structures, relationships not easily grasped, long or involved sentences, superfine discriminations, parenthetical explanations—all of these have a tremendous effect on a large body of readers. True, they frequently hide poverty of idea and muddiness of intellect; yet they do have a legitimate use among shrewd or crafty authors. In mock-serious writing, they create a humorous incongruity between actual triviality of idea and the apparently intellectual style. In public life, they make simple facts appear important when policy demands that they appear so, or they take the edge off truths which would cut sharply if not framed in a laboriously intellectual style. And they impress the class of people who must be impressed sometimes, but who cannot be impressed by honest simplicity.

The following paragraph from Cabell's foreword to his *Figures of Earth* shows how a skillful writer may deliberately employ a labored, mock-serious style to create an effect of sententiousness:

To you (whom I take to be as familiar with the Manuelian cycle of romance as is any person now alive) it has for some while appeared, I know, a not uncurious circumstance that in the *Key to the Popular Tales of Poictesme* there should have been included so little directly relative to Manuel himself. No reader of the *Popular Tales* (as I recall your saying at the Alum when we talked over, among so many other matters, this monumental book) can fail to note that always Don Manuel looms obscurely in the background, somewhat as do King Arthur and white-bearded Charlemagne in their several cycles, dispensing justice and bestowing rewards, and generally arranging the future, for the survivors of the outcome of stories which more intimately concern themselves with Anavalt and Coth and Holden, or even with Sclaug and Thragnar, than with the liege-lord of Poictesme.[2]

This next paragraph, taken from an editorial in the daily paper, garbs a few simple truths in a highly laborious style:

The resignation of Judge L——— affords a revelation of the unwisdom of the legislature in making an excessive reduction in the salaries of members of the judiciary. Rejecting the advice of prominent members of the bar of the State, of many other responsible citizens, and of most of the newspapers, the last session of the legislature cut the compensation of judges to such an extent that it was inevitable many of the abler judges would leave the service of the State. Unfortunately, Judge L——— is one of those who find it impossible to

[2] Copyright, 1921, by James Branch Cabell. Reprinted by permission of Mr. Cabell's publishers, Robert McBride and Company.

make the financial sacrifice that is required of judiciary members who serve under the new schedule of salaries.

This could be translated:

Judge L———'s resignation shows the unwisdom of the legislature in reducing the salaries of judges. Rejecting the advice of prominent lawyers, other responsible citizens, and most newspapers of the State, the legislature cut salaries of judges so sharply that withdrawal by many of the abler judges became inevitable. Unfortunately, Judge L——— was one of the judges who could not afford to serve under the reduced salary schedule.

The first version contains 111 words; the second, 67 words—a reduction of 40 per cent. The editor who wrote the first version was excusable only because he wanted to make his editorial sound as important as possible to people who care little for style.

The following paragraph, describing a crisis in the London Economic Conference in 1933, softens and obscures a perilous fact behind a cloud of words. That is, it does so until the last sentence, where the truth slips out in a blunt statement in extraordinary contrast to the preceding elaborately intellectual sentence:

The official announcement to the meeting said that the formula to be submitted to a plenary conference was only in nebulous form, but that it would include provision for indefinite adjournment of the monetary side of the conference and all the phases of the economic side which were in any way contingent upon money matters. That would leave little.

To call the passages quoted above vigorous writing would be false, and to call them intellectual would be flattering. But they do have a spurious sort of intellectuality that deceives a certain type of reader. And the kind of writing they represent is worth knowing about if only for the sake of its being avoided.

Yet in their deliberate shamming of intellectual vigor, they are, perhaps, superior to the writing which is so intellectual as to be incomprehensible. For instance, the abstruse intellectuality of the following passage, taken from a public lecture by a philosophy professor, is inexcusable:

That which is given at any moment is a perceptual perspective with an organism at the focus or center. The perspective called "mine" is mine only in virtue of the fact that the body called "mine" is, although only one factor among others, the focal factor of the perspective. It is the focal factor because even though at times the body is not given (as when we are said not to be self-conscious but absorbed in the "objective world") it can easily be "recovered," and because while the body varies with the other factors of the perspective, the other factors of the perspective seem to vary in an even greater degree with changes in the body.

When the reader of average intelligence cannot quickly understand what a writer is talking about, it is the writer's fault. If the reader must ponder, wonder, reread, and then at last remain in doubt, the writing is bad.

The following passage from an essay of Pater's on Wordsworth is not so bad as that just quoted, but is typical of the sort of thing which of late years has brought Pater into disrepute:

Sometimes as he dwelt upon those moments of profound imaginative power, in which the outward object appears to take color and expression, a new nature almost, from the prompting of the observant mind, the actual world would, as it were, dissolve and detach itself, flake by flake, and he himself seemed to be the creator, and when he would, the destroyer, of the world in which he lived—that old isolating thought of many a brain-sick mystic of ancient and modern times.

b. *True Intellectuality.*—Leaving this false or deceiving sort of intellectuality, we may pass on to a kind of style which shows an authentic intellectual vigor. Description of this style is difficult, and advice about how to achieve it almost futile. A seed catalogue I pick up is definitely non-intellectual in style:

The popularity this plant has gained in the short time since its introduction is simply marvelous. It is one of the finest decorative plants ever introduced. It grows rapidly under all conditions, and its inexpensiveness places it within the reach of everyone. The plant has often been called "Fountain Fern" on account of its gracefully drooping habit. It has matured fronds that often attain a length of four feet.

Nobody can justly complain about the clarity and the simplicity of this passage. It serves its purpose of conveying information, and it is in keeping with its lowly position in the world of letters. But nobody would think of it as having an intellectually vigorous style. Let us analyze it to try to discover what characteristics it has, and what it lacks.

In idea, it is concrete rather than abstract; it states simple, unoriginal facts of observation such as anybody might make; it really *develops* no idea; it gives no obviously independent personal opinions; it draws no inferences and makes no generalizations from presented data; it delves into none of the complexities of idea which might suggest themselves; and it deals with obviously unimportant ideas.

In structure, its sentences are short; only two sentences are complex; and one sentence is compound only by having two unrelated ideas joined by the ever useful "and." It has no transitional devices, no transpositions, no parallel structures indicating a synthetical intelligence at work, no variety of structure suggesting variety of idea.

Now contrast the passage from the seed catalogue with the following paragraph from Matthew Arnold:

I am going to ask whether the present movement for ousting letters from their old predominance in education, and for transferring the predominance in education to the natural sciences, whether this brisk and flourishing movement ought to prevail, and whether it is likely in the end it really will prevail. An objection may be raised which I will anticipate. My own studies have been almost wholly in letters, and my visits to the field of the natural sciences have been very slight and inadequate, although those sciences have always strongly moved my curiosity. A man of letters, it will perhaps be said, is not competent to discuss the comparative merits of letters and natural science as means of education. To this objection, I reply, first of all, that his incompetence, if he attempts the discussion but is really incompetent for it, will be abundantly visible; nobody will be taken in; he will have plenty of sharp observers and critics who will save mankind from that danger. But the line I am going to follow is, as you will soon discover, so extremely simple, that perhaps it may be followed without failure even by one who for a more ambitious line of discussion would be quite incompetent.

It sounds original because it is personal: it expresses personal opinions and personal experience. The first personal pronoun or adjective is used no less than seven times in the passage, and, in addition, it is implied in all the sentences about "a man of letters." The ideas presented are not mere concrete records of observation, but are ideas involving generalizations about facts. They are ideas with many complex facets of which the author is aware, and which he is willing to develop. And they are ideas of wide importance because they involve the thought and the conduct of great masses of human beings.

In structure, the sentences are long enough to avoid seeming childish: they average thirty-four words in length, whereas the sentences from the seed catalogue averaged only fourteen words. In the entire passage, there is no simple sentence, and no sentence compounded of only two simple independent clauses joined by "and." Throughout there are inversions for the sake of clarity, interpolations for the sake of completeness, and transitional devices for the sake of continuity. In a word, the author seems aware in the passage of the involved complexities, the many different points of view, the subtle significances which surround ideas. The world to him is not a lesson in the obvious. Moreover, he suggests the variety and complexity of the world by the variety and complexity of his sentence-elements; and yet he shows the power of his intellect by fusing these various aspects of the world into a coherent and unified piece of writing. When a student of composition can do all this, he will have an intellectually vigorous style.

A useful device making for a vigorously intellectual style is the *antithetical structure* offering mutually opposing views of the same idea. This device nearly always gives to writing a touch of sober strength, of rationality, of unhurried power. It shows a mind well balanced, unprejudiced, and unsparing. Dr. Johnson, the dominating figure of the Age of Reason, the ponderous philosopher whose opinions were like the heavy hand of law on a hundred years of literature—Dr. Johnson seldom penned a line which contained no judiciously balanced antithetical structure. Paragraph after paragraph unwinds in the manner of the following:

Of him that knows much it is natural to suppose that he has read with diligence; yet I rather believe that the knowledge of Dryden was gleaned from accidental intelligence and various conversation. . . . I do not suppose that he despised books, or intentionally neglected them; but that he was carried out, by the impetuosity of his genius, to more vivid and speedy instructors, and that his studies were rather desultory and fortuitous than constant and systematical. . . .

Criticism, either didactic or defensive, occupies almost all his prose, except those pages he has devoted to his patrons; but none of his prefaces were ever thought tedious. They have not the formality of a settled style, in which the first half of the sentence betrays the other. The clauses are never balanced, nor the periods modeled; every word seems to drop by chance, though it falls into its proper place. Nothing is cold or languid; the whole is airy, animated, and vigorous; what is little is gay, what is great is splendid. He may be thought to mention himself too frequently; but, while he forces himself upon our esteem, we cannot refuse him to stand high in his own. Everything is excused by the play of images and the sprightliness of expression. Though all is easy, nothing is feeble; though all seems careless, there is nothing harsh; and though since his earlier works more than a century has passed, they have nothing yet uncouth or obsolete.

This kind of writing is hardly to be imitated on a large scale; it is neither spontaneous, nor emotional, nor imaginative. But it is powerful. Nobody reading it can suspect the writer of having a weak intellect or undigested opinions. And one has only to contrast it with any book review in the Sunday newspaper to see why Dr. Johnson is immortal, and the reviewer is not.

So far we have dealt with the studied and elaborate sentence structure of vigorous intellect. But, on the other hand, a vigorously intellectual style may be just the opposite in its simplicity from the complex passages quoted above. When a writer is sure that his ideas in themselves are powerful, he need have only a *direct*, *straightforward style* which pounds away at the reader with simple, powerful logic, and simple, powerful facts.

Let love be without dissimulation. Abhor that which is evil; cleave to that which is good. Be kindly affectioned to one another with brotherly love; in honour preferring one another; not slothful in business; fervent in spirit; serving the Lord; rejoicing in hope; patient in tribulation; continuing instant in prayer; distributing to the necessity of saints; given to hospitality. Bless them which persecute you: bless, and curse not. Rejoice with them that do rejoice, and weep with them that weep. Be of the same mind one toward another. Mind not high things, but condescend to men of low estate. Be not wise in your own conceits. Recompense to no man evil for evil. Provide things honest in the sight of all men. If it be possible, as much as lieth in you, live peaceably with all men. Dearly beloved, avenge not yourselves, but rather give place unto wrath: for it is written, Vengeance is mine: I will repay, saith the Lord. Therefore if thine enemy hunger, feed him; if he thirst, give him drink: for in so doing thou shalt heap coals of fire on his head. Be not overcome of evil, but overcome evil with good.

In this passage from Paul's Epistle to the Romans is so much meat, so much weight of idea and power of logic that the writing needs no subtlety of style, no complexity of structure, no variety of form to give it vigor.

In this next (a letter from the anonymous Junius to Sir William Draper, who had taken it upon himself to reply to Junius's attacks on political abuses of the day) strength of idea and of feeling like-wise makes superfluous any style but the most straight and hard-hitting:

25. September, 1769.

SIR,

After so long an interval, I did not expect to see the debate revived between us. My answer to your last letter shall be short; for I write to you with reluctance, and I hope we shall now conclude our correspondence for ever.

Had you been originally and without provocation attacked by an anonymous writer, you would have some right to demand his name. But in this cause you are a volunteer. You engaged in it with the unpremeditated gallantry of a soldier. You were content to set your name in opposition to a man, who would probably continue in concealment. You understood the terms upon which we were to correspond, and gave at least a tacit consent to them. After voluntarily attacking me under the character of Junius, what possible right have you to know me under any other? . . .

You cannot but know that the republication of my letters was no more than a catchpenny contrivance of a printer, in which it was impossible I should be concerned, and for which I am in no way answerable. At the same time I wish you to understand that if I do not take the trouble of reprinting these papers, it is not from any fear of giving offense to Sir William Draper.

Your remarks upon a signature, adopted merely for distinction, are unworthy of notice; but when you tell me I have submitted to be called a liar and a coward, I must ask you in my turn, whether you seriously think it any way incumbent on me to take notice of the silly invectives of every simpleton, who writes in a news-paper; and what opinion you would have conceived of my discretion, if I had suffered myself to be the dupe of so shallow an artifice? . . .

JUNIUS

These, then, are the two styles which may be justly said to have intellectual vigor. One style is involved, the other direct; one is complex, the other simple; one is subtle, the other forceful; one is studied and various, the other is plain and uniform. One expresses ideas important for their originality, for their discriminating perception, for their keen intuitiveness, for their nice logic. The other expresses ideas important for their sincerity, for their open clarity, for their blunt power, for their obvious truth. One is the result of an astute mind at work on difficult and intricate problems; the other is the result of a strong mind at work on elemental truths.

2. Emotional Vigor.—In real life we convey ideas to one another by means of words, and we convey emotions not merely by means of words, but also by gestures, tones of the voice, expressions of the face, movements of the body sometimes quite unconscious. But in writing, we must convey emotions to one another by means of words alone. To accomplish this, we have, first of all, to convince the reader that we ourselves feel emotion. For people are like a herd of animals: fright, curiosity, or anger on the part of one is conveyed subtly to the whole herd. All that is necessary is that the herd be aware of the emotional state of one of its members.

The first business, therefore, of a writer who wishes to make his reader have an emotion, is to make the reader feel that the writer has the emotion. It is not sufficient that the writer merely *have* the emotion; he must make readers believe he has it, and thus *convey* the emotion to them. The devices by which readers are made to believe that the writer feels emotion are so varied that they can be discussed in only the most general way. It is obvious, however, that all emotions may be divided into two groups: those which are not in harmony with the intellect, and those which are aided and abetted by the intellect. Thus, a man may be so angry with his child that he would wish to harm the child seriously. That is a feeling not in harmony with the intellect. On the other hand, the man may be angry at an example of injustice and oppression in his daily life, and he may find that the more he weighs and considers the condition, the angrier he becomes. Here his feeling harmonizes with the intellect, and grows the more powerful for intellectual influence.

a. *Uncontrolled Emotion.*—To convince the reader that the writer feels the first sort of emotion, a writer would use certain forms of expression that he would not use in trying to convey the second sort of emotion. For instance, he would not employ long, involved sentences, elaborate sentence structures, devices for effecting smooth continuity, and so on. His writing would be rough, breathless, exclamatory—sentences short or incomplete, relation between sentences obscure, transition from sentence to sentence, idea to idea, and image to image abrupt and unplanned. This sort of violent incoherence is Carlyle's chief trick in writing. The following paragraph, chosen almost at random, is an excellent example of his vigorously emotional style. The semicolons and colons in the passage help deceive the reader's eye; but they have actually the effect of periods, as reading the passage aloud will prove:

No *Dilettantism* in this Mahomet; it is a business of Reprobation and Salvation with him, of Time and Eternity: he is in deadly earnest about it! Dilettantism, hypothesis, speculation, a kind of amateur-search for Truth, toying and coquetting with Truth: this is the sorest sin. The root of all other imaginable sins. It consists in the heart and soul of the man never having been *open* to the Truth;— "living in vain show." Such a man not only utters and produces falsehoods, but *is* himself a falsehood. The rational moral principle, spark of the Divinity, is sunk deep in him, in quiet paralysis of life-death. The very falsehoods of Mahomet are truer than the truths of such a man. He is the insincere man: smooth-polished, respectable

in some times and places: inoffensive, says nothing harsh to anybody;
most *cleanly*,—just as carbonic acid is, which is death and poison.

Ruskin has a passage of similar emotional incoherence which,
except that it is more subdued, might have been written by Carlyle:

Their labor, their sorrow, and their death. Mark the three. Labor:
by sea and land, in field and city, at forge and furnace, at helm and
plough. No pastoral indolence nor classic pride shall stand between
him and the troubling of the world; still less between him and the
toil of his country,—blind, tormented, unwearied, marvellous England.

Also their Sorrow: Ruin of all their glorious work, passing away of
their thoughts and their honor, mirage of pleasure, FALLACY OF
HOPE; gathering of weed on temple step; gaining of wave on deserted strand; weeping of the mother for the children, desolate by her
breathless firstborn in the streets of the city, desolate by her last sons
slain, among the beasts of the field.

And their Death. That old Greek question again;—yet unanswered.
The unconquerable spectre still flitting among the forest trees at
twilight; rising ribbed out of the sea-sand;—white, a strange Aphro-
dite,—out of the sea-foam; stretching its gray, cloven wings among the
clouds; turning the light of their sunsets into blood.

The short, sharp style of Dr. Johnson in his letter to Macpherson
is another example of the same sort of emotionally vigorous
writing:

I received your foolish and impudent letter. Any violence offered
me I shall do my best to repel; and what I cannot do for myself, the
law shall do for me. I hope I shall never be deterred from detecting
what I think a cheat, by the menaces of a ruffian.

What would you have me retract? I thought your book an imposture; I think it an imposture still. For this opinion I have given my
reasons to the public, which I here dare you to refute. Your rage I
defy. Your abilities, since your Homer, are not so formidable; and
what I hear of your morals inclines me to pay regard not to what you
shall say, but to what you shall prove. You may print this if you will.

This sort of writing is not common anywhere except in short passages. Carlyle, indeed, is the only important English writer who consistently used it on a grand scale. The following extract from Hazlitt, though fundamentally in the same vein as the preceding passages, is less extreme, and is more the usual thing in writing. It shows emotional vigor not much weighted by intellect or by intellectual considerations; yet it lacks the incoherence and the violence of the other passages:

> The florid style is the reverse of the familiar. The last is employed as an unvarnished medium to convey ideas; the first is resorted to as a spangled veil to conceal the want of them. When there is nothing to be set down but words, it costs little to have them fine. Look through the dictionary, and cull out a *florilegium*, rival the *tulippo-mania*. *Rouge* high enough, and never mind the natural complexion. The vulgar, who are not in the secret, will admire the look of preter-natural health and vigour; and the fashionable, who regard only appearances, will be delighted with the imposition. Keep to your sounding generalities, your tinkling phrases, and all will be well. Swell out an unmeaning truism in a perfect tympany of style. A thought, a distinction is the rock on which all this brittle cargo of verbiage splits at once. Such writers have merely *verbal* imaginations, that retain nothing but words.

b. *Governed Emotion.*—Much more frequent than the style represented in these passages is emotional writing showing a strict harmony between feeling and intellect. This harmony manifests itself in two ways—in pattern and in imagery.

(1) *Pattern* consists, essentially, of repeats. One line (thus: /) does not make a pattern; nor do two different kinds of lines (thus: —/) make a pattern. But a series of similar lines repeated (thus: /////) makes pattern. Likewise, a series of similar structures, sounds, or accents makes a pattern in sentences.

For some psychological reason too complex to be discussed here, the human mind under emotional strain tends to express itself in patterns, usually of sounds. The simple beat of tom-toms, the keenings of Celtic women over their dead, the waving of garments, the repetition of exclamations, the steps of a dance—and so on up to the complex repeats and rhythms of meter, alliteration, and rhyme in poetry—all these are patterns in which human emotion expresses itself. In prose, these patterns consist of rhythms (which will be discussed more fully later), parallel structures, and repetitions.

Hebrew poetry consists of parallel structures expressing over and over again different aspects of the same idea. Since much of the Bible is poetry, much of it is made up of such parallelisms. For example:

Give unto the Lord, O ye mighty, give unto the Lord glory and strength.

Give unto the Lord the glory due unto his name; worship the Lord in the beauty of holiness.

The voice of the Lord is upon the waters: the God of glory thundereth: the Lord is upon many waters.

The voice of the Lord is powerful; the voice of the Lord is full of majesty.

The voice of the Lord breaketh the cedars; yea, the Lord breaketh the cedars of Lebanon.

He maketh them also to skip like a calf; Lebanon and Sirion like a young unicorn.

The voice of the Lord divideth the flames of fire.

The voice of the Lord shaketh the wilderness; the Lord shaketh the wilderness of Kadesh.

This trick of repetition is carried over into the prose parts of the Bible. Paul writes:

Though I speak with the tongues of men and of angels, and have not charity, I am become as sounding brass, or a tinkling cymbal.

And though I have the gift of prophecy, and understand all mysteries and all knowledge: and though I have all faith, so that I could remove mountains, and have not charity, I am nothing.

And though I bestow all my goods to feed the poor, and though I give my body to be burned, and have not charity, it profiteth me nothing.

Charity suffereth long, and is kind; charity envieth not; charity vaunteth not itself, is not puffed up,

Doth not behave itself unseemly, seeketh not her own, is not easily provoked, thinketh no evil;

Rejoiceth not in iniquity, but rejoiceth in the truth;

Beareth all things, believeth all things, hopeth all things, endureth all things.

It is natural for writers laboring under a strong emotion which is at the same time validated by intellect to speak in these patterned structures; but it is particularly true that writers of the Anglo-Saxon tradition, whose style has been influenced for centuries by the King James Bible, resort continually to this style. Hardly a paragraph from any great English stylist is free of it, and seldom any great emotional moment is without it.

De Quincey writes:

These are the Sorrows; and they are three in number, as the *Graces* are three, who dress man's life with beauty; the Parcæ are three, who weave the dark arras of man's life in their mysterious loom, always with colors sad in part, sometimes angry with tragic crimson and black; the *Furies* are three, who visit with retributions called from the other side of the grave offences that walk upon this; and once even the *Muses* were but three, who fit the harp, the trumpet, or the lute, to the great burden of man's impassioned creations. These are the Sorrows, all three of whom I know.

The passage from Junius, quoted above, is another example of powerful emotion formulating itself into parallel structure. And the following from Huxley is an excellent example of a style manifesting in its complex and long-sustained elements a genuine intellectual vigor, and at the same time manifesting in its patterned structures an extraordinary emotional vigor:

The improver of natural knowledge absolutely refuses to acknowledge authority, as such. For him, scepticism is the highest of duties;
blind faith the one unpardonable sin. And it cannot be otherwise, for
every great advance in natural knowledge has involved the absolute
rejection of authority, the cherishing of the keenest scepticism, the
annihilation of the spirit of blind faith; and the most ardent votary of
science holds his firmest convictions, not because the men he most
venerates holds them; not because their verity is testified by portents
and wonders; but because his experience teaches him that whenever
he chooses to bring these convictions into contact with their primary
source, Nature—whenever he thinks fit to test them by appealing to
experiment and to observation—Nature will confirm them. The man
of science has learned to believe in justification, not by faith, but by
verification.

Very similar is Dr. Johnson's letter to Chesterfield, which should
be contrasted with the letter to Macpherson already quoted. The
last two paragraphs of the Chesterfield letter follow:

Is not a Patron, my Lord, one who looks with unconcern on a man
struggling for life in the water, and when he has reached ground,
encumbers him with help? The notice which you have been pleased
to take of my labours, had it been early, had been kind; but it has
been delayed till I am indifferent, and cannot enjoy it; till I am solitary, and cannot impart it; till I am known, and do not want it. I
hope it is no very cynical asperity, not to confess obligations where no
benefit has been received, or to be unwilling that the Publick should
consider me as owing that to a Patron, which Providence has enabled
me to do for myself.
Having carried on my work thus far with so little obligation to any
favourer of learning, I shall not be disappointed though I should conclude it, if less be possible, with less; for I have long wakened from
that dream of hope, in which I once boasted myself with so much
exultation,

My Lord,
Your Lordship's most humble,
Most obedient servant.

This next, from Ruskin, almost too long to quote, is a supreme example of a powerfully intellectual style which flames with a transcendent emotion. It shows that the two types of vigorous writing—intellectual and emotional—need not be mutually exclusive:

Stand upon the peak of some isolated mountain at daybreak, when the night mists first rise from off the plains, and watch their white and lake-like fields, as they float in level bays and winding gulfs about the islanded summits of the lower hills, untouched yet by more than dawn, colder and more quiet than a windless sea under the moon of midnight; watch when the first sunbeam is sent upon the silver channels, how the foam of their undulating surfaces parts and passes away, and down under their depths the glittering city and green pasture lie like Atlantis, between the white paths of winding rivers; the flakes of light falling every moment faster and broader among the starry spires, as the wreathed surges break and vanish above them, and the confused crests and ridges of the dark hills shorten their gray shadows upon the plain. . . . Wait a little longer, and you shall see those scattered mists rallying in the ravines, and floating up towards you, along the winding valleys, till they crouch in quiet masses, iridescent with the morning light, upon the broad breasts of the higher hills, whose leagues of massy undulation will melt back and back into that robe of material light, until they fade away, lost in its lustre, to appear again above, in serene heaven, like a wild, bright, impossible dream, foundationless and inaccessible, their very bases vanishing in the unsubstantial and mocking blue of the deep lake below. . . . Wait yet a little longer, and you shall see those mists gather themselves into white towers, and stand like fortresses along the promontories, massy and motionless, only piled with every instant higher and higher into the sky, and casting longer shadows athwart the rocks.

(2) It is to be noted that one source of emotion in this passage is its magnificent *imagery*. Indeed, it is characteristic of human beings not only to create patterns of sound or form in times of emotion, but also to vision forth images. We have only to read

Browning's short poem, "In a Gondola," to observe how the agony of emotion under which the young gallant labors brings to his mind a thousand fancies and conceits which the normal, placid mind could never conceive. This next, from Tennyson, shows the same glowing of the imagination in the fire of emotion:

From the meadow your walks have left so sweet
  That whenever a March-wind sighs
He sets the jewel-print of your feet
  In violets blue as your eyes,
To the woody hollows in which we meet
  And the valleys of Paradise.

The slender acacia would not shake
  One long milk-bloom on the tree;
The white lake-blossom fell into the lake
  As the pimpernel dozed on the lea;
But the rose was awake all night for your sake,
  Knowing your promise to me;
The lilies and roses were all awake,
  They sighed for the dawn and thee.

Queen rose of the rosebud garden of girls,
  Come hither, the dances are done,
In gloss of satin and glimmer of pearls,
  Queen lily and rose in one;
Shine out, little head, sunning over with curls,
  To the flowers, and be their sun.

There has fallen a splendid tear
  From the passion-flower at the gate,
She is coming, my dove, my dear;
  She is coming, my life, my fate.
The red rose cries, "She is near, she is near;"
  And the white rose weeps, "She is late;"
The larkspur listens, "I hear, I hear;"
  And the lily whispers, "I wait."

In the well-known Twenty-third Psalm, note the wealth of imagery which pours from a mind undergoing emotion:

The Lord is my shepherd; I shall not want.

He maketh me to lie down in green pastures: he leadeth me beside the still waters.

He restoreth my soul: he leadeth me in the paths of righteousness for his name's sake.

Yea, though I walk through the valley of the shadow of death, I will fear no evil: for thou art with me: thy rod and thy staff they comfort me.

Thou preparest a table before me in the presence of mine enemies: thou anointest my head with oil; my cup runneth over.

Surely goodness and mercy shall follow me all the days of my life: and I will dwell in the house of the Lord for ever.

The characteristic of these passages is not so much completeness and accuracy of observation, as it is *richness of imagination.* Not one complete and colorful picture appears, but a teeming variety of pictures which follow, one after the other, in rapid procession. The truly emotional mind seldom lingers on one object and describes it meticulously, detail by detail. Such a mind leaps, rather, from one object to another, vivifying each in a bold flash of imagination, suggesting each with a single phrase or epithet, and then passing on quickly so that in the end a score of images flash in and out of the mind of the reader. This wealth, variety, and abundance of complete images is what chiefly distinguishes descriptive writing which is truly emotional from that which is merely intellectual.

These images are often figurative. The imagination is not content to restrict itself to the presentation of pictures as they exist, but transforms the pictures into something different, and yet similar. This ability to transform, this facility in creating a multitude of comparisons, this high emotion which sees resemblances where

the commonplace mind sees only separate and distinct existences
—this is the trait in a writer which makes for the highest poetry
and the most stirring prose. Francis Thompson, the mystic poet,
is remembered chiefly for the daring leap of his imagination which
marks breath-taking resemblances between objects never before
spoken of in the same breath. Thus, in his poetry, God becomes a
hound pursuing his quarry; a poppy is a "yawn of fire"; the
poet's thought runs "before the hooves of sunrise"; and the setting
sun becomes a "globed yellow grape" which Evening "bursts
against her stained mouth."

Good prose writers use figurative language much more than the
average person believes. Following is a paragraph from Washington Irving, with the figures in italics:

Whoever has made a voyage up the Hudson must remember the
Kaatskill mountains. They are a *dismembered branch* of the great
Appalachian *family*, and are seen away to the west of the river,
swelling up to a *noble* height, and *lording* it over the surrounding
country. Every change of season, every change of weather, indeed,
every hour of the day, produces some change in the *magical* hues
and shapes of these mountains, and they are regarded by all the good
wives, far and near, as *perfect barometers*. When the weather is fair
and settled, they are *clothed* in blue and purple, and *print* their bold
outlines on the clear evening sky; but sometimes, when the rest of the
landscape is cloudless, they will gather a *hood* of gray vapors about
their summits, which, in the last rays of the setting sun, will *glow
and light up like a crown of glory*.

This next simple piece of description (from Stevenson) does not
necessarily show emotional vigor; but it does indicate a mind
vividly alive and strenuously alert to catch and translate every
image in nature:

While I was thus delaying, a *gush* of steady wind, *as long as a
heavy sigh, poured* direct out of the *quarter* of the morning. It was

cold, and set me sneezing. The trees near at hand *tossed their black plumes* in its passage; and I could see the thin distant *spires of pine* along the edge of the hill rock slightly to and fro against the *golden* east. Ten minutes after, the sunlight *spread at a gallop* along the hillside, *scattering* shadows and sparkles, and the day had come completely.[3]

In this next, by H. M. Tomlinson, the scene described excites a vigorous emotion which manifests itself in picturesque figures of speech:

The berg rose out of the level forest by the river, and to Colet it was anomalous. It was an isolated mass of white limestone, a lofty *island* in the *ocean* of jungle. Its pale cliffs *fell* sheer to the *green billows*. Its summit was flat, but was so near to the clouds that its trees were but a dark *undulating strip*. Its *walls*, when glimpses from below through breaks in the *roof* of the forest could be found, appeared to overhang, but there were *scarves* and *girdles* of green on their *bare ribs*. An eagle soaring athwart its loftier crags *was a drifting mote*. Stalactites were pendent before the black *portholes* of caves in *upper stories, like corbels over the outlooks of a castle of the sagas*. If the number of those dark apertures meant anything, then the berg was hollow, was *honeycombed* with cavities. This enormity was not inviting, even in a morning light; not in such a land as that. The unexplored *dungeons* of such a *castle* might hide anything.[4]

With this we shall leave the problem of emotional vigor in writing. Other devices, perhaps—other methods than those mentioned in this section—may give an impression of emotional vigor; but these are the most important. Abrupt and incoherent writing, patterned writing, profuse images, original and vivid figures of speech—these are the best indications of emotional vigor in writing.

[3] From *Travels with a Donkey* (1879). Reprinted here by permission of Charles Scribner's Sons.
[4] From chap. xxxi of *Gallions Reach* (1927). Reprinted here by permission of the publishers, Harper & Brothers.

EXERCISES

1. Intellectual Vigor.

a. Write in an intellectually laborious style a mock-serious account of some trivial campus or local happening.

In the same kind of style, write a serious account of the same happening. Try to make it seem of genuine importance.

Suppose you are the editor of your college newspaper. You wish to make a sharp criticism of some campus occurrence or custom, but you do not wish to offend anyone. By means of an editorial written in an intellectual style, accomplish your purpose.

b. Write an essay on some subject which has many purely reflective rather than merely informational complexities, and which will demand much original thinking on your part. Try to do justice to the complexities by developing them properly in a mature and thoughtful style. Choose such subjects as the following:

What have we a right to believe?
An examination of the philosophy of optimism.
Culture and a democracy.
The nature of man.
Property.
Must the right triumph?
A new economic plan.
What is art?
Tragedy and the tragic.
Comedy and the comic.
What one loses in going to college.
Education as an end in itself.
If I could educate a boy (or girl) as I wished.

Write paragraphs composed of antithetical sentences on the following subjects:

Undergraduate enthusiasms.
The evils of examinations.
Dangers of business success.
Americanism.
The lecture method of instruction.

Choose any of the subjects given in this set of Exercises, crystallize your opinion about it into a short thesis sentence, and then write a theme on the subject. Use a straightforward, terse, pounding style in which you express elemental truths simply.

2. Emotional Vigor.

a. Write two emotional paragraphs on each of the following topics. In one paragraph, try to give the impression that emotion is beyond intellectual control, and, in the other, that emotion is in harmony with the intellect:

A description of the death of some friend or relative.

A description of a flood, a fire, a windstorm, or some other natural disaster.

An account of some battle which figures in the history of your state.

An argument against some political abuse now agitating your section of the country.

A characterization of a favorite historical (or contemporary or fictional) hero.

b. Employing series of images, portray emotionally each of the following:

Trees after a rain.

The coming of winter.

The geological history of your home state.

The song of a street musician.

The grief of an animal over the death of her young.

The grief of a wife over the death of her husband.

The delight of a convalescent walking in the woods (or along the seashore or over a meadow) for the first time after a long and dangerous illness.

The love of a timid girl for some man whom she regards as a hero.

The hatred of a petty employee for his foreman.

The fear of discovery on the part of a murderer.

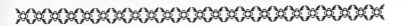

Chapter IV

VIGOR IN STYLE (*continued*)

3. Vigor of Wording.—We have spoken of the way in which involved and closely woven sentence structure, blunt and straight-forward sentence structure, abrupt and exclamatory sentence structure, and patterned sentence structure make for intellectual and emotional vigor. It remains now for us to examine the smaller elements of composition to discover how they, too, may contribute toward a vigorous style.

a. *Brevity*.—One of the first principles a writer ought to remember is the principle of *brevity*. In general, it is a sound doctrine which demands the greatest number of ideas in the shortest space. This does not mean that writing should be sketchy, incomplete, or hasty. Important ideas deserve to be elaborated, dwelt on, and discussed fully. The doctrine means merely that, however many ideas enter into a composition, the statement of each of them should consume as little space as possible.

The disease of wordiness has two quite different forms. One shows a general swelling involving the entire organism of the composition, and the other shows only small local abnormalities in the individual members of the composition-body. The one is ostentatious, the other secretive; the one is easily detected and, in most patients, easily cured; the other is insidious and hard to cure.

(1) The first kind has two symptoms: the *bookishly artificial use of unnecessarily long words*, and the deliberate use of too many words. Sometimes one of these symptoms predominates over the

other, and sometimes both are pronounced. Dr. Johnson's famous revision of his remark about a certain comedy "which had not wit enough to keep it sweet" is a good example of the first symptom. Dr. Johnson corrected himself: "A play which does not possess enough vitality to preserve it from putrefaction." The fault here is not too many words, but too many syllables. At another time the Doctor assured a "little thick, short-legged" printer's devil: "When you consider with how little mental power and corporeal labour a printer can get a guinea a week, it is a very desirable occupation for you." Boswell has the same habit of profuse syllabification:

However confident of the rectitude of his own mind, Johnson may have felt sincere uneasiness that his conduct should be erroneously imputed to unworthy motives, by good men; and that the influence of his valuable writings should on that account be in any degree obstructed or lessened.

This sort of wordiness is seldom seen nowadays except where its purpose is humorous—cheaply humorous, most often. O. Henry's use of long words, however, for a humorous effect is extraordinarily adroit:

Mrs. Hopkins was like a thousand others. The auriferous tooth, the sedentary disposition, the Sunday afternoon wanderlust, the draught upon the delicatessen store for home-made comforts, the furor for department store marked-down sales, the feeling of superiority to the lady in the third-floor front who wore genuine ostrich tips and had two names over her bell, the mucilaginous hours during which she remained glued to the window sill, the vigilant avoidance of the instalment man, the tireless patronage of the acoustics of the dumbwaiter shaft—all the attributes of the Gotham flat-dweller.[1]

Much more common is the other symptom, but much harder to describe. It is the stiff-starched, *now-I-take-my-pen-in-hand style;* the padded style of the student who feels that he must be scholarly

---

[1] From *The Voice of the City*, by O. Henry, copyright, 1904, by Doubleday, Doran and Company, Inc. Reprinted by permission.

and formal in his writing; the patronizingly careful style of textbook writers; the stiffly personal style of prefaces; the painfully
impersonal style of learned articles; the gravely sententious style
of editorials. In a word, it is a style affected by writers too much
aware of the seriousness of their missions, and too eager to make
other people likewise aware. As Dr. Johnson said, it is a style which
tries to appear dignified by walking on tiptoe.

At some time in life [a freshman theme begins] we all stop for a
moment and ask ourselves what this world of ours really is, what its
true meaning may be, and toward what unknown destiny it is tending. From that moment, we become aware that we are philosophers
in the deeper sense of the word.

Another freshman puts it:

What is the meaning of life? When I am asked this all-important
question, I do not make some visible motion with my arms or body,
but I search the invisible recesses of my mind.

Another more oratorical youngster ends his theme:

Give these United States today a man of Washington's integrity,
Lincoln's will, and Wilson's perseverance, and he will guide us out of
the pit into which we have fallen, and peace and prosperity will
reign supreme.

Probably the best way to correct all these examples of wordiness
is to cross them out entirely. They say the obvious, and use too
many words to say it in.

A little different is the next, the beginning of the Preface to a
freshman composition book by two great American scholars:

With the student in an attitude of confidence in the worth of his
own thinking and of eagerness to learn the methods by which his
thought can be conveyed to others in words, the problem of teaching
the use of English reduces to the balancing of constructive practice

over against the corrective drill necessary to eradicate the bad habits due to foreign birth, defective training, or indifference.

This formal sentence may be re-rendered:

When the student believes his own thinking is valuable, and is eager to learn how to convey his thoughts to others in words, teaching him the use of English becomes merely a problem of balancing constructive practice against drills necessary to correct bad habits due to foreign birth, defective training, or indifference.

The original sentence contained 67 words, the altered one only 52—a saving of 22 per cent.

A group of three English instructors wrote this for the benefit of freshmen:

It is often necessary for a writer, in the course of preparing a composition, to obtain information from books, periodicals, or other publications. When such sources are used by the writer, the fact must be made clear to the reader, and this is done by a system of reference called *documentation*.

A less formidably textbookish statement would be:

In preparing a composition, a writer must often obtain information from books, periodicals, or other publications. When he does so, he should tell the reader so by a system of reference called *documentation*.

The original passage contained 51 words, the revised 33—a saving of 35 per cent.

A scholarly paper which I have at hand starts off:

The average Elizabethan saw in astrology a subject which for the most part was incomprehensible to him. He believed in the efficacy of the stars to foretell human events to those who could read them, but he did not understand by what means these matters were discovered.

The passage might be rewritten like this:

To the average Elizabethan, astrology was mostly incomprehensible. He believed the stars could foretell human events to the initiated, but he did not understand how.

The original passage contained 47 words, the revised 25—a saving of almost 50 per cent.

(2) These examples, together with the excerpt from an editorial quoted in the previous chapter, are enough to show how the conscious desire for a stiff-starched tone results in wordiness. But another kind of wordiness creeps with malign ingenuity into even the most informal writing. It is a *wordiness due to grammatical construction* rather than to downright bombast. For example, a writer may use a long dependent clause or a long phrase where a short phrase or a single word might express his meaning quite as well, and be briefer.

"I watched the man as he swam across the river," might be rewritten, "I watched the man swim across the river," or, "I watched the man swimming across the river."

"A quality which he lacks is politeness," might be rendered, "He lacks politeness."

"Cosmic rays constitute a phenomenon which no one has yet been able to understand," might be rendered, "No one has yet been able to understand cosmic rays."

"He is a man whom no one should trust," might be rendered, "He is an untrustworthy man," or, "He is untrustworthy."

"Lincoln was a man endowed by nature with extraordinary abilities," might be rendered, "Lincoln was a man of extraordinary natural abilities," or, "Lincoln had extraordinary natural abilities."

"Men who have no principles should not be chosen to fill positions in the legislative halls of this nation," might be reduced to, "Unprincipled men should not be elected to Congress."

This sort of wordiness is extremely common in the work of young writers, for young writers have not learned to give each sentence that last instant of observation and consideration without which a concise style is impossible.

Even the practiced writer may sometimes neglect this last instant's survey, and may as a result construct such a sentence as this, found in an excellent textbook on writing:

But the break with convention being touched upon here is not an extreme one.

The sentence would be much better if it read:

But the break with convention touched upon here is not extreme.

Further on in the same book is an almost identical lapse: "A style which is distinguished by exactness in the meaning of words used is evidently an economical one."

The word "one" is the source of many an offense against brevity. In the following sentences, it might profitably be omitted:

That horse is the most beautiful *one* here.

He is a man whom you can trust and *one* whom you can believe.

The farm which he owns is a large *one*.

The term "hurricane" is used when the storm is *one* of marked intensity.

The question of states' rights *is one which* still troubles the country.

Another frequent offender is "there is" or "there are." Naturally there are times (as in this sentence) when no other word or structure could convey the same shade of meaning or perform the same function. In the following sentence, for example, any revision to omit "there is" would give the sentence a different implication:

There is no doubt that Sylvester's concept of verse was much influenced by that of Poe.

But in other sentences the form makes for wordiness:

There are many palaces which are as beautiful as this.

There are many good writers who have used slang.

There were two men killed in the wreck.

Five minutes ago there were no clouds in the sky.

There were several books which had to be read carefully.

There is one thing to be remembered.

The passive voice is another structure which sometimes results in wordiness. Many teachers of composition have an almost unreasoning horror of this voice, not only because it is wordy, but because it is psychologically weak. Yet the passive voice is useful. It discriminates between an important receiver and an unimportant agent, as, "My brother was shot by a highwayman." It helps an author be impersonal in a work (such as this book) where openly personal opinions would sound too much like personal prejudices. It draws the reader's attention from the personal equation to the concrete fact, as when a scientist writes, "It was found that this serum halted the disease," instead of, "I found that this serum halted the disease." It keeps statements indefinite where definiteness is impossible, as, "Nagging wives may be blamed for many domestic troubles," or, "This type of bird has been noted in nearly all parts of the world." It enables writers to say things which prudence or ignorance would prevent their saying in the active voice, as, "College football has been commercialized in this state." But notwithstanding these excuses for the passive voice, it is too often weak and wordy.

The theme of the play is artistically developed by the young author.

If this read,

The young author develops the theme of the play artistically.

the sentence would be 16 per cent shorter. Moreover, it would be direct and pointed instead of circuitous. In most of the following sentences, the active voice would be briefer, and in all of them it would be stronger:

Passive: A great game was played by both sides.
Active: Both sides played a great game.

Passive: When the passive voice is shunned, a few words are usually saved.
Active: Shunning the passive voice usually saves a few words.

Passive: As soon as the trench was abandoned by our troops, it was taken over by the enemy.
Active: As soon as our troops abandoned the trench, the enemy took it over.

Passive: The automobile was driven into the shade of a tree which had been chosen as the picnic site.
Active: We drove the automobile into the shade of a tree which we had chosen as the picnic site.

In all but the last example from two to four words are saved. In the last example, the active voice is obviously more effective than the passive.

b. *Apologies.*—The passive is indirect; and indirect writing of any sort is weak. When a writer has something to say, he should say it (unless he has excellent reasons for doing otherwise) as directly as possible. He should avoid halfway statements, apologies, and palliatives.

He should not say, "She *seemed* to dance like a woodland fairy," but, "She danced like a woodland fairy."

He should not say, "My head *seemed* to be bursting," but, "My head was bursting."

He should not say, "He was, *if I may use the term,* a man of destiny," but, "He was a man of destiny."

He should not say, "*It looked as if* the fountains of heaven had opened," but, "The fountains of heaven had opened."

He should not say, "His life hung, *so to speak,* by a thread," but, "His life hung by a thread."

c. *Static Verbs.*—These expressions are weak because they hint at an indecisive and somewhat timid nature in the writer. A few words, however, are weak in themselves. One of them is the verb "to be" in its various forms. A writer should not say, "Here is a field," but, "Here lies—or stretches—or extends a field." He should not say, "Here is a building," but, "Here stands—or towers—or squats—or huddles a building." He should not say, "Here is a path," but, "Here runs—or winds—or wriggles a path." In other words, whenever a writer can gracefully avoid the static "is" in favor of a more active verb, he should do so.

d. *Vague Words.*—Another offender is "very." The word has been used so much to intensify other words that it has lost its own strength. Nowadays, indeed, "He is a good man," is a stronger statement than, "He is a very good man." "It was a delightful party," is stronger than, "It was a very delightful party." And, "This is an interesting book," is stronger than, "This is a very interesting book."

"Great" is the next culprit on the list. It is not descriptive, not exact, not concrete. "A great door" tells us nothing about the door; "a great storm" does not make us visualize the storm; "a great event" does not distinguish the event in any particular way; "a great bargain" does not tell us whether the price is $4.98 or $4.90; "a great undertaking" does not tell us whether it is a worth-while undertaking, or a difficult undertaking, or an undertaking too big for the man who begins it; "a great number of people" does not tell us whether the number was five hundred or five thousand.

"Wonderful," "nice," and "splendid" are three old offenders who

have been escaping the gallows erected by judges of writing for
the last fifty years. They have been used so much that they have
lost their original meanings. Observe: "He is a wonderful/nice/
splendid man." "It is wonderful/nice/splendid weather." "We had
a wonderful/nice/splendid time." "This is a wonderful/nice/
splendid cake you have cooked." "It is very wonderful/nice/splen-
did of you." It makes no difference which of the three one uses,
or in what connection one uses them. Words that mean so many
things mean nothing.

e. *Hackneyed and Trite Words.*—This brings us to the problems
of hackneyed phrases and jargon. Any good handbook of freshman
English will give a list of the more common hackneyed or trite
terms which a writer should avoid. Many of them are included in
the following piece of doggerel:

> When will we cease to write in books
> Of murmuring, gurgling, twisting brooks,
> Of winds that sigh and moan and beat,
> Of the beautiful maiden's dainty feet,
> Of crowds that surge and wagons that clatter,
> Of waters that swirl and birds that chatter,
> Of his firm jaw and his modest ties,
> Of her sunlit hair and her heavenly eyes,
> Of fleeting clouds that fleck the sky,
> Of loves that wait but never die,
> Of lips that tremble and quiver and curl,
> Of bosoms that heave, and teeth like pearl,
> Of engines that puff and throb and groan,
> Of the villain's hiss, and his low, tense tone,
> Of the dying sun's last flickering beam,
> Of the pale moon's mellow, tender gleam?
> —When, my friend? When the universe is dead,
> When the brooks are dry, or gone instead,
> When the sun doesn't shine and the moon doesn't show.
> There you have it, my friend—and now you know.

This list contains others likely to escape detection:

along these lines	paramount issue
artistic temperament	passed away
brilliant career	picturesque scene
captain of industry	powers that be
close to nature	profound silence
come in contact with	promising future
deadly earnest	proud possessor
depths of despair	ruling passion
discreet silence	sea of faces
dominant issue	self-made man
dull thud	simple life
each and every	skeleton in the closet
equal to the occasion	snow-capped mountains
evolutionary process	soul of honor
familiar landmark	struggle for existence
fiber of his being	student body
force of circumstances	suddenly
harked back	thunderous applause
heart's content	true meaning of the word
in great profusion	untoward incident
iron constitution	vast concourse
last analysis	venture a suggestion
last but not least	walk of life
myriad lights	wrapped in mystery
of the earth earthy	wrought havoc
Old South	

f. *Jargon.*—Jargon is a form of speech a little different from anything we have yet encountered. Sir Arthur Quiller-Couch, in his book, *The Art of Writing,* has a chapter on jargon which is the prototype of what all essays on the subject should be. If the reader has not seen this shrewd and whimsical study of Quiller-Couch's, he should look it up in the library and read it at once. What will be said here is only a pale and vapid summary of what Quiller-Couch has said supremely well.

The jargoneer dislikes to say things directly. In the eighteenth century he would not call a fish a fish, but the "scaly breed" or the "finny tribe." He would not call sheep, sheep, but the "gentle tribe" or the "fleecy kine." He would not say, "The flowers are blooming," but, "Blushing Flora paints th' enamel'd ground." And on one fearful occasion, he would not call snow, snow, but "wooly rain!" Nowadays the jargoneer resorts to circumlocutions and euphemisms. *Near* is *in the environs of*; being *born* is *first saw the light of day*; *dying* is *passing away*; *no* is *in the negative*; *several years* is *over a period of years*; *good weather* is *favorable climatic conditions*; *studied hard* is *pursued his studies with great diligence*; *love* is *amorous advances*; *grew up* is *reached man's estate*—and so forth, and so forth.

Thus, we could say of a young man: "He first saw the light of day in the environs of New York. After pursuing his studies with great diligence over a period of years in the educational institutions of the metropolis, he reached man's estate, and shortly thereafter began making amorous advances to a member of the opposite sex. Though she long turned a deaf ear to his proposals, or answered them in the negative, she at last yielded, being under the spell of the favorable climatic conditions of spring. Forthwith the happy pair entered into the state of matrimony, and lived for a considerable period of years in a state of connubial bliss, though at last our hero's better half passed away."

Special groups of "vague, wooly, abstract nouns" are mentioned in the following warnings by Quiller-Couch: "Whenever in your reading you come across one of these words, *case, instance, character, nature, condition, persuasion, degree*—whenever in writing your pen betrays you to one or another of them—pull yourself up and take thought. . . . Train your suspicions to bristle up whenever you come upon '*as regards,*' '*with regard to,*' '*in respect of,*' '*in connection with,*' '*according as to whether.*'" The following sen tences illustrate these examples of jargon, together with a revision of the objectionable phrases:

In case it rains, we shall not go.
If it rains, we shall not go.

In the first instance, I must speak to you of, etc.
First, I must speak to you of, etc.

A book of this character (or nature) is useless.
A book like this is useless.

The condition of his health forbids his removal.
His bad health forbids his removal.

Our Mohammedan friend worshiped with others of like persuasion.
Our Mohammedan friend worshiped with other Mohammedans.

He assented with some degree of reluctance.
He assented reluctantly.

As regards his honesty, I am not at all doubtful.
I do not doubt his honesty.

In connection with (or with regard to, or in respect to) your last offer, we cannot just now accept.
We cannot just now accept your last offer.

We shall employ him or not according as to whether he answers the questions correctly.
We shall employ him if he answers the questions correctly.

One other sort of jargon which Quiller-Couch discusses is Elegant Variation, that is, a squeamishness about the repetition of words already used. For example, the school symbol of the local university is an owl. When the sports editor of the local paper describes a football game in which the team of this university participates, we hear in successive sentences of the "home team," the "Owl gridsters," the "feathered flock," the "feathered warriors," the "doughty Owlmen," and so on, with all the adjectives switched about to go with other nouns and carry on the elegant variation *ad infinitum*. In many a theme the death of some individual becomes "this unhappy event," "his unexpected demise," "his un-timely end," "this shocking occurrence," and whatever else the ingenuity of the author may contrive to circumvent (as he would call it) the Grim Reaper. Such elegant variation looks self-con-scious, as if a writer were too timid to use the same word twice, or too eager to show the resources of his vocabulary. Affected and overwrought, it can never be vigorous writing.

This section has consisted, up to now, of admonitions about what a writer should not do. From this point on, the section will consist of more positive advice about what a writer should do to attain vigor of wording.

g. *Specific Words.*—The elementary rule, Prefer the specific to the general word, is still sound. Instead of, "The birds were loud in the trees," write, "The jays were screaming among the pines." Instead of, "Flowers were blooming everywhere," write, "Red gaillardias and yellow cosmos glowed over the whole prairie." In-stead of, "The many kinds of books scattered about showed the diversity of his interests," write, "Gibbon's History on the desk, a volume on electricity lying open on the lounge, and a shelfful of modern novels showed the diversity of his interests."

h. *The Exact Word.*—The other elementary rule, Choose the exact word, is equally sound. Walter Pater regarded the language as an immense hoard of treasure to which writers resort for words. In this accumulated hoard is hidden one word for every purpose, and only one word. All others besides the one are mere makeshifts with which no self-respecting writer could be content. Thus, if one is *pleased* with something, he may put it that he is *delighted, charmed, gladdened, warmed, rejoiced, taken, captivated, fasci-nated, enchanted, enraptured, transported, bewitched, ravished, satisfied, gratified, tickled, regaled, refreshed, enlivened, attracted, allured, stimulated,* or *interested* by the thing. Which of the store to choose, the writer's meaning must determine. To give another example, people move in other ways besides by mere *walking* or *running*. They may *travel, journey, flit, migrate, perambulate, circumambulate, tour, peregrinate, wander, roam, range, prowl, rove, ramble, stroll, saunter, gad about, patrol, march, step, tread, pace, plod, promenade, trudge, tramp, stalk, stride, strut, stump,* or *toddle*. Nor should an author rest until he has chosen the very gem of a word in all these which suits the meaning he has in mind. Note how different are the meanings and the feelings conveyed by the following sentences:

> He sauntered into the room.
> He strutted into the room.
> He stalked into the room.
> He stumped into the room.
>
> He journeyed about the country.
> He flitted about the country.
> He prowled about the country.
> He tramped about the country.

A word always exists to match a thought, and nearly always to match a feeling. It is the writer's business to seek out this matching word as if it were a lost piece in a jig-saw puzzle. No other word is so satisfactory; no other word makes *quite* so perfect a fit.

i. *Short and Saxon Words.*—These two elementary rules about the specific word and the exact word are beyond stricture. But one or two other rules often quoted should be brought before the bar of good judgment and retried. The first of these is, Prefer the Saxon word to the Latin—together with its companion, Prefer the short word to the long. These precepts we should take with reservations. A simple, direct, and swift style, dealing with simple, clear, and nimble ideas, quite obviously demands a vocabulary much sharper and quicker than does a more elaborate style dealing with involved, heterogeneous, and deliberate ideas.[2] Further-more, long Latin words give to writing a sonorous dignity never attainable by the crisp Anglo-Saxon. How inferior is Tyndale's pure English translation, "I am the again-rising and the life," to the Latinized, "I am the resurrection and the life!" And how poor would be the following much-quoted and well-loved passage from St. Paul if all the underscored Latin words were replaced by their English equivalents:

Who shall *separate* us from the love of *Christ*? shall *tribulation*, or *distress*, or *persecution*, or *famine*, or nakedness, or *peril*, or sword?

As it is written, For thy sake we are killed all the day long; we are *accounted* as sheep for the slaughter.

Nay, in all these things we are more than *conquerors* through him that loved us.

For I am *persuaded*, that neither death, nor life, nor *angels*, nor *principalities*, nor *powers*, nor things *present*, nor things to come,

Nor height, nor depth, nor any other *creature*, shall be *able* to *separate* us from the love of God, which is *in Christ Jesus* our Lord.

Representative passages show that the following use words of one syllable to the extent indicated:

Somerset Maugham	75%
Katherine Mansfield	74%
John Galsworthy	70%
Willa Cather	69%
Sinclair Lewis	78%
Thomas B. Macaulay	70%
R. L. Stevenson	71%
Charles Dickens	73%
Walter Pater	65%
Matthew Arnold	66%
The daily newspaper	61%
This book	68%

[2] In this very sentence, notice how (without conscious design by the author) the two contrasting ideas have shaped themselves into two contrasting modes of diction. On the one hand, "simple," "direct," "swift," "clear," "nimble," "sharp," and "quick"; on the other hand, "elaborate," "involved," "heterogeneous," and "deliberate."

Narrative writing usually has the largest number of monosyllables; expositions of processes next; descriptions of sight-images next; descriptions of sound-images next; and expositions of ideas least. Modern writers tend to use more monosyllables than did the writers of the eighteenth and nineteenth centuries.

The figures just given show what a large percentage of modern English writing consists of monosyllables. Indeed, when other things are equal—when cadence, sonority, and euphony are not concerned; when complex and abstract ideas are not involved; when a stately, formal, dignified tone is not required; when no relief from a long succession of short words is necessary—when all these provisos are made, the short and Saxon words are to be preferred to the long and Latin words. Thus, in the old humorous examples, "I must go home," is better than, "I consider it necessary that I retire to my domicile." And, "I think he is a good man," is better than, "I am convinced of the rectitude of his principles."

Sometimes (as in the paragraph from O. Henry already quoted) a rare or sesquipedalian word will break the sameness of monosyllabic and commonplace diction. Perhaps Shakespeare had this effect in mind when he wrote these three dull lines, and then finished off with the amazing fourth line:

> What hands are here? Ha! they pluck out mine eyes.
> Will all great Neptune's ocean wash this blood
> Clean from my hand? No, this my hand will rather
> The multitudinous seas incarnadine.

The eighteenth-century critics made it a rule that no regular line of poetry should consist of monosyllables alone; and Pope illustrated the fault thus:

> And ten low words oft creep in one dull line.

Like many other eighteenth-century rules of writing, this went in the right direction, but went too far. "The one rule," said Stevenson in a famous passage, "is infinite variety." Too many short words, too many long words, too many Saxon words, too many Latin words—all are bad.

j. *Division of Labor.*—One of the commonly recommended means toward variety is what is called "division of labor." That is, the adjective should not bear the larger part of the burden of meaning and emotion in the sentence. Nouns and verbs are the backbone and the sinew of the language: they should carry the chief weight; and the adjective may often be transmuted, for the sake of strength as well as variety, into an adverb. All this does not mean that we ought to shun adjectives altogether, for adjectives have an indispensable place in all good writing—particularly in descriptions of colors or colored objects. But we ought to be wary of using adjectives to the exclusion or the subordination of other parts of speech. Mark Twain gave the excellent advice years ago, "When in doubt, omit the adjective." And Emerson counseled, "Let the noun be self-sufficient" (using an adjective, be it noted, in the sentence). These precepts will raise many a dubious sentence into respectability, and many a weak sentence into sound health. "He was an enormous man" has not the vigor of "He was a monster of a man." "The flashing guns were visible in the darkness" has not the vigor of "The guns were flashing visibly in the darkness." "The breeze became fresh" has not the vigor of "The breeze freshened." And "A cheerless wind was blowing" has not the vigor of "A wind blew cheerlessly."

k. *Coinages.*—Another means toward variety not accounted for in Pater's conservative scheme is the coining of new words and new compounds. The outright coining of absolutely new words can never proceed on a grand scale except for the purposes of outlandish, gargantuan humor such as that in Rabelais. Even there, however, it gives vigor to the writing. But in general, a sober writer coins words for their onomatopœic or their tonal ef-

fect. "Slurp!" "Blip!" "Tonk!" "Pfitt!"—these and their verb-forms
are examples of onomatopœic coinage. On the other hand, "He
went *galumphing* down the street" is chiefly intended to give to
the action a certain feeling. And so with, "The wind wheemed
eerily through the forest." Or, "He woozled me out of five dollars." Such coinages have an undeniable flavor of originality, an
atmosphere of vigor; and though they can never be used abundantly, they are often worth the trouble it takes to make them.

Another sort of coinage which we may mention in passing is the
deliberate creation of new words to fit new ideas, new inventions,
or new discoveries. These words differ from the preceding in having legitimate root-words, generally Latin or Greek. Often they
fill a want or an absolute need. The automobile, the airplane, and
the radio, for example, have brought into the language hundreds
of new words naming new objects such as *carburetor, magneto,
heterodyne, capacitance, hydroplane,* and *ailerons.* Biology and
psychology have brought new words naming new ideas and
processes such as *patroclinous, phenotype, introvert, libido,* and
schizophrenia. Physics and chemistry have an entire vocabulary
incomprehensible to the uninitiated. And a few trade-marks or
trade-names have supplied new and now reputable words—for example, *mercurochrome, vaseline, fabrikoid, Bakelite, cellophane,*
and possibly *victrola.* With all such words we can have no complaint. But the impudence of high-pressure advertising and the
eagerness of a certain kind of scientist to invent long hard words
to replace old easy ones—these we should resist. *Realtor, groceteria,
healthatorium, dactylogram, macrograph,* and *radiogoniometer,* to
mention a few examples, are without excuse.

1. *Compounds.*—A more important source of new words lies in
the combination of old words. Such combinations or compounds
are characteristic of Teutonic languages, and are in the best line of
English tradition. The introductory ten lines of Beowulf contain

these combinations: *spear-Danes, yore-days, people-kings, mead-settle, tore-away, little-owning, honor-worth, every-one, dwellers-around,* and *whale-road.* A single scene from Shakespeare's *The Tempest* yields *virgin-knot, sour-eyed, lass-lorn, pole-clipped, rocky-hard, grass-plot, many-coloured, honey-drops, short-grassed, dove-drawn, bed-right, waspish-headed, marriage-blessing, ever-harmless, sickle-men, rye-straw, cloud-capped, red-hot, calf-like, filthy-mantled, foot-licker,* and *pinch-spotted.* A page of John Galsworthy has *sub-golden, silver-coloured, silvery-necked, high-collared, red-coated, sword-hilt, week-end-run-to,* and *dark-lashed.* Nearly all these last, however, are compounded of adjectives, which are not to be compared in vigor with noun-compounds such as those from Beowulf and Shakespeare.

The chief value of both sorts of compounds is their brevity and their freshness. Thus, in Galsworthy, "with dark lashes" would be neither so short nor so original as "dark-lashed." The same would be true of "one willing to lick another's feet" instead of "foot-licker" as Shakespeare wrote it, or "spotted from the effect of pinches" instead of "pinch-spotted." "The window glass covered with a mist from his breath" is inferior to "the breath-misted window glass"; "a man who often sits on his lawn" is more commonplace than "a confirmed lawn-sitter"; "with lips drawn in" is a less notable phrase than "in-drawn lips"; and "people who live on a farm" is longer than "farm-dwellers."

m. *Original Meanings.*—To people who know a "little Latin and less Greek," the use of words in their original etymological sense may be a source of extraordinarily vigorous diction. In English, words attach to themselves through the centuries an incrustation of acquired meanings which writers conventionally accept; yet the core of the word, the original meaning at the center of the conventional meanings, still persists as a vague contour apparent in spite of the incrustation. If a writer can unearth this original meaning, he can present his readers with words elemental and powerful. When Shakespeare refers to the ghost of Hamlet's father as "the extravagant and erring spirit," he is getting back to the elementals of words. He does not mean a "spendthrift and sinful spirit" but a "strayed and wandering spirit." In a good dictionary, the original meaning of a word is given either in the etymological note or in the first definition of the word. By referring to these places, we may construct sentences such as the following:

> The castle was a towering *fabric* of stone.
> *Damp* spirits overcame him.
> I shall *keep* the Christmas holiday.
> A *vagrant* wisteria vine climbed over the porch.
> He came from a *gentle* family.
> He proved himself a truly *Laconic* warrior.

n. *New Uses.*—But the chief source of fresh and vigorous diction lies in the new uses of words. For example, we are accustomed to see the word *plump* used with definite material objects; but Kipling applies it to an action in "plump obeisances." We are accustomed to see the word *staring* used with *eyes*; but J. B. Priestley says, "She talked in a kind of idle, staring voice." We are accustomed to see the word *blur* used with images of sight; but de la Roche writes, "The music became by degrees blurred."

The attainment of this freshness of diction is not easy. It comes from the same almost philosophic spirit from which comes the power to make figures of speech—that is, the mind which sees similarities in things which to the average mind are quite different. When Conrad describes a swimmer immersed "in a greenish cadaverous glow," he recognizes the similarity between two things so unlike as sea-water and a corpse; when Poe speaks of "thy hyacinth hair," he recognizes the similarity between the curls on a woman's head and the curls of hyacinth petals, and when Wilbur Daniel Steele writes of "little houses scrambling up the length" of a street, he recognizes the similarity between houses and living things. Not quite so obviously, but just as surely, a writer who says, "She was one of those *frankly* sanctimonious persons," is employing a word usually associated with something very different from sanctimonious. Jane Austen has a similar description: "He possessed a countenance of strong, natural, sterling *insignificance*." When O. Henry says, "The girl *penetrated* the restaurant to some retreat in its rear," he uses a word associated with solids because he sees the likeness between the crowded restaurant with its thickly aromatic atmosphere, and a material substance. When Conrad says that light "fell from above on the heads of the three men, and they were *fiercely* distinct in the half-light," he sees the likeness between distinct vision and strong passion. And when Ellen Glasgow writes of "eyes fixed in a pathetic *groping* stare," she sees the likeness between searching eyes and searching hands.

To perceive likenesses in things different, to apply to one idea or image words most frequently used with another—this may require a certain quick, almost mystical intuition which every writer may not possess. But almost every writer has at least a spark of intuition; and by proper care, one may fan the spark into quite a warm blaze. At any rate, one can try. He can avoid saying "green grass," and say instead "poisonous grass," or "pallid grass," or "delicious grass," or "cheerful grass." He can avoid saying "blue sky," and say instead "livid sky," or "purple sky," or "dead sky," or "living sky," or "brazen sky," or "hovering sky," or "huddling sky," or "still sky," or "weary sky," or "glad sky." And he can vivify such a commonplace statement as "He glanced toward her" by saying instead, "His glance slid toward her—or slipped toward her—or rushed toward her—or wandered toward her—or bounded toward her."

So far, everything which has been said about style in this book has been advice which any intelligent person with some capacity for taking pains might follow—with the intensity of the pains depending on the individual student's adaptability and interest. But what is to be said in the next two parts of this discussion of style is not advice which anybody or everybody can follow. Indeed, much of it is not even advice. It is merely an analysis of some of the elements which create the vague abstractions "personality" and "beauty" in style. Some writers will find the analysis useful for their own writing; others will not.

EXERCISES

3. Vigor of Wording.
  a. Make the wording of the following sentences more vigorous. In addition, change the structure wherever it is weak. Explain all changes you make:

  (1) We come to college with the expectation of being able to increase our practical knowledge to such an extent that we shall be able to make a living for ourselves.

  (2) We may taste of many things in college, and thus acquire a wonderful fund of knowledge which, in our future life, will help us to understand the world and to enjoy it.

  (3) We make judgments in the same manner in which the business man makes his.

  (4) It is not the circumstance that we have a college education, or willingness, or ability, or personality, or any other one quality that assures success for us; but it seems to be a happy combination of all these qualities.

(5) We must not permit the importance which attaches itself to one phase of college life to overshadow the possibilities which are encompassed within the other.

(6) The plays that college students have assigned to them as required reading are read very hurriedly, and with the one idea in mind that an examination is to be passed.

(7) My first day at college was one of wonderful surprises and great disillusionments.

(8) The professor was a young man of seemingly athletic build. His eyes were bright and his manner was alert. The splendid character of this man was a great influence over all with whom he came in contact.

(9) He at once instituted an inquiry through the advertising columns of the daily paper in order that he might learn something of the whereabouts of his missing son.

(10) He was very glad to part with a large portion of his savings in order that his son might be able to train himself in the profession of law.

(11) The prisoner is charged with murder in connection with the killing of Q. R. Bronson in a hold-up which is known to have occurred on November 10.

(12) There is a considerable portion of the population which still harbors suspicion concerning the nature of the American banking business.

(13) Although marriage ceremonies and funerals seem to be entirely different things, they are similar in many respects.

(14) He thought that he could not remember having spent such a wonderful evening.

(15) The walk was postponed, but only after the promise of one for the next evening was given to him.

(16) The morning dawned clear and bright; in fact, it suffices to say that it was a typical Palm Beach morning.

(17) The moonlight reflected on her hair made her resemble some ancient Greek goddess.

(18) He was very much attracted to this beautiful young lady who seemed to exert something of a spell over him, though he felt that he was powerless to do anything about it.

(19) But alas! A rude awakening from a dream of splendor lay before him.

(20) There might be a few people who would pretend to be his friend as long as he had money.

(21) This nest is rather different from most I have seen, as it appears to be much more bulky than is usually the case.

(22) It would be audacious of me to appear to speak with authority on the more technical aspects of the printer's profession.

(23) Mr. D. believes the model to prove it possible to build a yacht to the limits of the length to which sheet aluminum of the correct quality can be rolled, without any cross-seams whatsoever on the hull.

(24) Mrs. Van Kosh had an utter horror of physical punishment in any capacity.

(25) She insisted that persuasion was the most efficient, cultured, and human manner in which to rear a child.

(26) Standing there, he presented an appearance that reminded one of a fish.

(27) In rescuing the unfortunate canine and bearing it off with me to my home, I succeeded in smothering all apprehensions as to family reactions relative to what they would invariably term an additional nuisance.

(28) There is a new color called Briar Brown, which is a dark, rich shade of brown, and which is very attractive, to say the least.

(29) In Coleridge's case a boy of truly extraordinary qualities was father to one of the most remarkable of men.

(30) Sedate, composed, and courteous, she presented a wide contrast to her little brother.

(31) He was a large man who had hair which was the color of a carrot; but though he was grotesque in appear-

ance, he was, I think, almost the kindest man I have ever known.

(32) Throughout my high school career, I selected subjects that gave promise of preparing me for college; and in those subjects I tried to stand out in scholastic rating—that is, I studied a great deal.

(33) When he came out into the light, I could see that he was very tall; but the dark eyes appeared to have a sinister light in them, and seemed to be able to see right through me.

(34) Sophistication and poise (both of them qualities essential for beauty) are evident in her entire bearing.

(35) The physical aspects of this great educational institution are in keeping with its scholastic attainments.

b. Make the diction of the following sentences more specific:

(1) The child was pleased by the many Christmas presents.
(2) It was a disorderly room.
(3) Bright colors were to be seen everywhere at the game.
(4) The entire village disliked seeing its minister wear shabby clothes.
(5) His whole appearance was grotesque.

c. Substitute as many synonyms as you can for each of the italicized words in the following sentences:

(1) He *came* toward us.
(2) The wind was *cold*.
(3) He is too *servile*.
(4) He is a *wonderful* man; it is a *wonderful* book; the weather is *wonderful*.
(5) A *light shone* in the west.

d. Write a paragraph on each member of the following groups of subjects, and then compare the number of Latin words in one paragraph with the number in the other:

(1) The necessity for internationalism.
The necessity for nationalism.
(2) The death of an old country grandmother.
The death of a great warrior or statesman.
(3) The love of Paris for Helen.
The love of a high school boy for a girl.

(4) A criticism of some ultra-modern painting.

A criticism of a painting by one of the old masters.

e. Make adjectives bear less of the burden in the following descriptive passages:

A small, cowering boy of ten stood before a huge man who held a long leather whip in his hand. An ugly scowl was on the man's swarthy face as he leaned toward the small boy with a threatening attitude.

An old and tottering man was trying to pick his feeble way along the crowded street. His shaking hand would now and then touch a wall for support; and now and then he would pause as if he were afraid to go farther through the dangerous traffic. "Can I help you, mister?" a shrill voice cried as a ragged urchin ran toward the old man. Taking the trembling hand in a close grip, the boy led the old man across the street, and left him safe on the other side. This kind act showed that, for all his ragged clothes, the little boy was at heart gentlemanly.

f. Substitute compound words for phrases in the following sentences:

(1) He entered the gate to the field.

(2) The chickens had littered the earth with the rubbish they had scratched up.

(3) He moved off down the road leading to the mill.

(4) He wore a black mustache which was cropped short.

(5) He came into full view on the slope of the hill.

(6) Daffodils grew in boxes at the windows.

(7) The farm was about a mile from the edge of the wood.

(8) We passed two outlandish vessels with high sterns.

(9) The owner of the boat came toward us.

(10) He rode a horse marked with sweat.

g. Write sentences in which you use the following words in their original meanings:

concur	artful	eager
capital	trivial	indifferent
apprehend	character	countenance
insinuate	prevent	quick
fond	virtue	conceit
infantry	nominate	accost

h. Try to find more notable words for the following ideas:

full face	windy day
puffy face	green trees
blue eyes	thick foliage
bright eyes	clear stream
rosy cheeks	high mountain
full lips	rolling country
weak chin	shady path
strong jaw	bright sunlight
receding forehead	sweet song
bald head	swaying vines

Chapter V

BEAUTY OF STYLE

B EAUTY is that which gratifies the eye or the ear independently of other considerations. But since writing (exclusive of good penmanship or good printing) consists of ugly black wriggly figures spread across white pages, it cannot gratify the eye as a beautiful image. Accordingly, writing which is beautiful must symbolize sounds gratifying to the ear. In this sense, therefore, we shall discuss beauty in style. It means beautiful sound, pleasing sound, in writing. Moreover, it ought to involve, and it shall involve in our discussion, fitness of sound to sense.

In the following pages we shall discuss beauty under three heads: beauty of pure sounds, beauty of patterned sounds, and beauty of rhythm.

1. Pure Sounds.—In some way, and for some reason, a few sounds please us in themselves, irrespective of their meaning or context, and a few displease us.

a. *Beautiful Sounds and Ugly Sounds.*—Among the vowels, *a* as in *art*, *o* as in *ode*, *oo* as in *moon*, and the two *u* sounds in *tuneful* are the most pleasing. Next come *a* as in *ale*, *e* as in *well* and in *eve*, and *i* as in *white* and in *ill*. And positively displeasing are *a* as in *bat*, *a* as in *all*, *o* as in *pod*, *u* as in *up*, and *ou* as in *out*. The pleasingness of *oi* depends on the consonants which accompany it; for example, *voice* and *moil* are beautiful words, but *choice* and *coil* are not.

The consonants may probably be arranged something like thi in descending order:

Beautiful: *l, m, n, r, v, s, d.*
Negative: *t, f, w, y.*
Ugly: *k, b, p, h, g, j, z.*

This order is only approximate, it would differ with differen individuals. But in a list made out by a score of people, the firs half-a-dozen sounds here given would probably appear first in on order or another on all lists. An Italian musician pointing out th beauty of the English language gave as an example of perfec beauty the words "cellar door"; Poe thought *v* was the most beau tiful letter, and he said that the saddest words in the language were "no more." In his great poem he used with tremendous effec the word "nevermore." In all the phrases quoted, the beautiful *l's m's, n's, r's,* and one *s,* together with the long *o's,* occur again and again.

S and *d,* however, are problems. They seem to be beautiful when they occur alone, but are ugly when prominently repeated in suc cessive words. Likewise all the negative letters and their partners (mentioned below) become ugly if too much repeated. Indeed, a sentence in which the number of consonants is disproportionately large is rough, no matter what the consonants may be:

Midst thickest mists and stiffest frosts,
With strongest fists and stoutest boasts,
He thrusts his fists against the posts,
And still insists he sees the ghosts.

Moreover, some consonants sound so much alike that a reader must be careful to pronounce them very distinctly when he finds one of them at the end of a word, and another at the beginning of the next word. Such pairs make unpleasant reading. They are *b* and *p; d* and *t; f* and *v; g* and *k; m* and *n; s* and *z.* To be added

o the list is any consonant repeated from the end of one word to
he beginning of the next word, as "deep places." Some ugly sen-
ences showing the *liaison* (as it is called) of pairs of consonants
ollow:

The big king kicked Tim.

A plain man must drink good tea.

Hop up behind his sister.

Pop broke glass on market days.

The next few quotations illustrate the beautiful and the ugly
effects produced by certain letters:

Fat black bucks in a barrel-house room[1]

This is an ugly-sounding line. Notice the flat *a's* and the flat *u*, the
b's, the *k's*, the *h*, the *f*, the ugly *ou* in *house*. *Room* is the only
beautiful word in the line.

This next is from that consummate master of word-music,
Tennyson:

> O, hark, O, hear! how thin and clear,
>   And thinner, clearer, farther going!
> O sweet and far from cliff and scar,
>   The horns of Elfland faintly blowing!
> Blow, let us hear the purple glens replying;
> Blow, bugle; answer, echoes, dying, dying, dying.

Notice how the long *o's*, the *i's*, and the *n's*, *l's,* and *r's* echo and re-
echo through the lines; and how every ugly sound (like *h*, *k*, *g*,
and *p*) is immediately modulated by a following beautiful sound.
The single exception is "how."

Shakespeare's early and poor play, the *Comedy of Errors*, has
lines such as these:

[1] In the original poem, the word is "wine-barrel" instead of "barrel-house"; the
latter word is the first in the next line.

Back, slave, or I will break thy pate across.

Hence, prating peasant, and fetch thy master home.

If I last in this service, you must case me in leather.

It would make a man as mad as a buck to be so bought and sold

Turning to prose, we find this in Kipling: "shrimp-pink pris-
oners of war bathing." Not quite so bad is, "The shutter of the
room next mine was attacked, flung back." Carlyle writes, "Thus
your Actual Aristocracy have got discriminated into Two Classes,"
and, "The Ant lays-up Accumulation of Capital, and has, for
aught I know, a Bank of Antland." Here is a sentence from
Galsworthy, with the purely unpleasant sounds capitalized, and the
unpleasant repetitions or *liaisons* italicized:

HiS *KicKS* *A*nd *CrowS A*nd sPlAsHingS HA*d t*he Joy of a gn*A*t'S
d*A*nce or a J*A*cKdAw's GAmBols.

But it should be remembered that the sense or the feeling of a
passage may often demand ugly sounds. The sentence just quoted
from Galsworthy (in which the bathing of an infant is described)
would be absurd if it were dignified and beautiful; and the line
from Lindsay's *Congo* ("Fat black bucks," etc.) is purposely ugly
because the author tries to create an unpleasant reaction in the
reader. The following from Tennyson's *Morte d'Arthur* is likewise purposely harsh for its onomatopœic effect:

Dry clashed his harness in the icy caves
And barren chasms, and all to left and right
The bare black cliff clanged round him, as he based
His feet on juts of slippery crag that rang
Sharp-smitten with the dint of armed heels.

b. *Feeling and Letter-sounds.*—Not only are certain sounds beautiful or ugly in themselves, but certain sounds convey certain feel-

ings. In the following paragraphs, we shall very briefly describe the feelings excited, first, by vowels, and next, by consonants.

O, especially long *o,* gives sonorousness, solemnity, power, and often mournfulness to words.

I, especially long *i,* gives a feeling of quick brightness, delight, and happiness.

A as in *fate* often has about it a feeling of lazy deliberation, or stateliness, or undeviating straightness, or weight.

Long *e* usually implies feeling keen rather than powerful.

Long *u* and long *oo* make a tuneful, crooning sound that is soothing, smooth, and curative.

Short *a, e,* and *u* are dull words, heavy, flat, platitudinous, and sometimes depressing. They occur in words like *wet blanket, mud, smut, fat, nap,* and *death.*

The Biblical sentence, "Arise, shine, for the light has come, and the glory of the Lord is upon thee," is a perfect example of joyous long *i's* which grow into the more solemn emotion of the long *o's,* which in turn end with a hint of excited feeling in the long *e.*

"Give ye ear and hear my voice; hearken and hear my speech." This, with its long *e's,* almost screams at its reader. The next verse, however, at once mounts into true solemnity: "Doth the plowman plow all day to sow? Doth he open and break the clods of his ground?"

Some consonants have definite emotional connotations, or excite definite feelings or ideas. The long-drawn *m* and *n,* for example, bring about in the sound-progression a momentary suspension which is lulling and soothing. Tennyson uses these letters, together with long *o,* most skillfully in *The Lotos-Eaters*:

> "Courage!" he said, and pointed toward the land,
> "This mounting wave will roll us shoreward soon."
> In the afternoon they came unto a land
> In which it seemed always afternoon.

All round the coast the languid air did swoon,
Breathing like one that hath a weary dream.
Full-faced above the valley stood the moon;
And, like a downward smoke, the slender stream
    Along the cliff to fall and pause and fall did seem.

R with long vowels creates a calm, clear, star-like music, as in this stanza from *The Lady of Shalott*:

Only reapers reaping early
In among the bearded barley,
Heard a song that echoes cheerly
From the river winding clearly,
    Down to towered Camelot;
And by the moon the reaper weary,
Piling sheaves in uplands airy,
Listening, whispers, " 'Tis the fairy
    Lady of Shalott."

But with a profusion of other consonants, *r* becomes harsh and rasping—as in the lines from *Morte d'Arthur* already quoted.

L is liquid, light, translucent; it is pale like twilight; it is soft like the glow of a pearl. In his descriptions of the sea, Conrad invariably calls on this letter to assist him, as in this:

I saw it suddenly flicker and stream out on the flagstaff. The Red Ensign! In the pellucid, colorless atmosphere of that southern land, the livid islets, the sea of pale, glassy blue under the pale, glassy sky of that cold sunrise, it was, as far as the eye could reach, the only spot of ardent color.[2]

S is a swift and agile letter if it is not bound up with long vowels. Thus, Tennyson's "So strode he back slow to the wounded king," is slow and deliberate because of the long *o's* which impede the flow of the *s's*. But Pope's lines,

Not so when swift Camilla scours the plain,
Flies o'er the unbending corn or skims along the main,

[2] From *A Personal Record*, by Joseph Conrad, copyright, 1912, by Doubleday, Doran and Company, Inc. Reprinted by permission.

show the *s* in its true nature. The old tongue-twister, "She sells sea-shells by the seashore," is all the more difficult to say because the *s's* invite—indeed, almost compel—hasty utterance. If the line were slowed up by long *o's*, we should not be tempted to say it fast, and should find it no more difficult than Tennyson's line quoted above. Thus: "Sol soaks so-and-so's in soapsuds."

B, t, p, and *d* (especially the first three) give an impression of abruptness—of a chopped-off sound, an idea bitten through, a sentence pat and proper.

F also gives a cleaving edge to sound, as in this line from Chesterton, wherein abrupt *t's* mingle with forceful *f's*:

> White founts falling in the courts of the sun.

This sentence from Kipling (with one word omitted) contains all these cutting letters. If it contained, instead, many long *o's, m's, n's,* and *r's,* we should feel sorry for the sheep; but as it now stands we do not think of him twice: "A fat-tailed sheep who did not want to die, bleated at my tent-door."

G, h, and *j* are ordinarily regarded as rough, savage letters with none of the refinement of *l, m, n,* and *r.* A look into a thesaurus shows all these words with *g's* and *h's* as synonyms of *horrible*: *ugly, homely, misshapen, shapeless, hard, hard-visaged, haggard, grim, ghastly, ghostly, gristly, gruesome, ungainly, gross, hulking, horrid,* and *hideous.*

Poe's poem, *The Bells,* is a remarkable exercise in letter-sounds and letter-feelings which the reader may study with profit.

In the following experiment, notice how the sense and the feeling change with the changing of dominant letters:

> With *o*: A bullet moaned slowly across the hollow.
> With *i*: A bullet trilled swiftly from cliff to cliff.
> With *e*: A bullet screeched fiercely, deep in the ravine.
> With *a*: A bullet wailed past the face of the palisade.

With *n*: A bullet sang along the canyon between pinnacles of stone.
With *r*: A bullet from far off rang its clarion through the gorge.
With *l*: A bullet leapt lightly across the valley.
With *s*: A bullet sped swiftly from side to side of the abyss.
With *b*, *f*, *p*, and *t*: A bullet cleft the space between lip and lip of
     the gulf.
With *g*, *h*, and *j*: A bullet hurtled savagely from jagged crag to
     crag.

So far, we have dealt with pure sounds as units, irrespective of their relation to the sentence as a whole. In the next section, we shall examine them as they appear in the sentence itself.

2. Patterned Sounds.—The essence of pattern is repeat. A single beat of a tom-tom is not a pattern, but a series of similar beats is; one soldier in uniform is not a pattern, but a whole squadron is; one row of corn is not a pattern, but a field of rows is.

These primitive types of patterns, however, consisting as they do of mere repeats, soon grow monotonous to the eye or ear. To be permanently gratifying, therefore, a pattern must have variety, change, relief from sameness; and yet all the while it must maintain its identity as a system of repeats. Good sentences have this variety within sound-patterns. One sound repeats itself over and over, and yet just before it becomes monotonous, this sound gives way to another. Then, after a bit, the first sound may be taken up again, carried on, blended with the second, made a part of the special pattern formed by the second, and eventually wrought into a harmony.

Within the sentence, only those sounds which occur in accented syllables and in important words form a part of the sound-pattern. But the very fact of repetition gives importance to sounds which would be ignored if they were not repeated. Any sound, therefore, repeated several times becomes a part of the sound-pattern almost independently of its accentuation or sense-importance.

In the following paragraphs, vowel-patterns are first discussed, and then consonant-patterns.

a. *Vowel-patterns.*—A sentence already quoted is a good example of simple pattern:

> Arise, shine, for thy light has come,
> . . i . . . . . i . . . . i . . i . . . . u . . .

> and the glory of the Lord is upon thee.
> . . . . o . . . . o . . . . o . . . . . e

Expressed symbolically, according to the grammatical balance of the sentence, the pattern looks like this:

> iiiiu
> oooe

This next is a little more intricate:

> Or ever the silver cord be loosed,
> o . . e . . . . i . . . . . o . . . . e . u . . . .

> or the golden bowl be broken,
> o . . . . . o . . . . . . o . . . . e . . . o . . .

> or the pitcher be broken at the fountain,
> o . . . . . i . . . . . . e . . . o . . . . o . . . . . .

> or the wheel broken at the cistern.
> o . . . . e . . . . o . . . . i . . . .

It may be expressed

> oeioeu
> oooeo
> oieoo
> oeoi

Observe the beautiful weaving back and forth between the dominating *o* and the less emphatic *e's* which gradually reach a climax in the word *wheel*; and observe the minor *i* sound reappearing in all the components but one.

One more example from the Bible before we turn to modern prose:

> Intreat me not to leave thee,
> ...e....e..o....e.......e
>
> or to return from following after thee:
> o......u....o...o.o.....a.......e

for whither thou goest,	I will go;
......i.......o..o...	i...i...o

and where thou lodgest,	I will lodge.
.......e.....o.o.....	i...i...o...

This is

```
eeoee
ouoooae
ioo — iio
eoo — iio
```

The entire passage is a pattern of only three elements—*e, i,* and *o* —with two discords (*u* and *a*). Notice, moreover, the additional pattern in the last two elements of the passage.

This sentence from Conrad has different pattern-elements:

> He is the war-lord
> ..e........a..o..
>
> who sends his battalions
> .....e........a..a....
>
> of Atlantic rollers
> ...a..a.....o....
>
> to the assault of our shores.
> ......a..a......o.....o...

There may be some question as to whether the passage is divided correctly; but the interplay of *a's* and *o's* is obvious. The last element of the sentence, containing two *a's* and two *o's,* forms a perfect conclusion by repeating the two dominant elements of the sentence and by having the less important of these dominant elements (*o*) acquire importance by coming at the end of the sentence.

One more example will reveal additional complexities of these vowel-patterns:

> Oh, moonlit night of Africa,
> o.....u...i...i.....a....a
> and orchard by those wild sea-banks
> ....o.......i...o....i...e...a...
> where once Dido stood;
> ......u.....i.o..u..
> _____
>
> oh, laughter of boys
> o...a..........o..
> among the shaken leaves,
> ...u........a.....e....
> and sound of falling fruit;
> ....o........a......u..
> _____
>
> how do you live alone
> .o.......u.i....o..
> out of so many nights
> o......o..a....i....
> that no man remembers?
> ......o..a.....e...e..
> _____
>
> For Carthage is destroyed, indeed,
> .o...a...a........o.......e..
> and forsaken of the sea,
> .....o..a...........e.
> _____
>
> yet that one hour of summer
> .....a .u....o......u.....

is to be unforgotten
......e.u..o..o....

——————— .

while man has memory
...i....a...a...e....

of the story of his past. [3]
o......o...o......a..

In outline form, the pattern goes like this:

$$
\left\{
\begin{array}{l}
\text{ouiiaa} \\
\text{oioiea} \\
\text{uiou} \\[6pt]
\text{oao} \\
\text{uae} \\
\text{oau} \\[6pt]
\text{ouio} \\
\text{ooai} \\
\text{oaee}
\end{array}
\right.
$$

$$
\left\{
\begin{array}{l}
\text{oaaoe} \\
\text{oae} \\[6pt]
\text{auou} \\
\text{euoo} \\[6pt]
\text{iaae} \\
\text{oooa}
\end{array}
\right.
$$

A more perfectly balanced, patterned, and harmonious arrangement is hard to imagine.

Perhaps there is no better way to get music in prose than by the use of vowel patterns such as those analyzed. With vowels alone can a writer work out close-knit and intricate patterns which, despite their intricacy, the reader can *feel* as patterns.

b. *Consonant-patterns.*—It is true that consonants can be molded

[3] From Andrew Lang's *Adventures among Books.* Quoted by W. E. Williams in *Plain Prose*, Longmans, Green and Company, 1929, p. 110.

into patterns quite as complex; but except for a few consonants and a few simple patterns, consonant-patterns have little real effect on the reader. He usually sees them as mere repetitions of a unit without relation and without variety. Furthermore, except with three or four consonants (*m, n, l,* and sometimes *r*), these repetitions become displeasing before they have worked themselves into a notable pattern. About the best a writer can do, therefore, after he has made the simple consonant-patterns, is to be content with repeating consonants only for the psychological effects already mentioned. He should leave most of the business of pattern-making to the vowels.

Some consonants can be worked into pleasing arrangements of repeats. In the stanzas from *The Lady of Shalott* and *The Lotos-Eaters* we have seen how the repetition of *r, m,* and *n* gives real pleasure. And in a passage from Conrad we have seen *l* used pleasingly. Moreover, these repeats are not merely alliterative; they weave at random in and out of the syllables. This next passage of prose, from Kipling, illustrates the musical use of the same four letters. It begins with *l* and *r,* passes on to *m* and *n,* and concludes with *r* once more. (The vowels make a pattern of *o's* and *i's.*)

The *n*ight had c*l*osed i*n* *r*ain, and *r*o*ll*ing c*l*ouds b*l*otted out the *l*ights of the vi*ll*ages i*n* the va*ll*ey . . . The *m*onkeys su*n*g so*rr*ow-fu*ll*y to each other as they hu*n*ted d*r*y *r*oots i*n* the fe*rn*-d*r*aped trees.

But (omitting these four) consonants can usually be felt as patterned only when they are alliterative. Furthermore, if the alliteration involves more than two or three syllables, it is nearly always distinctly unpleasant to the reader.

The sentence lacks a proper proportion of parts.

The water washed the watchdog away.

Girls gain their growth less gradually than boys.

All these sentences sound bad.

The best sort of alliteration for prose is that which is an intricate crisscross of sound that is felt rather than intellectually perceived. Let us see it working out in verse and then in prose. Swinburne, that master of patterned language, writes:

> *Th*ere go *the* *l*oves *th*at *w*ither,
>   *Th*e old *l*oves *w*ith *w*earier *w*ings;
> And *a*ll *d*ead years *d*raw *th*ither,
>   And *a*ll *d*isastrous *th*ings.

The pattern is

Th	th	l	th	w
Th	l	w	w	w
a	d	d	th	
a	d	th		

In the following passage from Pater's *Marius the Epicurean*, note how *s* and *m* are the primary alliterative elements, and how alliterations of *l, f,* and *h* weave like three threads in and out of the fundamental pattern:

*S*o, *l*ittle by *l*ittle, they *s*tole upon the *h*eart of their *s*ister. *S*he, *m*eanwhile, bids the *l*yre to *s*ound for their de*l*ight, and the *p*laying is *h*eard: *s*he bids the *p*ipes to *m*ove, the choir to *s*ing, and the *m*usic and the *s*inging come invisibly, *s*oothing the *m*ind of the *l*istener with *s*weetest *m*odulation. Yet not even thereby was their *m*alice put to *s*leep: once *m*ore they *s*eek to know what *m*anner of *h*usband *s*he *h*as, and *wh*ence that *s*eed. And P*s*yche, *s*imple over*m*uch, *f*orgetful of *h*er *f*irst *s*tory, answers, "My *h*usband *c*omes *f*rom a *f*ar *c*ountry, trading *f*or great *s*ums. *H*e is already of *m*iddle age, with *wh*itening *l*ocks."

In the following highly rhetorical passage from Ruskin, the reader should notice how the first half of the first sentence is dominated by a constantly recurring *w*; how the second half is dominated by couplets or triplets of alliteration (*b, b, b; p, p; l, l, l*); and how the two halves are woven together by the *f* and *k*

sounds repeated at intervals throughout the sentence. The next
sentence follows the same scheme, with variations. The first half
is dominated by *s*; the second half is dominated by groups of other
alliterations (*g, g, g; b, b, b, b; r, r, r, r; b, b*); and the two halves
are woven together by the *l* sound repeated at intervals throughout
the sentence:

And then you *w*ill hear the sudden rush of the *aw*akened *w*ind,
and you *w*ill see those *w*atch-towers of vapor swept a*w*ay *f*rom their
*f*oundations, and *w*aving *c*urtains of opaque rain let down to the
valleys, swinging from the *b*urdened *c*louds in *b*lack *b*ending *f*ringes,
or *p*acing in *p*ale *c*olumns a*l*ong the *l*ake-*l*evel, grazing its surface into
*f*oam as they *g*o. And then, as the *s*un *s*inks, you *s*hall *s*ee the *s*torm
drift for an instant from off the hills, *l*eaving their *b*road *s*ides
*s*moking and *l*oaded yet with *s*now-white, torn, *s*team-*l*ike *r*ags of
capricious vapor, now *g*one, now *g*athered a*g*ain; while the *s*moulder-
ing *s*un *s*eeming not far away, but *b*urning like a red-hot *b*all *b*eside
you, and as if you could *r*each it, plunges through the *r*ushing wind
and *r*olling cloud with headlong fall, as if it meant to *r*ise no more,
dyeing all the air a*b*out it with *b*lood.

To summarize all this about patterned sounds:
Prominently repeated vowel-sounds (interspersed occasionally
with variant vowel-sounds) constitute the easiest, and often the
most effective kind of sound patterns.

L, m, n, or *r* prominently repeated make easy and effective
sound-patterns.

The other consonants seldom make noticeable or pleasing sound-
patterns unless they occur in alliterations. These alliterations themselves are not pleasing unless they occur in the intricate crisscross
formations described above.

c. *Rhyme.*—One other subject remains to be discussed, though
briefly. It is *rhyme*. We may say at once without any hesitation
that rhyme has no regular place in prose. It usually looks like an
accidental error made by an unskilled writer; and sometimes it

looks like cheap sensationalism. Yet once in a while rhyme is effective. It may be onomatopœic, as in Bierce's "a grumble of drums," and in such phrases as "a growling, howling pack of dogs," "a sputtering, stuttering, frightened little boy," "rushing through the bushes," "chattering about matters of no consequence," "lapping at the platter" (approximate rhyme), "wailing in the jailhouse," and so on. Or it may sometimes, in this day of advertising and political slogans, make a catchy phrase which will draw attention and perhaps be memorable: "gangsters shooting and looting in the cities," "lovers sighing and crying in the parks," "people wailing and railing against fate," "politicians snug in their offices and smug in their conceit," "portraits of office-seekers staring and glaring from every billboard," "the smart, tart bright young people," and so on.

Up to this point, we have discussed only letter-sounds and word-sounds as units or repeated units. We have not discussed the larger groupings of words, the blocks made up of many different syllables forming complex bursts of sound and related harmoniously to other such groups. Our next section will deal with such sound-clusters.

3. Rhythm.— The problem of prose rhythm has been the subject of some studies in physics, many studies in psychology, and countless studies in rhetoric. But probably no writer has ever been able to satisfy anybody but himself with his analysis of prose rhythm. Accordingly, it will be extraordinary if the following paragraphs seem to the reader at all correct or helpful. The chief virtue that the author would claim for them is that they add another point of view, another method of analysis, to those already known. Through synthesizing the various points of view, through picking up a hint here and following a suggestion there, somebody may sometime come to a real understanding of prose rhythm. Till that time, all

suggestions, hints, and points of view of whatever kind will be valuable.

Furthermore, in the course of this study, the student writer may happen upon some bits of information which he had not known, or upon some problems which he had never thought about. If he does, the study will be worth while.

Rhythm in prose is not rhyme; it is not meter (which is a regular succession of alternating accented and unaccented syllables); it is not mere parallel structure (like *I came, I saw, I conquered*); it is not groups of sounds having the same number of syllables; it is not patterns of vowel-sounds and consonant-sounds. Rhythm is like ocean waves breaking on the shore. No two waves are alike; the sounds made by no two waves are alike; and the intervals between no two waves are the same. Yet a rhythm exists in the beating of the surf; and the rhythm changes with changes in the tide and weather.

a. *Rhythm as a Sound Wave.*—The essence of rhythm, like that of pattern, is repeat, although the repeated units need not be identical. Moreover, the repeat consists of two elements instead of one. The wave comes in, and it goes out; comes in, goes out; comes in, goes out. Sounds rise and fall; rise and fall; rise and fall. A sentence with rhythm rises to a crest of sound, and then falls away— only to be followed by another such rise and fall, rise and fall.

<pre>
                    the sea;
        run into   yet the sea
      All the rivers   is not full.

                  come,
          the rivers   thither
      from whence   they return
    Unto the place   again.
</pre>

of labor;

are full   man cannot

All things   utter it.

with seeing,

is not satisfied   nor the ear

The eye   filled with hearing.

been,

which hath   it is that

The thing   which shall be;

done,

which is   it is that which

And that   shall be done.

Notice in this passage just quoted that the rise to the crest and the fall away from it are of about the same length; and that each of the differents crests, from beginning of rise to end of fall, is about the same length as each of the others. Contrast the passage with a piece of non-rhythmic prose such as the following. Writing such as this conveys information clearly, but it is not beautiful.

today,

throughout India   due to

were reported   monsoon storms.

and heavy property damage

Hundreds of deaths

were homeless.

of families

Thousands

over a cliff.

a train was thrown

In southern India

was buried

of fifteen   when a house

a wedding party   collapsed.

In the United Provinces

reported

Most deaths   were caused

by similar

accidents.

Rhythm has many more complexities, however, than those just indicated. In considering them, we should keep in mind a fundamental rule-of-thumb, which is: Include as many words as reason allows in each of the two fundamental elements of a wave. In the following sentences, for example, breaks in thought and in sound come at the places indicated by single bars; but the real crests of the sentences come only at the double bars.

As I sat there, / two clergymen, / each with a magazine in his hand, / seated themselves, // one on one side of the fire, / and one on the other, / close to me.

They soon began / to abuse what they were reading, // and each was reading some part / of some novel / of mine. The gravamen of their complaint / lay in the fact // that I reintroduced the same characters / too often.

We may ignore the minor breaks just now, and keep in mind only the two larger elements of the sentences.

We need not follow punctuation (always variable and often arbitrary) in analyzing passages into sound waves. Sometimes several sound waves may occur in a single sentence, as in the Biblical passage already quoted. On the other hand, one sound wave may involve more than one sentence:

We were in an ecstasy. // We were possessed.

The sun was glorious in the sky. // The sky was of a blue unspeakable.

A great deal of steam! // The pudding was out of the copper. A smell like a washing day! // That was the cloth.

b. *Rhythm as Balanced Sound.*—So far, we have been speaking of the larger rhythmic unit as a wave. Suppose, now, that we abandon that figure, and speak of it as a balance of sound. As in poetry there are the strophe and antistrophe, the stanza and the refrain, the word and its rhyme, so in prose there are sound-units which cry aloud for other sound-units to complete them. In a word, many a sentence-element demands another balancing sentence-element before the sentence as a whole can be satisfying.

Various forces within one sentence-element may impose the necessity of a corresponding sentence-element for the sake of completion.

Grammatical structure is one of the forces:

Though I wanted to go, . . .

If he speaks to me, . . .

When he was writing this book, . . .

All these sentence-elements demand by their structure an answering element.

Logic may also require an additional sentence-element:

I was about to second his remarks.

When I first spoke, he did not answer.

This might have gone on forever.

Such sentences point inevitably toward something more to follow.

And finally, a certain *rhythm in preceding sentences* may point to a like rhythm in subsequent sentences. Thus:

He tried five or six professions in turn without success. He applied for ordination; but as he applied in scarlet clothes, he was speedily turned out of the episcopal palace. He then became tutor in an opulent family, but soon quitted his situation in consequence of a dispute about play. Then he determined to emigrate to America.

The last sentence cannot possibly remain thus without a completing sentence. The rest of the passage has imposed a certain rhythm on the entire paragraph which the last sentence cannot ignore.

c. *Types of Balance.*—But to get back to our fundamental point. Rhythm involves a balancing of sound-groups. Now, balance does not mean symmetry. Balance, indeed, does not necessarily require that both elements have the same general structure. The sketches (Figs. 1 and 2) show a balance between identical parts. But such a balance is primitive and crude. The next sketch (Fig. 3) shows a balance made up of one heavy mass and three light masses. This balance is more complex and more interesting than the others. The final sketches (Figs. 4 and 5) show what any artist knows— that well-isolated small objects balance a large object or a group of objects. This is the most interesting of all balance-combinations.

These are the fundamental types of balance. All other types are but variations of these. In sentences, sound-elements of different lengths take the place of the figures in the drawings. Otherwise the principles of balance are the same in both pictorial and literary art. It should be clearly understood, however, that since spatial isolation is not usually possible in writing, it is replaced by weight of meaning. Thus a short sound-element must have a powerful significance before it can balance a long one, or before it can balance several sound-elements.

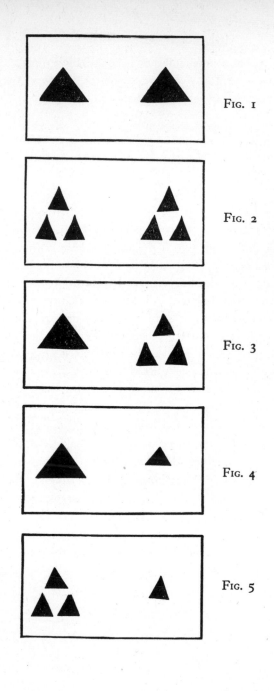

FIG. 1

FIG. 2

FIG. 3

FIG. 4

FIG. 5

Examples of the various types of balance follow, along with a graphical analysis of each:

(1) Two sound-elements of the same length balance each other.

_____ // _____

Stolen waters are sweet, // but bread eaten in secret is pleasant.
Hatred stirreth up strifes: // but love covereth all sins.
He is my brother, // but I do not love him.

(2) Several sound-elements may balance several other sound-elements of the same length:

_____   // _____
_____   _____
_____   _____

He that hath pity on the poor / lendeth unto the Lord; // and that which he hath given / will He pay him back again.
Then said the princes / and all the people / unto the priests / and unto the prophets: // This man is not worthy to die: / for he hath spoken to us / in the name of the Lord / our God.
Such as it [Milton's character] was when, / on the eve of great events, / he returned from his travels, / in the prime of health and manly beauty, / loaded with literary distinctions, / and glowing with patriotic hopes // —such it continued to be when, / after having experienced every calamity / which is incident to our nature, / old, poor, sightless, and disgraced, / he returned to his hovel / to die.

(3) One long sound-element will balance several short sound-elements. (The long element may come last, as shown, or first.)

_____
_____   // _____
_____

Wrath is cruel, / and anger is outrageous; // but who is able to stand before envy?
What shall we say then to these things? // If God is for us, / who is against us?
Neither blindness, / nor gout, / nor age, / nor penury, / nor domes-

tic afflictions, / nor political disappointments, / nor abuse, / nor proscription, / nor neglect, // had power to disturb his sedate and majestic patience.

(4) A short sound-element may balance several other sound-elements of any length—provided the short one expresses a more weighty idea than the others, and (most often) comes at the important end-position of the sentence:

$$\underline{\qquad\qquad} \quad // \quad \underline{\qquad}$$

I tell you further, / and this fact you may receive trustfully, / that his sensibility to human affliction and distress / was no less keen / than even his sense for natural beauty // —heartsight deep as eyesight.

We shall attempt to speak of them, / as we have spoken of their antagonists, // with perfect candor.

Be not deceived: // evil communications / corrupt good manners.

Till I come, // give attendance to reading, / to exhortation, / to doctrine.

(5) Occasionally one short sound-element, weighty in its meaning, will balance a longer element:

$$\underline{\qquad\qquad} \quad // \quad \underline{\qquad}$$

He labored long and faithfully, // but failed.

The first man is of the earth, // earthy.

A philosopher might admire so noble a conception; // but not the crowd.

All these illustrations are sufficient to show the general nature of balance in prose. These general principles, however, are subject to infinite variations. Balanced elements may fall within larger balanced elements; and a whole paragraph may consist of a complex interweaving of balance within balance. The following paragraph from Huxley, for example, is one large rhythmic unit:

If these ideas be destined, / as I believe they are, // to be more and more firmly established / as the world grows older;. if that spirit be fated, / as I believe it is, // to extend itself into all departments of human thought, / and to become co-extensive with the range of knowledge;. if, as our race approaches its maturity, / it discovers, / as I believe it will, // that there is but one kind of knowledge / and but one method of acquiring it;. // then we, / who are still children, / may justly feel it our highest duty to recognize the advisableness of improving natural knowledge, // and so to aid ourselves and our successors / in our course towards the noble goal / which lies before mankind.

Graphically analyzed, the passage would look like this:

The distinctiveness of a writer's style, the prevailing temper, form, and sound which make him what he is, issues, for the most part, from the rhythms which he adopts. It may be a simple rhythm of parallel and antithetical structures composed of two, four, or six sound elements, as in entire books of the King James Bible. Or it may be the complex symphonies of Ruskin, Newman, and Pater.

d. *Harmony of Rhythm and Idea or Feeling.*—But whatever the rhythm they use, good writers fit it to the sense of their work. Simple and plain ideas demand simple and obvious rhythms; involved and difficult ideas demand involved and intricate rhythms. Moreover, letter-sounds must harmonize with the rhythm and with the idea. Certain subjects require certain letter-sounds for their proper transference to the reader; and both subjects and letter-sounds require certain tempos of rhythm. A funeral oration, for example, would not have sprightly *i*-sounds nor would it have a quick and tripping rhythm; instead, it would be filled with long *o*-sounds, and would fall into a slow, stately tempo full of long periods, long sound-elements, and large groupings of well-balanced parts. One would not say in the oration, "He died of angina"; but, "Having long suffered an acute affection of the heart, he at last succumbed to his ailment." (Of course, this second version is wordy; but its rhythm is right—it means right. That a child may understand.) Of a boxing-match, on the other hand, no one would seriously write, "During an encounter notable for its rapidity as well as for its vigor, the present holder of the championship title succeeded in decisively conquering the challenger"; but one would write, "In a hard, fast match the champion knocked out the challenger."

The whole purpose of rhythm, from the beat of the Zulu's tom-tom to the measures of Shakespeare's blank verse, is to create some sort of *feeling* in the listener. Feeling expresses itself in pattern (for rhythm is but a pattern); and pattern, in turn, rouses feeling. The whole business of a writer, therefore, if he wishes to make his reader feel, is to formulate a rhythm which will be consistent with the ideas conveyed by words and the feeling stimulated by word-sounds.

EXERCISES

1. Pure Sounds.

a. Write two short descriptions on each subject suggested below. Try to fill the first description with pleasant, and the second with unpleasant, sounds.

The traffic passing your home at a certain hour.

A touchdown made by your school, and one made by the
opposing school.

A conference with a professor.

Food on the table ready to be eaten.

A crowd at a bathing beach.

An automobile ride through a hilly country.

A modernistic picture you have seen.

A dog sleeping in the sun.

Children playing in the street.

A large person dancing.

b. Experiment with the different emotional effects you can obtain by varying the letter-elements of the sentences below. Alter the meanings slightly whenever you wish.

The old lady was sitting up in bed.

The cat was crying to be admitted.

A bird was singing beautifully from a nearby bush.

He is always complaining about his troubles.

You can always find him reading a book in the library.

2. Patterned Sounds.

a. By describing different kinds of winds at different seasons of the year, try to make the following kinds of vowel-patterns:

With long *a*.

With long *e*.

With *i*.

With *o*.

With *oo* as in *moon*.

Do the same with descriptions of different cloud effects.

Do the same with the different expressions a child's face assumes as the child passes through different emotional states.

Do the same with different incidents in a football game.

b. Using whichever of the consonants *l, m, n,* or *r* seems most suitable, write short, patterned descriptions of the following:

An opal.

An emerald.

A clear winter night.

A spring morning.

Dawn.

A cat stalking a bird.

A woman singing her baby to sleep.

Morning services in a country church.

c. Using a subject suggested in any of the Exercises of this book, try to construct a few paragraphs having pleasing alliterative patterns such as that in the passage by Ruskin quoted in the text above.

3. Rhythm.

a. Read aloud long passages from the King James Bible, Macaulay, Walt Whitman, and Stevenson. Try to find the rhythm in each group of sentences you read, and try to express this rhythm with your voice until you get the "feel" of rhythm.

b. With the purpose of getting appropriate rhythmic effects, write

A somewhat poetic description of the movement of the planets and other heavenly bodies through space.

A description of the movement of traffic as seen from a tall building.

A character sketch of a dignified old scholar.

A character sketch of an energetic and mentally powerful figure such as Mussolini.

An account of a train trip taken at night.

A short essay on Lincoln's place in history.

A short essay on Augustus Cæsar's place in history.

A short emotional argument against child labor.

A short emotional argument in favor of universal military training.

GENERAL EXERCISES ON STYLE

Improve the following sentences or passages, and explain your changes:

1. That man is spiritless who mildly sinks into senility merely because he believes he is irrevocably growing old when the years slip by, for he should know that youth is merely a mental state.

2. His hair was curly, and two small locks stood above his fore-

head like the horns of a faun. He was seated at the soda fountain waiting for his order, and he ran his fingers through his hair.

3. In desiring to go to college I had an ideal to attain, and in order that I might not fail before I reached the goal, I prepared myself.

4. The same punishment which in one age and country is effective may, in another age or country, be wholly without effect.

5. We received an unusually long "town-permission" in order to see O'Neill's *Strange Interlude* because it lasted from two-thirty in the afternoon until six; then a forty-five-minute intermission was given for dinner, and the play was over at ten.

6. However, his coma was soon broken into by the grinding of the steel wheels of the streetcar.

7. Thorsen was happy: he was going to die, and he had found in death a strange beauty.

8. The crowd was quiet, disdaining even the small whisperings and rustlings often attendant where people gather together in groups.

9. In the light of the torches he was strangely impressive. Wisps of light danced about his white hair with a curious effect.

10. He was praying, his voice mingling with the sounds of river and wind, and then winging upward to Him by whom words were heard before they were spoken.

11. In the shadows at the old man's feet I perceived a cripple, and I realized that the prayers were for him, and there came to me a startling thought.

12. Individual prayers sprang up among the crowd, and often these rumbling undertones were broken by loud shouts of "Amen!"

13. The sufferer trembled as he listened to the whispering of the figure in white, and then he did what he had never done before— he walked.

14. Already I was the possessor of one dog of sorts.

15. That evening the two hunters met in the cabin, and a discussion of the day's luck followed.

16. Both in England and in the United States constant efforts are being made to reduce the number of capital offenses.

17. The power of the state over the life of law-breakers should be exercised with great discretion. The age, the country, and the state of society should be taken into consideration, and punishment should be delivered accordingly.

18. It may be added that the Scriptures clearly recognize and justify the infliction of capital punishment in certain cases.

19. His mother was conscientious, thoughtful, and did her best to quell her unruly offspring.

20. Neither of these opportunities is taken advantage of in high school.

21. All types of psychological devices had been lavished on Wee Willie without the slightest trace of improvement in him.

22. Afterward, his habit of fibbing became annoying, even exasperating, as he neared his fifth birthday.

23. Choking and sputtering, he overturned Marjorie's salad, broke his tea glass, and almost blinded Mr. Rover with his spluttering, enjoying himself immensely.

24. Dave's thoughts were evidently far from his situation, and a peculiar expression stole over his features.

25. As far back as I can remember, I have always had an intense dislike for them.

26. I had just received my report card, but I was very disappointed to find that I had made no better than a D in my English. At first I thought that there must be some mistake; so I averaged my grades and found that the grade was correct.

27. In personally diagnosing myself, I believe that of my traits and characteristics, both good and bad, the outstanding one is self-consciousness.

28. Science has greatly increased our power of affecting the lives of distant people, without increasing our sympathy for them.

29. The qualities which produce a man of great eminence in some one field of endeavor are such as might often be undesirable if they were universally distributed.

30. The creed of efficiency for its own sake has become somewhat discredited in Europe since the War, which would never have taken place if the western nations had been slightly more indolent.

31. He fed red corn to his hogs, and stored the white corn in his barn.

32. The summer evening was closed, and Janet, just when her longer stay might have occasioned suspicion and inquiry in that jealous household, returned to Cumnor Place, and hastened to the apartment in which she had left her lady.

33. But it soon appeared that fate intended to turn the incident which he had so gloried in into the cause of his utter ruin.

34. Somewhat to his surprise, the countess said nothing further on the subject, which left Wayland under the disagreeable uncertainty whether or no she had formed any plan for her own future proceedings, as he knew her situation demanded circumspection, although he was but imperfectly acquainted with all its peculiarities.

35. The throng and confusion was of a gay and cheerful character, however.

36. Whenever the senses are impinged on by external objects, whether by the rays of light reflected from them, or by effluxes of their finer particles, there results a correspondent motion of the innermost and subtlest organs. This motion constitutes a representation, and there remains an impression of the same, or a certain disposition to repeat the same motion.

37. In the application of these principles to purposes of practical criticism as employed in the appraisal of works more or less imperfect, I have endeavored to discover what the qualities in a poem are, which may be deemed promises and specific symptoms of poetic power, as distinguished from general talent determined to poetic composition by accidental motives, by an act of the will, rather than by the inspiration of a genial and productive nature.

38. On the night of his arrival in London, Alexander went immediately to the hotel on the Embankment at which he always stopped, and in the lobby he was accosted by an old acquaintance, Maurice Mainhall, who fell upon him with effusive cordiality, and indicated a willingness to dine with him.

39. Henri was very poor, his clothes were torn and dirty and his shoes full of holes, but Sophie felt proud to be with him, although usually she would have been much put out by such things; for several years she had not followed the fashions, but she had always been scrupulously clean in herself and her linen.

40. Miss B., who suffered much from gastric catarrh, had saved a little money out of her dress allowance, and driven from the house by her mother's ill-treatment, went to study in Cracow.

41. She finds her way here by the same creative process by which our feet find the familiar way home on a dark night by accounting for themselves for roots and rocks which we have never noticed by day.

42. We think that it is possible that when these novels written by Miss Cather have little left in them but historical interest, there will still be readers who will find in the three brief novels we have already mentioned and in one long one some flashes of truth about men and women that is universal.

43. When the act was over, they strolled over to the drug-store to drink a Coca-cola.

44. He checked himself abruptly, throwing up his hands in what seemed to be a convulsive gesture.

45. Smith, who had by this time made his sales-connection, swallowed the pride which contrasted so strangely—yet not, after all, unusually—with his lack of chin, and went to see his father and his older sister, who were the last of his close relatives.

46. There she stayed, not happy, and yet not unhappy, making some friends, until she was eighteen, and had graduated with honors, making up for lost time with a vengeance which astonished her teachers, filling in the gaps with a fortitude and determination which won their admiration, and taking a tremendous interest in chemistry.

47. Inflation is among the many subjects about which I disclaim any pretension to real comprehension.

48. Perhaps the greatest danger which is involved in the growing assumption of power by the federal government is the possibility that when rugged individuality has been eliminated as a vital factor in our life the indomitable fighting spirit that made America what she is today may also have been crushed to earth, so that instead of the old do-or-die initiative we may continue to pass the buck in placid resignation.

49. Poor thing! It seemed to be an effort for her to move; her pink, checked gingham dress seemed to make her appear fatter than she really was, and her sunbonnet made her head look too large for her.

50. The statement just made is in accordance with the known facts. Something must be done about the industrial situation which confronts us today. The fate of the nation hangs in the balance; we cannot afford to delay action any further. Everything depends on the willingness of the citizens of this great nation to pull together in one concerted effort to set the wheels of prosperity spinning once more.

Chapter VI

PERSONALITY IN STYLE

THIS part of the discussion on style will be short because the subject is vague, and because good advice about how to acquire personality in style is about as useless as good advice about how to acquire it in real life. The only thing really worth stating is that all writing pretending to literary merit *should* have personality. But what is personality? The dictionary says that it is "that which constitutes distinction of person." This helps a little, for it implies that personality in style is individuality of style; it is what distinguishes one author's work from another's, and gives to each work of one author a certain unity which brands it as distinct.

What constitutes this distinction, however, is another problem. When we look about at our friends and acquaintances, we find ourselves classifying them as *straightforward, earnest, serious, idealistic, emotional, nervous, changeable, melancholy, sophisticated, excitable, stupid, clever, brilliant,* and so on. We classify them according to their morals, their intelligence, and their emotions. But the first of these three standards is obviously useless in our investigation of personality in style; for though a writer or his thoughts may be virtuous or wicked, his style cannot be. We have left, therefore, the two categories of intelligence and emotion.

1. Intellectual Personality.—Concerning the first of these, something has already been said in the section on Rationality in Style; accordingly, little remains to be mentioned here. One of the most

important items contributing to intelligence of personality in style is the presence of an *objective* in every piece of writing. That is to say, every piece of writing should have a central thought, a fundamental idea, a unified theme around which all the other thoughts in the writing are grouped, and toward which they all point. Writing which has no such central objective is certain to convey the impression of a maundering, flaccid intellect which allows itself to talk on and on without point or purpose. Furthermore, this objective must be made clear to the reader by means of repetitions, summaries, references, and proportional lengths of discussion; for if the objective is not obvious to the reader, having an objective is useless.

Next, every non-fictional composition of any length should be divided into a few major parts. Readers cannot and will not follow long, unbroken discussions. But these parts should not be divided and redivided into a vast number of interrelated subdivisions which confuse the reader and make him lose the main objective or the main divisions of the composition. Such dismemberment of ideas is a German habit foreign to the best English tradition. Superfine distinctions and complicated analyses indicate a careful but not a brilliant personality; they might well give place to broad groupings and original syntheses.

As a kind of transition between intelligent personality and emotional personality in style, the value of *impartiality* may be mentioned. Unpracticed writers are likely to think that the most telling criticism and the most powerful satire consist of slashing adjectives, forceful epithets, and scathing denunciations hurled with passionate vigor against the thing attacked. But practiced writers know that no criticism and no satire is effective unless it sounds coolly impartial. Accordingly, practiced writers are always careful to mention a few good traits of their victims. The practiced writer says, "No one ever doubts that Mr. Hoover was as honest as the day is long, sincere, hard-working, and business-like. BUT . . ." Or, "No one ever doubts that Mr. Roosevelt is vigorous, progressive, courageous, and earnest. BUT . . ." And the concession that each man has many real virtues only makes the criticism that follows seem the more calmly judicious, and therefore the more tellingly hurtful. Even if the writer believes that the object of attack has no virtues at all, he should not say so, but should rack his brain to discover some plausible excellence with which to drape the victim. Furthermore, two or three words like "unutterably stupid," "idiotic bungler," "nincompoop," "block-head," "lunatic," and so on, will undo the effect of entire pages of seemingly impartial writing. They are the cloven hoof showing an essentially passionate rather than intellectual personality.

2. **Emotional Personality.**—This brings us to emotion in the personality of style. *Emotion,* however, is a vague word. As used here, it means general disposition, habit of spirit, temperament. The emotion which appears in a style may be of a thousand sorts: *violent* in Carlyle; *playful* and *whimsical* in Charles Lamb; *genial* and *bantering* in Arnold Bennett; *exaggeratedly humorous* in Mark Twain; *austerely but passionately logical* in Matthew Arnold; *enthusiastic but careful* in Huxley; *graceful, familiar,* and *well-bred* in Stevenson; *painstaking, plain,* and *sincere* in Defoe; *cocksure, manly,* and *hearty* in Kipling.

Different subjects and different audiences may demand a variety of personalities at different times from the same author. A social-ist talking to a group of miners would have a style flaring with indignation; talking to a board of mediation, he would have a forceful, logical style; talking to an audience made up from the general public, he would have a persuasive, good-humored style; and writing a book about the economic condition of the poorer classes, he might have a sympathetic, compassionate, warm-hearted style. Which style he adopts depends entirely on his judgment of the fitness of things.

Before setting pen to paper, a writer ought to decide quite methodically what personality he intends to adopt in his contemplated work. Doing so is not admitting duplicity or insincerity. Dickens could write half-a-dozen books like the *Pickwick Papers* and *David Copperfield*, and then adopt an entirely new manner in the *Tale of Two Cities*; Scott could write the swashbuckling *Ivanhoe* and the tender character-study, *Heart of Midlothian;* Poe could write the Gothic study in madness and the supernatural *The Fall of the House of Usher*, and then turn to a "story of ratiocination" like *The Gold Bug*; and George Eliot could write realistic studies of English village life such as *Silas Marner* and *Adam Bede*, and then turn to an historical novel of the Italian Renaissance, *Romola*. Different subjects and different occasions demand different styles.

A writer should deliberately adopt a style which seems to him to fit the subject, the occasion, and his own purpose. If his purpose is to ridicule chivalry, he will adopt one style; if it is to glorify chivalry, he will adopt another. If his purpose is to write a delightful essay on raising vegetables, he will adopt one style; if it is to give information about raising vegetables, he will adopt another. If his purpose is to write a thrilling account of a Civil War battle, he will adopt one style; if it is to criticize the strategy employed by General McClellan, he will adopt another. His writing personality will shift like a windmill with every change of the wind; and, like a windmill, it can do valuable work only if it is able to shift.

One caution must be voiced. Some writers are versatile enough to possess many writing personalities; some can have only two or three; and some can have but one. By experimenting, every writer should determine which personalities serve him best, and which make him ridiculous (or worse). Those which he can assume convincingly are, of course, those which he should adopt. The others he should attempt only for his own private edification. Just here it is that teachers and advisers may be of genuine assistance. They may give a writer impartial judgment on his different personalities. They may tell him to preserve and develop one, reform another, and do immediate execution on a fourth. Counsel such as this is almost indispensable. Literary groups give it among themselves; composition classes encourage it; teachers and personal advisers should take it as their chief business.

The very first duty of a writer of anything but textbooks is to develop some sort of personality in his style. Without it he will not be read; with it, and even with little else besides, he will be read by even very wise people.

Chapter VII

IMAGERY

1. Art.—From the hundreds of definitions of art which have been written, the definition which seems best, and which is certainly the most useful for our present purposes, is that of the Italian philosopher, Benedetto Croce. To Croce, art is "intuition." That is to say, art is " 'vision,' 'contemplation,' 'imagination,' 'fancy,' 'figurations,' 'representations,' and so on."

Art is derived from the artist's power to conceive and bring forth images. These images are not an accumulation of parts; they are not a series; they are not a group of interdependent organs. But each image is a *oneness*, a *totality*, a *nexus* of parts. It is an *intuition* conceived and brought forth perfect. When we see a man, we do not see an accumulation of arms, legs, ears, hands, feet, and so on; we see a *man*. Art is like that. The artist conceives images complete, and (if he is a true artist) he conveys them to other people complete.

These two principles—imagination and completeness—are the bone and sinew of art. Historical fiction differs from history in that the one makes the reader *see* the past, and the other makes him *know* it. Architecture differs from mere construction in that one makes an observer *see* a building as an image, and the other makes him *know* it as something to be used. Painting differs from photography in that one creates a *unified image*, while the other creates a *collection of unselected images*.

Art need not be beautiful; it need not teach a lesson; it need not be true or untrue; it need not be moral or immoral; it need not be useful or non-useful; it need not be realistic or unrealistic. That which is perceived as a complete and unified image—merely that is art.

With this conception of art as intuition, or perfectly conceived image, Croce includes another idea. It is that the real source of the image is feeling; that, indeed, the image is but a symbol of feeling—that art is feeling made image. Suppose we give a concrete illustration. The neighbor owns a police dog. To me the dog is a useless, noisy, meddlesome animal; to the neighbor he is a joyous, faithful, courageous friend; to the casual passerby he is a dangerous and detestable creature who may bite unoffending strangers without provocation. The three of us, therefore, if we described the dog or painted a picture of him, would create three quite different images. Our individual feeling about the dog would determine what he would look like in our artistic efforts.

In the same way, the Middle Ages, for example, may be imaginatively conceived as dashing and adventurous (as in Sir Walter Scott), superstitious and ridiculous (as in Mark Twain), gentle and beautiful (as in Maurice Hewlitt), or mysterious and supernatural (as in Cabell). A story of the South may be romantic and gallant (in Thomas N. Page) or sordid and ugly (in William Faulkner). Negro life may be gently humorous (in Joel Chandler Harris), burlesque (in Octavus Roy Cohen), grimly tragic (in Eugene O'Neill), or broadly farcical (in Roark Bradford). Feeling alone determines what the image is to be.

As we proceed, we shall see how these principles of Croce may help a writer elevate his work from the level of mere exposition to the level of art.

2. Kinds of Images.—We have been speaking of images as if all of them were pictures. And as a matter of fact, the great majority of images do appeal to the sense of sight by being made up of de-

tails of color, form, and motion. Yet other sorts of material are equally the material of art—images of sound, of taste, of touch, of smell, of temperature, of sensations in the vital organs and in the muscles. Except for images of sound, most of the list seldom play a part in writing. They deserve attention not only because they are neglected, but because when they *are* used, they are generally effective.

An appeal to the senses is the only way to create images. Mere factual knowledge is worse than nothing so far as art is concerned. To say that a building faces south; that its reception hall is forty-five feet long and twenty-two feet wide; that the hall contains three tables and fourteen chairs—this means nothing at all to one looking for artistic writing. And no more does it mean anything that a man is about five feet and ten inches tall; that he weighs about one hundred and fifty pounds; that his eyes are blue and his hair dark. Such exact details are not imaginative. They are scientific. They have no place in artistic writing.

3. Imaginative Words.—Some words, or patterns of words, make pleasing or suggestive sound-images irrespective of their meaning. But since we have already spoken of these sound-images made by words, we must confine ourselves here to the images called to the reader's mind by means of words which themselves are inconsiderable as sound-images. That is, we must talk of words that recall sense impressions.

a. *Concrete Words.*—It is an old principle that concrete words are preferable to abstract. They are preferable because they are imaginative.

"It was autumn," is not so imaginative as, "The last of the leaves were falling, and the ground was spread with brown and gold."

"The sun rose," is not so imaginative as, "The red and swollen sun lifted itself over the eastern wall."

"In winter," is not so imaginative as, "When icicles hang by the wall."

The entire Bible, a book of precept, philosophy, and theology, where, of all places, one might expect teeming abstractions, is instead a treasure-house of concrete imagery.

"Wickedness is vain," becomes, "He that soweth iniquity shall reap vanity."

"The froward shall have many hardships," becomes, "Thorns and stones are in the way of the froward."

"Life is better than death," becomes, "A living dog is better than a dead lion."

"There shall be peacefulness," becomes, "The lion and the lamb shall lie down together, and a little child shall lead them."

"They shall have no decent burial," becomes, "And their dead bodies shall be for meat unto the fowls of heaven, and to the beasts of the earth."

In every good writer there is a similar urge to transform the abstract into the concrete. Hardly a bald, factual statement exists but it can be dignified and vivified by concrete imaginative expression. The simple fact that it is dawn becomes in *Hamlet*:

> The morn in russet mantle clad
> Walks o'er the dew of yon high eastern hill.

In the same play, the simple fact that the player was much affected becomes concrete:

> All his visage wann'd,
> Tears in his eyes, distraction in 's aspect,
> A broken voice.

Nor does Hamlet say, "Who insults me?" but

> Who calls me villain, breaks my pate across,
> Plucks off my beard and blows it in my face,
> Tweaks me by the nose, gives me the lie i' the throat
> As deep as to the lungs, who does me this?

Stevenson does not say, "Death makes life lonely for the living," but, "There are empty chairs, solitary walks, and single beds at night."

Irving does not say, "It grew darker in Westminster Abbey," but, "The chapels and aisles grew darker and darker. The effigies of the kings faded into shadows; the marble figures of the monuments assumed strange shapes in the uncertain light; the evening breeze crept through the aisles into the cold breath of the grave."

b. *Polysymbolic Words.*—All words symbolize something; but some words symbolize several things. Naturally, a writer's meaning becomes richer if he can substitute the latter sort of word for words that symbolize only one object, idea, or emotion. The following is a list intended to suggest the possibilities of such substitutions. In the list, the first of each pair of words appeals to one sense only; the second word appeals to several senses.

Black	sight
Pitchy	sight and touch
White	sight
Snowy	sight and temperature
Gray	sight
Leaden	sight and weight
Sticky	touch
Gelatinous	touch and sight
Sore	touch
Raw	touch and sight
Hot	temperature
Fiery	temperature and sight
Soft	touch
Cottony	touch and sight
Weep	sight
Sob	sight, sound, and motion

```
Cut  . . . . . . . . . . . . . . . sight
Chop  . . . . . . . . . . . . . sight, sound, and motion
```

c. *Atmospheric Words.*—These words with their complex imagery are close kin to the next sort of words we shall consider, namely, words with atmosphere. To indicate what is meant by "atmosphere," we have only to recall the old joke about the foreign gentleman who complimented the American woman: "What a lovely hide you have!" *Hide* was just what the gentleman meant; but the atmosphere of the word is wrong: no lady would endure it. In the same way, we cannot write (as in the old example), "The lady held a lily in her fist," though that is what she did. We cannot write, "George III went crazy," but must say, "George III became insane." We cannot write, "Heifetz is one of the world's greatest fiddlers," but must say, "Heifetz is one of the world's greatest violinists." These illustrations explain *atmosphere* very well. It is the aura which surrounds a word, the associations linked to it, the ideas, images and emotions which come to the reader when he chances on the word.

The business of the writer is not merely to avoid such ludicrous errors as those mentioned above, but to find words which will enrich his meaning by adding clusters of appropriate images to his words. Thus, to use an example already mentioned in another connection, the sentence, "She lay between white sheets," tells the reader merely that the linen was clean. But if it reads, "She lay between snowy sheets," it tells the reader that the sheets are cool as well as clean.

To the sick man, the wrinkles in the bedclothes looked enormous.

To the sick man, the wrinkles in the bedclothes looked mountainous.

The last word has associations of vast irregularities spread over wide spaces, of laborious travel, of unfeeling ruggedness. Since these words fit the sick man's conception, the word *mountainous* enriches the simple idea of bigness.

He moistened the sick man's face with a damp cloth.

He swabbed the sick man's face with a soggy rag.

The first sentence does the sick man a kindness; the second abuses him. "Swab" is associated with mops roughly handled; "soggy," with solids left too long in questionable liquids; and "rag," with casual salvaging from dirty clothes.

Keats writes, "I set her on my pacing steed." Suppose he had substituted the plain word "horse" for "steed." How different would have been the effect. Sir Walter Scott writes, "He mounted his charger." What if he had written "pony" instead?

Shakespeare begins a sonnet:

> That time of year thou mayst in me behold
> When yellow leaves, or none, or few, do hang
> Upon those boughs which shake against the cold,
> Bare ruined choirs, where late the sweet birds sang.

The word "choirs" calls up far more images than the word itself actually signifies. It calls up a picture of the entire abbey ruined and desolate, with a winter wind wailing through it.

Diction such as this means more than it says. It makes use not only of the reader's knowledge of word-significance, but also of his experiences, his reading, his emotions, his imaginings. It is like music which calls a thousand pictures to mind, though each picture may be only half-perceived and half-comprehended. Tennyson had this kind of diction in mind when he wrote of Virgil's poetry:

All the charm of all the Muses often flowering in a lonely word.

d. *Figures of Speech.*—At this point we should logically include a full discussion of figurative language and its power to evoke mages. But since we have already discussed figurative language in one or two places, we need not pause over it here. That is, we need not pause except to reiterate that imaginative writing is all but impossible without figures of speech; that the best imaginative writers strew figures profusely over their pages; that figures have a charm in themselves and in their associated ideas; and that figures make for power, variety, and richness of imagery.

4. Imaginative Details.—The subject matter of the artist is not the general, as it is with the scientist, but the particular; not the class, but the individual. He is not to make us see what horses look like, but what *a* horse looks like—and *a* man, *a* train-coach, *a* lawn, *a* bird. Maupassant tells how Flaubert trained him to observe a tree until he found how that one tree differed from all other trees, and then to express in words the distinctive details of that particular tree. Finding distinctive and imaginative details should be the chief business of any artist.

a. *Familiar Details.*—The details need not be garnered from remote or visionary places, or from marvelous and romantic happenings. In general, they are more pleasing if they come from the realm of the commonplace and the familiar.

> For, don't you mark? we're made so that we love
> First when we see them painted, things we have passed
> Perhaps a hundred times nor cared to see.

Such images as the following, familiar as our own hand, delight us:

She put down the dish, wiped her palm along the side of her hip, and shook hands with the visitor.

Fantastically, as if ghosts were eating, she heard only the clinking of spoons touching glasses, and the low clatter of forks against plates; but no voices.

Putting his thumb to the side of his nose, and leaning far forward at the waist, he blew with a loud, fluid snort.

As she ascended the stairs before him, he noticed her cheap cotton stockings with tiny bits of lint sticking out all over them.

I watched her buy a package of gum, open the end of the cerise wax-paper wrapper, and extract a flat stick.

In preparing lemons for the tea, she first carefully sliced off the pithy nipple at the end of each lemon.

b. *Unfamiliar Details.*—Even when we are describing objects or scenes unfamiliar to the reader, we must translate them into terms of the familiar. Thus, Tennyson describes the dying King Arthur as

> > looking wistfully with wide blue eyes
> As in a picture.

And the boat on which the king is taken

> Moved from the brink like some full-breasted swan.

Kipling gives us:

Now and again a spot of almost boiling water would fall on the dust with the flop of a frog.

Willa Cather speaks of "the horny backbones of mountains," and describes sunset on the desert thus:

The scattered mesa tops, red with the afterglow, one by one lost their light, like candles going out.

In one sentence Ruskin pictures "the heaving mountains rolling against [the sunrise] like waves of a wild sea"; glaciers blazing in the sunlight "like mighty serpents with scales of fire"; and the "whole heaven one scarlet canopy . . . interwoven with a roof of waving flame."

All these figures make us perceive images beyond our experience by recalling to us images within our experience. Much image-making proceeds in this way.

c. *Incongruous Details.*—The matter of old images in new connections deserves further comment. We may call up particularly
vivid images by means of an incongruity between details as they
usually occur and as they appear in some newly imagined situation. Homer, for example, describes one of his warriors as having
forgotten his whip when he drove out in his chariot, and belabor-
ing the horses with the butt of his spear. The *incongruity between
the object and its use* makes the incident highly visual. Similar
descriptions follow:

The carpenter took up a sharp wood-chisel, and proceeded to pare
his nails.
As he sat in the chair, he bent over and scratched his shin with
a ruler.
His arms piled full of books, Dr. Watson gave directions to the
librarian, pointing here and there with his chin.
She stood at the kitchen table vigorously rolling out biscuit dough
with a short length of iron pipe.

Sometimes an *incongruity of environment* creates visual images:

The tops of a dozen parked automobiles showed above the parapet
on the roof of a six-story building.
A large yellow butterfly had drifted into the room through an
open window, and was hovering over a vase of cut-flowers at the
visitor's elbow.
The burro stood motionless, with head down and lower lip drooping, full in the blazing sunlight; two or three panting chickens had
taken refuge in the shadow of his body.

An *incongruity between the object and the thing of which it is
made* may serve the purposes of visualization:

The front gate was merely the ornamental head-piece of an iron
bed swung by one side to a fence post.
The sideboards of the Negro yard-man's small wagon were two
green Venetian blinds placed on edge.

The Negro chief had a pierced lower lip through which he had stuck a new yellow pencil stolen from the white men's camp.
He wore a finger ring of braided hair.

The types of details mentioned in this section do not by any means exhaust the possibilities of the imagination. Far from it! They constitute some of the most vivid types of details, but, after all, they are only suggestive. They are guideposts to imagery, not the entire kingdom.

5. Imaginative Construction.—Often a writer can construct complete images only by the use of several details, not just one like those mentioned above. What these details shall be, and what the writer's method of presenting them, depends entirely on the purpose of the writer. His first duty, therefore, in trying to create a full and unified image is to ask himself what his purpose is in presenting the image to the reader.

a. *Purpose in Imaginative Writing.*—The imaginative writer's purpose is always one of the following: to paint a picture, to convey an idea, or to convey or rouse a feeling. Most of the details cited in the last section attempted *to paint pictures.* This next, a longer description from Flaubert's *Salambo*, does the same:

The heavy mill-stones were revolving in the dust, two cones of porphyry laid one upon the other, the upper, which had a funnel, being turned upon the lower by means of strong bars which men pushed with their breasts and arms, while others were yoked to them and pulled. The friction of the straps had caused purulent sores about their arm-pits, such as are seen on asses' withers; and the ends of the limp black rags which barely covered their loins hung down and flapped against their hocks like long tails. Their eyes were red, the shackles clanked about their feet, and all their breasts rose and fell in unison. They were muzzled to prevent them from eating the meal, and their hands were enclosed in gauntlets without fingers so that they could not pick it up.

But some descriptions are meant *to convey an idea*. Shakespeare, in the following song, does not mean to paint a picture, but to convey an idea of winter and its cold:

When icicles hang by the wall,
  And Dick the shepherd blows his nail,
And Tom bears logs into the hall,
  And milk comes frozen home in pail,
When blood is nipped and ways be foul,
Then nightly sings the staring owl,
    Tu-whit, to-who,
    A merry note,
While greasy Joan doth keel the pot.

When all aloud the wind doth blow,
  And coughing drowns the parson's saw,
And birds sit brooding in the snow,
  And Marian's nose looks red and raw,
When roasted crabs hiss in the bowl,
Then nightly sings the staring owl,
    Tu-whit, to-who,
    A merry note,
While greasy Joan doth keel the pot.

This next, from George Eliot, is also intended to convey an idea of quietness on Sunday morning:

You might have known it was Sunday if you had only waked up in the farmyard. The cocks and hens seemed to know it, and made only crooning subdued noises; the very bull-dog looked less savage, as if he would have been satisfied with a smaller bite than usual. The sunshine seemed to call all things to rest and not to labour; it was asleep itself on the moss-grown cow-shed; on the group of white ducks nestling together with their bills tucked under their wings; on the old black sow stretched languidly on the straw, while her largest young one found an excellent spring-bed on his mother's fat ribs; and Alick, the shepherd, in his new smock-frock, taking an uneasy siesta, half-sitting, half-standing on the granary steps.

And this next, from Keats, does not attempt to give a picture of autumn—a thing manifestly impossible—but to convey an idea of what autumn does:

> Season of mists and mellow fruitfulness,
>   Close bosom-friend of the maturing sun;
> Conspiring with him how to load and bless
>   With fruit the vines that round the thatch-eaves run;
> To bend with apples the mossed cottage-trees,
>   And fill all fruit with ripeness to the core;
>   To swell the gourd, and plump the hazel shells
> With a sweet kernel; to set budding more,
>   And still more, later flowers for the bees,
>   Until they think warm summer days will never cease,
>   For Summer has o'er-brimmed their clammy cells.

The third purpose an imaginative writer may have, *to convey or rouse a feeling,* is often intermingled with the other two. Thus, both the George Eliot paragraph and the Keats stanza just quoted are probably intended as much to awaken a feeling of peace and lassitude in the reader as to convey idea. The following passage from Daudet, however, is written only with the purpose of conveying a feeling of sadness; it gives only the vaguest sort of picture:

The little Dauphin is ill; the little Dauphin is dying. In all the churches of the kingdom the Holy Sacrament remains exposed night and day, and great tapers burn, for the recovery of the royal child. The streets of the old capital are sad and silent, the bells ring no more, the carriages slacken their pace. . . . All the castle is in a flutter. Chamberlains and major-domos run up and down the marble stair-ways. The galleries are full of pages and courtiers in silken apparel, who hurry from one group to another, begging in low tones for news. Upon the wide perrons the maids of honor, in tears, exchange low courtesies and wipe their eyes with daintily embroidered handkerchiefs.[1]

[1] From Alphonse Daudet's "The Death of the Dauphin," in *Pastels in Prose,* copyright, 1890 and 1918, by Harper & Brothers. Reprinted by permission of the publishers.

This next, from *The Tempest*, likewise tries to rouse a feeling rather than convey a clear-cut image:

> Our revels now are ended. These our actors,
> As I foretold you, were all spirits, and
> Are melted into air, into thin air;
> And like the baseless fabric of this vision,
> The cloud-capp'd towers, the gorgeous palaces,
> The solemn temples, the great globe itself,
> Yea, all which it inherit, shall dissolve
> And, like this insubstantial pageant faded,
> Leave not a rack behind. We are such stuff
> As dreams are made on, and our little life
> Is rounded with a sleep.

Much imaginative writing, however, is concerned with both pure imagery and feeling. Poe, for instance, is famous for his passages which create pictures, and at the same time rouse emotions:

> During the whole of a dull, dark, and soundless day in the autumn of the year, when the clouds hung oppressively low in the heavens, I had been passing alone, on horseback, through a singularly dreary tract of country; and at length found myself, as the shades of evening drew on, within view of the melancholy House of Usher. . . . I looked upon the scene before me—upon the mere house, and the simple landscape features of the domain—upon the bleak walls—upon the vacant, eye-like windows—upon a few rank sedges—and upon a few white trunks of decayed trees—with an utter depression of soul.

Irving's description of evening in Westminster Abbey, already quoted, is another excellent example of imagery created and feeling roused in the same passage; and the first three stanzas of Gray's *Elegy in a Country Churchyard* are another.

b. *Selection of Details.*—Now, suppose a writer has determined definitely the purpose he has in mind in creating an image; his next step is to decide just which details of the image he is to use in writing. Obviously he cannot possibly use every detail; for if he did, he might, like Agassiz's student, spend days describing a three-inch fish, or write an encyclopedia on what he sees in walking across the campus. He must select, and select rigorously. Selection is so vital a business to the artist that it has given rise to many an aphorism—that art is but selection; that a piece of art is to be judged less by what it contains than by what it does not contain; and that the genius of the artist consists in his knowing what to leave out.

If, for example, the artist is trying to give an *idea* that the weather is very cold, he will not tell the reader that the cattle are tucked away snug and content in their barn, and that people are cozy on the warm hearthstone. If he is trying to give a *feeling* of sadness, he will not tell about the private balls, the parties, the gaiety, and the love-making which will occur no matter how many Dauphins die. And if he is a criminal lawyer trying to paint a *picture* of a murder, he will paint it far differently from the way the district attorney paints a picture of the same murder.

In all these descriptions, nobody is necessarily falsifying details; but each is selecting certain details and omitting others. A man may be a regular church attendant, he may be charitable, he may be a good husband and a kind father, he may have friends among the most honest people in his city—but he may falsify accounts in the bank of which he is president. A cold morning may be brisk and cheerful weather to some people, and it may be bitterly hard to others. The Negro yard-man may be a subject of humor to some people, and a subject of tragedy to others. Seldom in imaginative writing can any writer paint things just as they would appear to the scientist, to the camera, or to the impartial observer. Nearly always the image created depends on the writer's selection of certain details which affect him, and which, he hopes, will affect the reader, and on the omission of certain other details. And his selections and omissions depend altogether on his purpose.

This does not mean that the writer should give the impression of being biased and impartial. Quite the contrary! The reader must never be allowed even to think that other details exist, or that the writer is not being scrupulously exact in his description. Nevertheless, the fact remains that the entire responsibility for the image, the idea, or the feeling conveyed rests squarely in the writer's hands. What the image, the idea, or the feeling shall be depends on him, and not on what he is describing. If he is not willing to assume the responsibility, to fix the mark of his own personality on the image, he can never be a good artist.

c. *Arrangement of Details.*—Up to this point, we have seen that the fundamental requirement for good imagery is a certain purpose on the part of the writer, which purpose guides him in the selection of details. Furthermore, his purpose sometimes guides him in the arrangement of details after he has selected them. Thus, if his purpose is merely to convey an *idea* that a day is cold or hot, that a family lives in squalid surroundings, that a room looks neat, that a certain street corner is busy, or other such ideas, he need do no more than give a series of details selected for the purpose in mind and arranged more or less at random. Shakespeare's winter song, Keats's stanza on autumn, and Eliot's description of a Sunday morning (all quoted above) are examples of such random arrangement of details. In the last-mentioned, they occur in a roughly climactic order, with the most noteworthy detail coming last; such an arrangement, however, is not always necessary.

The same sort of random arrangement, with usually a more careful effort toward climax, is common in description the purpose of which is to rouse *emotion*.

But when the writer's purpose is to paint a *picture*, he can seldom resort to a mere series of details and depend on their cumulative effect. Instead, he must arrange his details with such care that the reader will receive a unified and complete image that will satisfy Croce's definition of *intuition*. Distortions, false impressions made and later corrected, details which refuse to coalesce, details out of harmony with one another, details which distract the reader from the main image, details out of all proportion to their importance, details out of their rational place—all such errors are stumbling blocks lying in the artist's path.

The following paragraphs will try to explain how these stumbling blocks may be removed or circumvented by the arrangement of details intended to form a picture.

(1) *If the subject of description is changing, or if the author's point of view is changing,* the chronological order of arrangement of details is usually best. The description of a butterfly emerging from its cocoon, of a tide coming in, of a boat race, of a prizefight, of a football game, of the emotion one feels during a battle, of inward sensations one has when he takes opium, of bodily pains—the description of all such changing subjects must almost necessarily begin with the first thing that happens, and proceed to the next, and the next, and so on to the end.

Similarly, a description of what one sees during a walk down the street, or an automobile ride into the country, or a canoe-trip down the river, or a tour abroad—such descriptions of objects observed while the writer's point of view changes must almost necessarily begin with the first thing that happens, and proceed to the next, and the next, and so on.

(2) Describing *changeless objects from a motionless point of view* requires a more elaborate technique in the arrangement of details. Various objects require different methods. But most of the methods may be included under one of two sorts of possible

arrangements: details as they are arranged in space, and details as they are observed.

As for the first of these—objects may be described according to their arrangement in *perspective*. For example, I may describe the lawn I see directly under my window, then the hedge on the far side of the lawn, then the street beyond the hedge, then the patch of woods beyond the street, then the houses beyond the woods, and then the fields beyond the houses stretching away to the horizon. Thus I should proceed from the nearest objects to those successively farther and farther away. Or I may reverse the process, begin at the horizon and work inward toward the lawn beneath my window. It makes little difference which method I follow as long as I stick to the order I have adopted.

Somewhat similar to perspective description is description of details according to their *arrangement in space regardless of perspective*. In describing a room, for instance, I may begin with objects on my right as I enter, and then proceed all around the room until I have made a complete circle back to the objects on my left. Or in describing a man, I may begin with his head and work downward to his feet. In this method, too, an order once adopted ought not to be changed without a warning to the reader.

Now about the other method of arranging changeless objects observed from a motionless point of view. *Details may be presented as they are observed*. For example, a person pictured as coming from the darkness into a brightly lighted room would not notice at first a book lying on a small table over in the corner of the room. Instead, dazzled for a moment, he would see only bright lights and people; he would observe next the larger pieces of furniture, the rugs, and the hangings; then he would become aware of more subdued colors here and there, and of smaller objects in the room; and finally he might perceive the book on the table. The same sort of gradual accommodation of vision would occur if the person went from light into darkness, or if he suddenly struck a light or extinguished one. The writer must accommodate his arrangement of details to the stages of accommodation which the person's eyes undergo.

But even where there is no change of light, an observer ordinarily sees certain details in an object before he sees others. Usually, he first gets a general impression, forms a large, vague image, and later on fills in his outline with particular details. Accordingly, a writer should usually follow this arrangement in his work by *proceeding from the description of general details to the description of particular details.* If he is describing a man, he says something about "a short fat man" (the general impression) and then adds details about "rolls of fat overhanging his collar," "a deep crease running around his wrist between hand and arm," "little dimples on each knuckle," and so on (the particular details). He says of a house, "a brick cottage of the English type" (general impression) and then adds something about "steep gables," "small-paned, casement windows," "a beam of timber over the door," and so on (particular details).

General details may be classified under various headings, the following of which are intended to be suggestive, though not exhaustive:

I. Type form.

The army was drawn up in a *horseshoe-shaped* bend of the river.

The house is *L-shaped.*

Our first impression was of an enormous *round man.*

The ship was *high fore and aft, and low in the waist.*

The valley lay between two straight cliffs, *flat like the floor of a long room with high walls.*

II. Type color.

She appeared in a *red* dress with a *black* sash.

The flowered hillside looked as if a *rainbow* had broken and splashed over it.

The *green* of the jungle was *intense* and *dark*.

A *bottle-green* cloud hung in the west.

More than half the houses in this seaport town were *yellow* with *red* roofs.

III. Type movement.

Woodpeckers fly with *wave-like undulations up and down.*

The main piston of the engine *shot forward and drew back* with tireless monotony.

Chinese girls, their feet bound, *minced and toddled* beside him.

A tropical hurricane is a vast *whirlpool* of air with *straight winds blowing furiously toward the center.*

The sick man *leaned forward* as he walked, and *took short, quick steps as if to catch himself before he should fall.*

IV. Type sound.

A machine gun *chattered* in the darkness.

Above the music, one could hear the vague *shuffling sound* made by the dancers' feet.

The inside of the factory was pervaded by a *vast humming roar.*

Traffic *clattered* over the brick pavement.

The tires of the big car made a *smacking noise* as they moved swiftly along the wet pavement.

V. Our sense of touch is limited to distinguishing between the following sensations:

Soft or hard; smooth or rough; sharp or blunt; wet or dry; large or small; heavy or light; thick or thin; hot or cold.

But we frequently use figurative words to express touch sensa tions—words such as *velvety, silky, icy, rasping, syrupy, glassy* and so on.

VI. Our sense of smell is confined to the following types of odors Spicy, flowery, fruity, resinous or balsamic, burnt, and foul.

VII. All taste-types are composed of salt, sour, sweet, or bitter. To these may be added irritants or caustics, such as pepper, alcohol, and vinegar; textures, such as greasiness, softness, toughness, and so on, and humidity (relative dryness or moistness).

The three last sense-types mentioned are so limited in number that writers must often resort to figures of speech in calling them to the reader's imagination.

It is only after he has given his type-image that the writer faces the problem of filling in with particular details. George Eliot writes, for example, "If ever a girl looked as if she had been made of roses, that girl was Hetty in her Sunday hat and frock." There is the general picture. Details of the girl's rose-likeness follow:

For her hat was trimmed with pink, and her frock had pink spots, sprinkled on a white ground. There was nothing but pink and white about her, except in her dark hair and eyes and her little buckled shoes.

Maupassant describes his Two Little Soldiers: "Being little and thin, they looked quite lost in their coats, which were too big and too long." There is the general picture. The author goes on to present particular details arranged in the descending order from the large and noticeable to the small and inconspicuous:

The sleeves hung down over their hands, and they were much both- ered by their enormous red breeches, which compelled them to walk vide. Under their stiff, high shakos their faces seemed like mere nothings—two poor, hollow Breton faces, simple in an almost animal simplicity, and with blue eyes that were gentle and calm.[2]

J. B. Priestley writes, "Miss Potter had a sleek, almost electro-plated blonde head." This detail describes Miss Potter's general appearance; we know at once that she is a blonde. Moreover, it is the first of a series of details presented according to their arrangement in space—from the head downward:

No eyebrows; very round blue eyes; a button of a nose, so small and heavily powdered that it resembled the chalked end of a billiard cue; and a mouth that was a perpetual crimson circle of faint astonishment. The upper half of her, her neck and shoulders and the thin arms ending so curiously in little dumpy hands, was poor; but her legs were really beautiful.[3]

These three paragraphs of description are enough to suggest the varied possibilities of arrangement of details after the type-image is presented. Rules to cover all images are out of the question; the writer must decide for himself what method he is to follow. Yet he will find it nearly always safe to begin with the large and the general, and to proceed, by any method that seems fit, to the small and the particular. This is a good working principle.

Nowadays, numerous details and elaborate descriptions in the Sir-Walter-Scott manner are out of fashion. Consequently, many writers content themselves with presenting only *the general type-image, followed immediately by one or two short, vividly imaginative, particular images.* Arnold Bennett presents M. Chirac:

Now a fragile, short young Frenchman, with an extremely pale face ending in a thin black imperial, appeared at the entrance.

A little more elaborately, in *Great Expectations*, Dickens describes Mrs. Joe Gargery:

> My sister, Mrs. Joe, with black hair and eyes, had such a prevailing redness of skin, that I sometimes used to wonder whether it was possible she washed herself with a nutmeg-grater instead of soap. She was tall and bony, and almost always wore a coarse apron fastened over her figure behind with two loops, and having a square impregnable bib in front, that was stuck full of pins and needles.

And Stevenson uses the same method here:

> In the dock, the centre of men's eyes, there stood a whey-coloured misbegotten caitiff, Duncan Jopp, on trial for his life. . . . He kept his head bowed and his hands clutched on the rail; his hair dropped in his eyes, and at times he flung it back; and now he glanced about the audience in a sudden fellness of terror, and now looked in the face of his judge and gulped.[4]

6. Interpretative Description.—The pure image, the way a thing looks, is not always sufficient. Croce's definition of art, if we recall it, has it that art is feeling made image—image symbolizing feeling. This definition is perfectly sound, for the best imaginative writing passes beyond pure description to interpretative description. That is, to description not only of the external appearance of objects, but also to the implications which the writer feels lie behind the surface. In passages quoted above, the writers read into details of their characters "faint astonishment," "animal simplicity," "irritable tension," "cold fire," and "fellness of terror." And daily people speak of a "weak chin," a "malicious smile," and a "brutal mouth." Even inanimate objects or natural scenes may be rendered interpretatively: the writer may read into his subject whatever he thinks it means, as George Eliot, in the description of Sunday morning already quoted, read peacefulness into farmyard objects, and as Poe, in the beginning paragraphs

[4] From *Weir of Hermiston*, chap. iii. Reprinted here by permission of the publishers, Charles Scribner's Sons.

of *The Fall of the House of Usher*, read nameless terror and desolation into scenes along the way. What the interpretation shall be depends, of course, on the personal feeling and the personal judgment of the writer: to one person, a mouth may look "brutal"—to another, "affectionate"; to one person a smile may look "malicious"—to another, "mischievous." But all this brings us back to where we started: the picture any reader receives from an imaginative description depends entirely on the writer's purpose, idea, and feeling in constructing the description.

EXERCISES

1. Art.

   a. By writing a few sentences on five of the following subjects, try to see how many descriptive details you can include and yet give a unified impression. Fifteen is a considerable number.

   An old lady.
   A man's (woman's) bedroom.
   A flock of ducks on a pond.
   Small boats tied up at wharves along a riverside.
   A view from a hilltop.
   A cloud effect.
   A house.
   A forest early in the morning or late in the evening.
   A city street at some particular hour of the day.
   A beach.

   b. Do the descriptions you have just written convey any feeling? If not, rewrite them in such a way as to make them convey feeling. Rewrite one description several times so as to make it convey a different feeling with each revision, but do not add more details.

2. Kinds of Images.

   Write a description of your breakfast this morning in terms of the following senses:

   Taste.

Smell.

Temperature.

Sound (include sounds made by yourself and by others at
the table).

3. Imaginative Words.

    a. Express concretely the following abstract statements:

        It was in the middle of summer.

        He is lazy.

        I feel gloomy.

        The wind is blowing.

        He walked rapidly.

        She is a shallow little thing.

        I dislike everything about him.

        The good life is not an easy life.

        He began to take a pride in his appearance.

        The entire nation was distressed about his death.

    b. Find a polysymbolic word or phrase for each of the italicized
words in the following sentences:

        Her face was *pale*.

        His eyes were *hard*.

        The jewels *shone* in the darkness.

        He *put* the book on the table.

        He looked out on the *soft* green of new leaves.

        A *cold* wind was blowing.

        The axeman *cut* off the victim's head.

        He *passed* me hurriedly.

        He marched *stiffly*, like a toy soldier.

        He *drank* tea and *ate* cookies.

        He *turned* the pages rapidly.

        He *held out* a *cold* hand.

        The roof *fell* in.

    c. Explain the connotations of the italicized words or phrases in
the following passage:

> To her right, she saw the *shattered array* of a dying
> cornfield. The stalks leaned *stiffly* at *infinite* angles, *flut-*
> *tering tattered* brown *pennants* in the wind. She gave a
> melancholy shudder as she *stared* at the corn-rows: this
> same field, only two months past, had been *gloriously*

green, flaunting its *plumed* tassels like *cloth of gold*. Then
it had been *heavy* and *pregnant* with imminent *fertility*,
but now it was the *graveyard* of summer. Life had *departed* from the field.

M. G. Williams

d. Use each of the following words in a figure of speech in a
sentence:

watchman	cloy	adorn	opulence
patrolman	glut	garnish	affluence
sentinel	gorge	whitewash	competence
sentry	sate	bedizen	riches

penurious
destitute
impecunious
beggared

4. Imaginative Details.

a. During the course of about two weeks, accumulate from your
observation a list of forty familiar details like those quoted in
Section 4 above.

b. Examine the descriptions you wrote under Sections 1 and 2
above to determine where you might have used figures of speech
effectively. Try to invent figures of speech which could be applied
to details in the descriptions.

c. During the course of two weeks accumulate from your observation a list of forty details which are imaginative because of
some incongruity.

5. Imaginative Construction.

a. Write three separate descriptive paragraphs about one of the
following topics. In the first paragraph, try to paint a picture; in
the second, try to convey an idea; and in the last, try to rouse a
feeling.

A mob attempting to secure and lynch a prisoner.

A hot summer day.

The home of a country relative.

A business office.

A horse (dog, cat, parrot).

A preacher in the pulpit.

A teacher before the class.

b. By selecting different details, rewrite the descriptive paragraph you have just done so as to have it convey an opposite idea; an opposite feeling.

Look about the classroom. What details would you select to suggest that it is efficiently constructed and arranged? Inefficiently constructed and arranged? Cheerful? Cheerless?

Do the same for some view of the campus and its buildings

c. List fifteen or twenty details which you can see from your window. Now (supposing that your purpose is to give a picture of the scene) arrange these details in all the orders suggested in the text above.

Do the same for the details which you can see from the window of a train passing through a plains country; or a farming country or a mountainous country; or a flat marshy country; or a forest country.

Express in a sentence the type-form of each of the following

A tree you know.

A flower.

Your favorite chair.

A strange bird in the zoo.

A building on the campus.

A lamp.

A town seen from an elevation.

An unusual breed of dog.

Express in a sentence the type-movement of each of the following:

An odd manner of walking which you have noticed.

The way a cat walks; runs; creeps.

The way a fly beats against a window pane.

The way a mathematics teacher writes a formula on the blackboard.

The way someone gets out of bed in the morning.

The way an orchestra-leader calls for a softening of the music.

Express in a sentence the type-sounds of the next ten noises you hear.

Tell in a sentence how each of the following feels to your touch:
> Different articles of your clothing.
> Leaves of different plants.
> The ground on a cold day; on a warm day; on a wet day.
> A bunch of keys.
> A bird which you hold in your hand.
> A dog's head when you pat it.
> The steering wheel of an automobile as you drive.
> An electric-light switch as you snap it on or off.
> A thin rug as you step on it.

Try to express the type-smells and the type-tastes of each article of food you can recall having eaten during the last day or two. Distinguish carefully between the two types of details. In addition, list and describe the next ten smells you notice.

If the class is not too large, the instructor may let each member come to the front of the room, one person at a time, and read for two or three minutes while the rest of the class writes a thumb-nail description of the reader in the manner suggested in Section 5 above.

6. Interpretative Description.

Enlarge two of the descriptions just written into longer, interpretative descriptions.

Write an interpretative description of one of the following:
> An automobile.
> A street.
> A house.
> A scene in nature.
> A river.
> An animal (cat, dog, horse, fish, bird, etc.).

PART TWO

The Writing of Exposition

Chapter VIII

THE NATURE OF EXPOSITION

1. **Definition.**—In trying to distinguish between exposition and other forms of writing, we may well parody Coleridge's famous sentence distinguishing between poetry and science: Exposition is that species of prose composition which is opposed to works of narration and description by proposing for its immediate object truth, not pleasure. That is, exposition conveys ideas for the sake of *instructing* the reader, not for the sake of *pleasing* him by emotional stimulation or imagination.

To be sure, exposition may avail itself of narration and description, and may try to stimulate emotion and imagination in the reader; but all this will be auxiliary to the main purpose of instruction. It will not exist for its own sake. For instance, a plain factual history of, say, England under the Hanovers will consist of quite as much narrative as any novel; yet the history will be narrative not for the sake of any pleasurable emotion it stirs in the reader, but for the sake of the instruction it gives him. And an account of the way a cotton gin or a cider press works may be almost pure description—the gleam of metal, the revolution of wheels, the meshing of cogs, the motions of the workmen; but the description will exist primarily to give the reader instruction, not merely to please his fancy by means of vivid imagery. Exposition is instruction.

2. **The Field of Exposition.**—An enormous proportion of all writing is expository. So vast, indeed, is the field of exposition

that any attempt merely to outline it is certain to fail. Exposition includes news items, news articles, special features, editorials, and advertisements; it includes magazine articles, book reviews, accounts of travel, descriptions of places in the day's news, and descriptions of social conditions; it includes political speeches, funeral orations, sermons, classroom lectures, and a large part of all conversation about people and opinions; it includes textbooks, reference books, compilations of statistics, criticisms, histories, and biographies; it includes laboratory directions, reports of experiments or observations, building specifications, auditors' reports, and business letters. Even poetry, when it becomes philosophic, is likely to be expository; and those portions of fiction which analyze character, explain motives, and describe situations are likewise expository. To put it negatively, whatever is not imaginative writing for the mere sake of imagination is exposition.

3. The Uses of Exposition.—The definition of exposition has already implied its use. Exposition is used to instruct. But instruction may be of three sorts. First, it may be instruction in facts; second, it may be instruction in the meaning of facts; and third, it may be instruction in a certain intellectual or emotional point of view.

By way of illustration, suppose a writer tells the number of men killed and wounded in the Great War, the value of property destroyed in the line of battle, the money spent by all nations conducting the war, and the money spent on pensions, hospitals, and reconstruction since the war. And suppose that, at the same time, he records the amount of profits made by certain businesses in the war, the wages made by workers supporting the combatants, the money made by American citizens supplying armies with food and clothing, and the millions in interest received by American financiers from foreign debtors. If the writer does nothing more than this, he will be merely giving instruction in facts.

But suppose he goes on to interpret his facts. He balances accounts; he shows how apparent assets are actually liabilities; he explains that even nations which profited most by the war during the 1920's have become bankrupt in the 1930's. His logical and impersonal conclusion, then, may be that the war was unprofitable to all concerned.

And now suppose he goes on to argue from the evidence he has educed and interpreted that all wars are not only murderous, but ruinous. He condemns wars from both the humane and the economic standpoints, and he tries to persuade his readers never again to sanction a war. In doing this, he is giving instruction in a certain intellectual and emotional point of view; he is not merely giving facts and trying to interpret them impartially. He is trying to influence opinion and inspire action. Mere facts and their clarification no longer satisfy him. He has become an *agitator* in the literal sense of the word—an individual attempting to stimulate others by instructing them in his own point of view.

4. The Requirements of Exposition.—Though instruction and not pleasure is the immediate purpose of exposition, a writer should not feel altogether relieved of the responsibility of trying to be interesting. Of course, some essays in exposition need no virtues except clarity and conciseness. On the other hand, all expositions are not mathematics textbooks, building specifications, and scientific articles on the chemistry of insect blood. Some expositions are book reviews, art criticisms, biography, histories of literature, articles on current social problems, philosophical or moral essays, sermons, public lectures, accounts of true adventure, essays on natural history, and character sketches. These expositions require

some other virtues besides clarity and conciseness: they require to
be interesting.

a. Macaulay censures the historian whose only object is to as-
semble facts: "While our historians are practicing all the arts of
controversy, they miserably neglect the art of narration, the art of
interesting the affections and presenting pictures to the imagination." This art of *interesting* need not be hostile to truth (as
Macaulay goes on to show). Furthermore, history which has made
use of this art will be read and will exercise influence while quite
as scholarly, but less interesting, books will be neglected.

That a writer may produce these effects [Macaulay continues] without violating truth is sufficiently proved by many excellent biographi-
cal works. The immense popularity which well-written books of this
kind have acquired deserves the serious consideration of historians.
Voltaire's *Charles the Twelfth*, Marmontel's *Memoirs*, Boswell's *Life
of Johnson*, Southey's account of Nelson, are perused with delight by
the most frivolous and indolent. Whenever any tolerable book of
the same description makes its appearance, the circulating libraries
are mobbed; the book societies are in commotion; the new novel lies
uncut; the magazines and newspapers fill their columns with extracts.
In the meantime, histories of great empires, written by men of
eminent ability, lie unread on the shelves of ostentatious libraries.

Macaulay's own devices for achieving interest in this very essay
are worth study. In the paragraph just quoted, he assumes the
aggressive, controversial tone which is so much more effective
than mere abstract statement; he gives examples of the sort of
history which he approves; he uses a set of hammering parallel
structures; he states the popularity of well-written biographies in
terms of vivid images; and he concludes with a powerful contrast.

In succeeding paragraphs he uses paradoxes: "A history in which
every particular incident may be true may on the whole be false."
Blunt, hard statements: "No past event has any intrinsic importance." Rhetorical questions: If Lord Clarendon had done so-

and-so, "Would not his work in that case have been more interesting? Would it not have been more accurate?" Similes: The merely factual historian is like a "gnat mounted on an elephant, and laying down theories as to the whole internal structure of the vast animal, from the phenomena of the hide." Metaphors: "The upper current of society presents no certain criterion by which we can judge of the direction in which the under current flows." Analogies: "The effect of historical reading is, in many respects, analogous to that produced by foreign travel"—and then an elaboration of the analogy through several hundred words. References to or indirect quotations from other authors: Bishop Watson, Sir Walter Scott, Hume, Tacitus, Lord Clarendon. And throughout the essay full lists of specific details are presented to support every large generalization.

All these devices, together with those mentioned in the first chapter of this book, the student may well employ to make his own work interesting. Occasionally these devices come naturally; but more frequently they hide away and must be sought out by conscious effort. Being interesting without effort is a gift of few people.

b. Being interesting is a requirement of all but the most coldly scientific sorts of exposition. But being *clear* is a requirement of all exposition. Exposition that is not clear is like a clergyman without morals or a teacher without learning. Endeavoring to clarify, it lacks clarity; and pretending to instruct, it confuses. Poetry may be obscure, description may be incomplete or only suggestive, and narrative may be the record of happenings the reader does not understand. But exposition can afford to leave no dark corners in the reader's mind, or to trouble the reader with no unexplained ideas and half-suggested facts. Exposition must be lucid, logical, complete; it must leave the reader with more knowledge, greater understanding, or new ways of looking at an issue. It must be so constructed that it has a clear meaning as a whole, and that each part of it has a clear meaning in relation to the whole and in relation to every other part. Lacking in either this general or this specific clarity, the exposition is, in some measure at least, a failure.

5. The Sources of Exposition.—To attain clarity in his exposition, a writer must have, first of all, knowledge about his subject. Like Frank Buck or any other world-traveler or adventurer, he may have gained his knowledge from personal experience; like Maeterlinck or Fabre, he may have gained it from long and careful observation; like Boswell or Trelawney, he may have gained it from associating with others; like Kittredge and Lowes, he may have gained it from reading; like Plato and Locke, he may have gained it from pure thought operating on rather obvious phenomena; or like Darwin, William James, and Spengler, he may have gained it from several of these processes working together.

a. Most young students are inclined to distrust their own *experiences* as possible sources of subject matter. Asked to write an exposition, a college youth who has worked during three vacations in a small factory which manufactures fishing tackle will invariably propose to write about "Buddhism in China"; and a college girl who works in a local library will believe that she must write about "The Case against the Sugar Tariff." The youth will not realize that he can be more original and interesting, and can convey more valuable information about the manufacture of fishing tackle than any other subject he might choose; and the girl will not believe that her inside knowledge of the way her library functions will be more interesting and valuable to readers than anything she could find out about tariffs. No intelligent person has reached the age of eighteen without having acquired some special knowledge about something. The giddiest flirt could write entrancingly on "How to Attract Men"; the slowest farm boy could write informatively on "How to Care for Milk Cows"; the most hurried New Yorker could write interestingly about "Subways as a Passenger Knows Them"; and the most childlike freshman could write a revolutionary exposition on "What I Think of My Parents." One of the very first lessons a writer should learn, therefore, is this: Value personal experience.

b. Careful *observation* and accurate recording of details observed makes worth-while exposition. The play of a child, the motions of a pole-vaulter, the behavior of a robin looking for worms, the typography of a book, the structure of a blossom— simple things such as these, if observed closely, can be the subjects of endless, and yet extraordinarily interesting exposition. All of us have seen cats begging for attention by rubbing about people's legs; but how many of us have observed this common occurrence with the minute attention that Darwin shows in the following paragraph?

Let us now look at a cat in a directly opposite frame of mind, whilst feeling affectionate and caressing her master. . . . She now stands upright with her back slightly arched, which makes the hair appear rather rough, but it does not bristle; her tail, instead of being extended and lashed from side to side, is held quite stiff and perpendicularly upwards; her ears are erect and pointed; her mouth is closed; and she rubs against her master with a purr instead of a growl.

In another place Darwin describes the act of weeping:

The corrugators of the brow (*corrugators supercilii*) seem to be the first muscles to contract; and these draw the eyebrows downwards and inwards towards the base of the nose, causing vertical furrows, that is a frown, to appear between the eyebrows; at the same time they cause the disappearance of the transverse wrinkles across the forehead. The orbicular muscles contract almost simultaneously with the corrugators, and produce wrinkles all round the eyes. . . . Lastly, the pyramidal muscles of the nose contract; and these draw the eyebrows and the skin of the forehead still lower down, producing short transverse wrinkles across the base of the nose. . . . When these muscles are strongly contracted, those running to the upper lip like-wise contract and raise the upper lip. . . . The raising of the upper lip draws upwards the flesh of the upper parts of the cheeks, and produces a strongly marked fold on each cheek—the naso-labial fold, —which runs from near the wings of the nostrils to the corners of the mouth and below them. . . . As the upper lip is much drawn up during the act of screaming, in the manner just explained, the depressor muscles of the angles of the mouth are strongly contracted in order to keep the mouth widely open, so that a full volume of sound may be poured forth. The action of these opposing muscles, above and below, tends to give to the mouth an oblong, almost squarish outline. . . . An excellent observer, in describing a baby crying whilst being fed, says, "it made its mouth like a square, and let the porridge run out at all four corners."

These passages describe what all of us could see if we would only observe; yet despite their commonplaceness of subject, they are both interesting and informative.

c. Contemplation of one's *associates* may furnish material for half-a-dozen kinds of exposition. The simple character sketch may grow out of long observation of a roommate, a professor, a janitor, a classmate, or any other individual of no greater importance. Indeed, it frequently happens that the most fascinating subjects for character sketches are those unobtrusive mouse-like people who so often are the bodily framework for a maze of tangled "complexes" and psychoses.

The religious youth who is troubled by scientific theories he has learned in college; the student leader who seeks popularity at the cost of independence; the pretty freshman girl who is in a flutter of amazed delight because the campus hero likes her; the girl who assumes the airs of a countess, though we know she does house-work to pay her way through college; the handsome elderly lady on the faculty who has never married; the awkward, gesticulating, timid young professor in the foreign language department—such people are interesting in themselves. A mere presentation of them as they reveal their personalities to their associates would make valuable exposition.

Even more valuable would be exposition attempting to show how heredity, early environment, education, certain crucial experiences, and certain significant people have worked together to fashion a character into the individual we know.

Yet the exposition derived from one's associations may concern no one individual. Instead, it may attempt to give the reader an understanding of some racial or social group with which the author is familiar. What are the racial characteristics of the German, the Jew, the American Negro, the Japanese, the Southerner, or the New Englander? What are the ideas and the thought-channels of the common sailor, the American banker, the middle-western farmer, the college student, the adolescent boy, or the high school girl? A well-considered exposition attempting to answer any of these questions would be both interesting and valuable.

The sort of exposition derived from personal associations may take a wider field than even a racial or a social group. It may develop a generalization which the student has constructed out of his knowledge of all humanity—a generalization which approaches a philosophy of life. "Most men are fundamentally honest"; "Young people are usually sad"; "The way to a woman's heart is to make her laugh"; "Women are always dissatisfied"— these are typical generalizations which may result from observation of people.

d. *Reading* is an ever fruitful source of material. Term themes in courses of history, literature, economics, and philosophy are usually typical expositions derived from the writer's acquaintance with other authors. The aim of such expositions is primarily to give information to people who have not the time or the opportunity to investigate as thoroughly as the writer can. Accordingly, fullness of information within certain specified limits, and clarity of expression are the chief things to be desired in this sort of exposition.

At the same time, the writer should remember that mere summaries or paraphrases, though these have a place in exposition, are seldom adequate in themselves for the proper explication of sources. Selection, from sometimes numerous possibilities, of sources to summarize or paraphrase, decisions as to which sources deserve the fullest treatment and the greatest amount of space, weighing of authorities, judgments on seemingly contradictory or conflicting sources, organization and arrangement of material—all this requires initiative and originality on the writer's part. He cannot be a mere parrot; he must practically always contribute something of himself. His exposition, consequently, though composed of materials taken from other writers and though often designed to give purely objective knowledge, will almost inevitably reflect the individual author's own personality. It will cover old materials; yet in its standards, its interpretations, its objective, and its purpose it will be, and it ought to be, a new contribution to recorded knowledge.[1]

e. Some of the very best and most useful exposition ever written has come from *original thought* about well-known facts. Most of the philosophers, from Plato to Bergson, have built intricate and fascinating intellectual systems on the basis of information common to all educated men. Burke impressed upon two or three generations his theories about beauty, though he had less experience with beauty than thousands of people who have walked through the corridors of the Metropolitan Museum a couple of

[1] The collecting of data on bibliographic cards, the use of footnotes and bibliography, the conventional symbols and abbreviations employed in footnotes and bibliography, and the most acceptable form and arrangement for footnotes and bibliography—these are matters of importance. Most of the handbooks and rhetorics used nowadays in freshman English courses contain information about such things. Consequently, they will not be studied in the present work. The student is referred to his freshman handbook instead.

times; Rousseau wrote a classic in the literature of education, though he had less concrete information about his subject than any college senior who expects to become a teacher; and Jefferson has influenced the destiny of a nation for a century and a half, though he probably knew less about history than any half-a-dozen college professors you know. These men were great because they thought —because they could draw inferences, judge conditions, and construct general laws from commonplace facts of no consequence to people less thoughtful.

Too much reading and too little thinking often suffocates the creative principle. Most good writers have been wide readers; but reading is no substitute for thought. A little knowledge well used is far more valuable than much knowledge never put to work. Schopenhauer, in his volume called *Chips and Scraps*, has an energetic essay on this very subject. He deserves to be quoted at some length:

Much reading deprives the mind of all elasticity; it is like keeping a spring continually under pressure. The safest way of having no thoughts of one's own is to take up a book every moment one has nothing else to do. It is this practice which explains why erudition makes most men more stupid and silly than they are by nature, and prevents their writings obtaining any measure of success. They remain, in Pope's words:

Forever reading, never to be read! . . .

Reading is nothing more than a substitute for thought of one's own. It means putting the mind into leading strings. The multitude of books serves only to show how many false paths there are, and how widely astray a man may wander if he follows any of them. But he who is guided by his genius, he who thinks for himself, who thinks spontaneously and accurately, possesses the only compass by which he can steer aright. A man should read only when his own thoughts stagnate at their source, which will happen often enough even with the best of minds. On the other hand, to take up a book for the purpose of scaring away one's own original thoughts is a sin against the Holy Spirit. It is like running away from nature to look at a museum of dried plants or gaze at a landscape in copper-plate.

f. The final source of exposition—that is, *a compound of all the sources previously mentioned*—doubtless produces more influential work than any of the others. We ask a writer not only to think, but to know what has already been written on his subject, and to have special knowledge gained from experiment or observation, from personal associations, or from personal experience. In a word, we ask him to have both a wide knowledge and a special knowledge of his subject, and in addition we like to see him organize his knowledge into a coherent system having a place in the larger system of things. If, for example, someone writes about coal strikes in America during the last fifteen years, we expect him to have read much on the subject, observed much, and (if possible) experienced much and known people connected with the strikes. Furthermore, we expect him to have thought about the strikes long enough to show us how they have fitted into the general social and economic scheme during the last fifteen years, and how they have influenced the present and may influence the future. We want learning in our writer, special knowledge, and a power to theorize. If he has only the first, he is a pedant; if he has only the second, he is a technical expert; and if he has only the last, he is likely to be a windbag.

An hour or two spent reading the articles in any of the better-class general periodicals will show how true it is that our best-known contemporary writers derive their materials from all the sources indicated. The learning may be neither esoteric nor all-inclusive; the special knowledge may be accidental; and the power to theorize may be limited. But if the three of them are used for all they are worth—if they are forced to yield up every droplet of expository attar they contain, they may be brewed into a really valuable piece of writing.

How good an essay may be constructed from fairly commonplace material many a good author demonstrates every month in the better-class magazines mentioned above. Analysis of an example will clarify this statement. In an excellent article called "Our Racial Amnesia," which appeared in *Harper's* some time ago, James Truslow Adams employs only the following information or theories:

General Information:

Jefferson and Hamilton were thoroughly grounded in history.

So were our own grandfathers. (Books read in childhood by "Uncle Joe" Cannon are mentioned.)

Henry Ford is ignorant of history.

Even our colleges fail to give students a thorough grounding in history.

Business men have no historical perspective; they are interested in personalities. (Roosevelt's, Harding's, and Coolidge's concessions to this interest are mentioned.)

Popular reading does not furnish a historical background. Neither does science, nor sport, nor motoring. (Examples of sportsmen who have been forgotten overnight are mentioned.)

Our ancestors wanted their reading matter packed with thought; we want ours "short and snappy." (Examples are mentioned from modern newspapers, motion pictures, and radio programs.)

Special Information:

A certain high school graduate could tell the author nothing about the *Federalist.*

A certain college professor told the author that colleges turn out a "low-grade, standardized product."

Living in a business man's club five months, the author never heard the "slightest mention of literature, art, economics, or national affairs."

The author knows nobody who has read Wells's *Outline of History* through.

The author mentions historical novels which he read as a child. The author mentions talking with relatives who recalled the days when there were no railroads.

Theories:

We are living in a world whose only interest is the present.
To ignore history endangers our social structure.
Common people have lost the power of thought.
We follow the fashion and yield to the emotion of the moment.
We are victims of "racial amnesia."

The average educated person knows all the general information Adams draws upon here or could discover it in an hour's research among old magazines and newspapers; he could substitute special information of his own quite as pointed as that given by Adams; and he has doubtless often thought or expressed the same theories Adams has written down here. In short, though general information, special information, and private theories have gone into the composition of this article, none of the three is so profound or so specialized as to discourage emulation. And yet the article is one of the best.

EXERCISES

1. Definition.
    a. Write paragraphs describing three of the following in an expository style; then write other paragraphs describing the same three in a non-expository style:
        Some bird or some dog.
        The house you live in.
        A restaurant you know.
        A friend.
        A classroom.

A piece of furniture.

A view of the campus.

b. Select three brief news items from the daily paper, and re-tell them in a non-expository style.

2. The Field of Exposition.

3. The Uses of Exposition.

Explain briefly how you could write three different expositions having three different uses about each of the following subjects:

The manners of college students.

Football and college finance.

The last ten movies I have seen.

Conservation measures enacted by the present federal ad-ministration.

Bird life on the campus.

Getting a book from the library.

The freshman's problems of adjustment.

The pre-medical (pre-law) course in college.

The English courses at this college.

Tuition and fees at this college.

4. The Requirements of Exposition.

Take some unsatisfactory exposition you have written, or let your instructor give you some poor expository theme one of his freshmen has written, or select a particularly uninteresting page in a history or philosophy textbook—and convert it into interesting exposition by using the devices mentioned in the foregoing dis-cussion. Do not change the fundamental ideas expressed in the original work.

In planning an exposition on "The Political Situation in My Home Town," suppose you think of the ideas mentioned below. Show how each of these in turn might be made the unifying idea of ten different expositions, and show how all the other ideas could be related to this central one:

1. The town is small.

2. The leading political faction is a group of merchants on X Street.

3. There is a demagogic political boss.

4. The liquor vote is influential.

5. Municipal funds have been used to help the trade of the leading faction.

6. The best-paved and best-lighted street is X Street.

7. The mayor of the town is a tool of the boss and of the leading faction.

8. There is some jealousy between the boss and the leading faction.

9. There has been corruption in the granting of contracts, in the appointment of officials, and in the administration of the law.

10. The reform element is divided into two groups, one of which wants merely a transfer of power to itself, while the other wants actual reform.

5. The Sources of Exposition.

a. Make a list of the experiences which have given you considerable knowledge about certain subjects. If you wish, or if your instructor suggests it, write an exposition on one of these subjects.

b. Write a paragraph or so describing in detail the appearance and the movements of three of the following:

Your father driving a car.

A professor giving a lecture.

Your dog greeting you when you return home.

A fish moving about an aquarium for a few minutes.

A baby just learning to walk.

A baby amusing itself playing on the floor.

Your mother as she makes a bed.

A friend eating a sandwich; eating ice cream; drinking; playing bridge.

An insect on a plant.

A sparrow struggling with a large tangle of straw.

c. Make a list of expository subjects that could be derived from your knowledge of people. Try to include subjects of each type mentioned in Section 5, Part c, of the text. Write expositions on any of these subjects that your instructor thinks promising.

(d. The individual interests or the special tasks of every student must determine the kind of exposition the student may create from reading other writers.)

e. Write a thoughtful and interesting exposition in which you try to answer one of the following questions.

What is sentimentality?

What is art?

What is tragedy?

What is the difference between a radical and a liberal?

What is a proper attitude toward sex?

When is a man (or a woman) educated?

Of what value are novels?

Of what value is poetry?

What should be the chief ideal of every nation?

How should we let tradition affect us?

f. Write an exposition on one of the following topics; include general information, personal information, and individual theories:

Changes in American political philosophy since 1930.

The social revolution of the 1920's.

Modern comedy.

College humor.

Victorianism in your college.

The drift of modern high school education.

How your college differs from another in the state.

Your own moral standards and those of your mother (or father).

American poetry since 1930.

Chapter IX

THE METHODS OF EXPOSITION

IN THIS chapter we shall discuss some of the most useful ways by which information may be conveyed, ideas clarified, or opinions influenced. Not every method here mentioned may be employed in every kind of exposition; on the other hand, certain kinds of exposition may employ several of these methods. Problems of application, however, we shall defer to an exercise in the next chapter. Just now our business is to examine the methods themselves.

1. The *Chronological Method* is used when we record events in the order of their occurrence in time. Obviously it is useless in expositions about static conditions where events occur neither to the writer nor to the thing written about. Just as obviously it is the simplest and most logical method for most expositions concerned with changes occurring in place or time or form.[1]

Changes depicted in the chronological order may be of two types: (a) unique and (b) habitual. For example, if I am telling about the events of, say, Gladstone's life, I am dealing with events which have happened only once and will never happen again. But if I am telling how Golden Plovers migrate up the interior of

---

[1] It should be added here that this method (often combined with the descriptive method discussed below) is the one we frequently employ in portraying cause-to-effect sequences. A cause and its effect do not often exist simultaneously, and even when they do we cannot write about them simultaneously. Consequently, writing which shows a cause acting to produce an effect later in time is actually narrative writing. At the same time the descriptive method may enter into the composition by the writer's depicting the nature of the cause and of the effect. For example, if we describe how a dog barks at a cat and the latter runs up a tree, we shall be portraying a cause-to-effect sequence by means of the chronological method, and at the same time we shall be using the descriptive method.

204

North America in spring, and then return to South America in autumn by an overseas route from southeastern Canada, I am dealing with events which occur habitually. In other words, though I am using the chronological method in both narratives, the first employs the method of *particularized narration,* and the second *generalized narration.*

2. The *Descriptive Method* may be used with either static or changing events. It is the method employed when we wish to give facts (size, color, weight, etc.) about the physical appearance or the construction of things. It differs from the imaginative method by not attempting to make the reader *see* the subject; it gives him information about the subject so that he may recognize it if he does see it. Like the chronological method, the descriptive method may be of two sorts: (a) description of particular things like a lost dog, a table to be built, a house to be recognized, or a man wanted for murder; and (b) description of general types like collie dogs, Queen Anne tables, gothic buildings, and Cherokee Indians. That is, the descriptive method may take the form of either *particularized description* or *generalized description.*

3. The *Method of Classification* involves the division of general concepts (concrete or abstract) into particular groups. Each of the preceding sections of this chapter, for example, resorts to the method of classification by dividing each of the general methods into an *a* and a *b* part. Cæsar begins his *Commentaries* with the famous declaration that "all Gaul is divided into three parts," and then proceeds to describe each part in turn. Edmund Gosse writes of Swinburne's lyrics, "We may well divide them into two large classes: those belonging to a pre-Christian and those belonging to a Christian age." And the old proverb classifies great men in the familiar way: "Some men are born great; some achieve greatness; and some have greatness thrust upon them."

The classification may be broad or detailed. For example, Gosse's classification just quoted is extremely broad; and the classification of expository methods in this chapter is rather detailed. But as long as the classification is *complete* enough to include every member of the group under examination, we need not complain.

We should be critical, however, of classifications which have no *unified basis of division*. If Gosse had divided Swinburne's lyrics into those belonging to a pre-Christian era and those written in anapestic tetrameter, his classification would have been absurd. The basis for division would not have been unified. The same would have been true if the maker of the proverb had said, "Some men are born great; some achieve greatness; and some go to Europe."

Nobody ever commits quite such ridiculous blunders as these except for a humorous effect. But young writers have been known to divide college students into the groups: "bookish, intelligent, friendly, and socially inclined." Having no unified basis for his classification, the writer who made this division of college students did not form them into mutually exclusive groups. A college student may belong to any one of the four groups mentioned, and yet belong to all the others as well. Such ununified standards of classification are fatal to clear exposition.

4. *Definition* is a fourth method of exposition. A formal definition states, first, the general class to which a thing belongs; and, second, the way in which it is distinguished from all other members of that class. A *hawk*, by way of illustration, is "any of a family of diurnal birds of prey—excepting eagles and vultures." A *laundress* is "a woman—whose employment is washing clothes."

Yet definition in this strict sense is not so common as a kind which is definition only by a liberal extension of the word's meaning. To tell the nature of a thing (like a razor or a political philosophy)—to tell what its appearance is, what it does, what it resembles, what it stands for in our minds (as a razor stands for shaving, and Fascism for a dictator)—this is to define. Some of the forms this kind of definition may take are briefly discussed in the following paragraphs.

a. *Synonyms* are used to define many simple words, especially verbs. *To mourn,* for example, is defined thus: "To grieve for; lament; deplore; bewail." And *to plague* is defined thus: "To vex; harass; torment; distress; annoy; tantalize; trouble."

b. *Examples* may be used as a means of definition. Thus *ungulate* is defined in Webster's *Dictionary* as "any of a group consisting of the hoofed mammals, as the ruminants, swine, horses, tapirs, rhinoceros, elephants, and conies." And *republic* may be defined by reference to the United States, France, Portugal, Spain, and the Spanish-American countries.

c. An *enumeration of its qualities* may define an object or a condition. A *greyhound* is a "slender dog, remarkable for swiftness and keen sight." Shakespeare defines Silvia by telling her qualities:

> Who is Silvia, what is she,
>   That all our swains commend her?
> Holy, fair, and wise is she;
>   The heaven such grace did lend her,
> That she might admirèd be.

And Ruskin thinks that people tell what they are by showing what they like:

Go out into the street and ask the first man or woman you meet what their "taste" is, and if they answer candidly, you know them, body and soul. "You, my friend in the rags, with the unsteady gait, what do *you* like?" "A pipe and a quartern of gin." I know you. "You, good woman, with the quick step and tidy bonnet, what do you like?" "A swept hearth and a clean tea-table, and my husband opposite me, and a baby at my breast." Good, I know you also. "You, little girl with the golden hair and the soft eyes, what do you like?" "My canary and a run among the wood hyacinths." "You, little boy with the dirty hands and the low forehead, what do you like?" "A shy at the sparrows, and a game at pitch farthing." Good; we know them all now. What more need we ask?

d. A thing may be defined according to its *work or uses*. A *bed* is "an article of furniture to sleep or rest in or on." A *ladybug* is "a small, roundish, often brightly colored [enumeration of qualities] beetle, mostly feeding on insects and insects' eggs." A *lady-killer* is "a man who captivates, or has the reputation of fascinating women." H. W. Garrod makes these offhand definitions: A good book is one which "addresses a large part of its appeal to imagination and emotion"; and "the best critic of books, in the long run, is the man who brings to the study of them a large charity."

e. Definition may be by means of an *historical survey*. No one can define the Constitution of England without an elaborate survey of history; and no one can define socialism without tracing it clear back to Marx. *Lager beer* (a name derived from the German word *lager*, a storehouse) is "so called from its being stored several months before use." And the words *extrovert, introvert,* and *libido* mean nothing to us unless we have a knowledge of Jung and Freud.

5. Strictly speaking, *Comparison and Contrast* may be used as means to define. But since they involve other elements than those belonging absolutely to the thing defined, they are treated here as a separate expository method.

We may best define *Fascism* by showing how it differs from a democracy; we may best portray political conditions in Wisconsin by showing how they differ from political conditions in other states; we may best tell something of President Franklin Roosevelt's policies by showing how they differ from those of Presidents Coolidge and Hoover. On the other hand, we may explain certain things by showing how they resemble other things. We may best describe English rooks by comparing them to American crows or grackles; we may best describe the government of Mexico by comparing it to our own government; and we may best describe the Argentine Pampas by comparing them to our own Great Plains.

6. *Analogy* is close kin to comparison. Indeed, it *is* comparison. But it is comparison between things not at all related in their fundamental natures, and yet parallel in many of their forms or activities. Thus a comparison between communism and socialism would not be an analogy, but a comparison between communism and a colony of ants would be. The purpose of analogy, like that of comparison, is to express the unknown in terms of the known, the obscure in terms of the clear, and the complex in terms of the simple. For accomplishing this purpose the analogy is a highly useful and interesting device; but if the analogy violates its fundamental purpose by becoming long, elaborate, and complicated, it is worse than useless. This caution is voiced because even experienced writers frequently abuse the analogy by overdevelopment. Carried away by their imagination, they wander into mazes of comparison that leave the reader confused and breathless. An example of such a labyrinthine analogy has already been quoted in the first chapter of this book.

7. *Presentation of Authority* is a method used often, but seldom exclusively, in exposition. By using this method, the writer does one of two things: He either renounces personal views in favor of the views of some authority, or else substantiates and supports personal views by reference to authority. The method is extremely useful because it gives the weight of important names or convincing workers to an unknown or inexperienced writer's work, because it gives the weight of numbers to a single writer's work, and because it shows that the writer is not ignorant. The method may take any of the following forms:

a. The simplest is *quotation*. Here the writer actually quotes what his authorities have said. By doing so, he has the very words of his authority (not mere interpretation) to vouch for an idea expressed. Quotation lends an interesting variety of style to a piece of writing, and, if properly selected, may be more effective than anything the writer himself can say. Yet no exposition should be a mere patchwork of other people's words. If it is, the reader is certain to think the writer a pedantic or timid soul who has not the courage of his convictions; and if the reader is a professor and the writer a student, the reader at once concludes that the writer has been padding the paper to avoid labor. In general, no more than one-fifth of an exposition, at the very most, should consist of direct quotation from other authors.

b. In place of quotation the writer may substitute *paraphrase*. A paraphrase renders the *sense* of a passage. It may, therefore, be either longer or shorter than the original, in the same or in a different language, and in similar or in different words. A paraphrase may amplify a terse or cryptic statement by expressing it in more familiar terms, or by giving brief illustrations that will clarify its meaning.

Thus the proverb, "Never look a gift-horse in the mouth," may be paraphrased, "Do not be too critical of things you receive free. For instance, if someone gives you a ride in his automobile, don't find fault with the way the motor works." Here the original passage has been amplified, and has been illustrated by an example more understandable than the original to a modern generation unacquainted with horses.

Sometimes the authority has written in a foreign language. If so, the writer who wishes to use the authority must either translate him directly (with a note, if the passage is vital, to the effect that the quotation is a personally translated version), or may paraphrase him in English. Such a paraphrase as this, however, is more likely to be a summary than a strict paraphrase.

Sometimes a paraphrase may use words much like those in the original passage. The proverb just quoted, for example, may be paraphrased, "Never look into the mouth to discover the age and value of a horse that has been given to you." But, in general, a paraphrase should avoid the phraseology of the original passage. Suppose the original passage read like this:

Radical critics of the American press are fond of saying that journalism is not, and under existing conditions cannot be, a profession. They point out that the American newspaper editor is usually only the hired employee of the owner, and that the ultimate authority always rests with the latter.

And suppose the student paraphrases the passage:

Radical critics of the American press say that journalism is not and cannot be a profession. They say that the newspaper editor is only an employee of the owner, with whom the ultimate authority rests.

This paraphrase is unfair to the original authority. It is made up almost entirely of his very words, and yet it purports to be an original paraphrase. The revised passage should be set in quotation marks with a row of dots to indicate omitted words. Or else it should be reworked to look something like this:

Radical critics say that since practically every newspaper editor in America derives all his authority from the owner of his paper, journalism is not and cannot at present be a profession.

As a rule, more than three or four important words (not articles, prepositions, conjunctions, etc.) quoted in the sequence of their occurrence in an original passage ought to be enclosed in quotation marks.

c. The *summary* differs from the paraphrase in purpose. Where the paraphrase merely tries to give the sense of a passage, the summary tries to give the sense in a briefer form than that of the original. Moreover, a paraphrase is always the re-rendering of a mere passage, whereas a summary may be a brief statement of

CREATIVE WRITING

the fundamental meaning of an entire volume. A writer paraphrases a paragraph and summarizes a chapter or a book.

A summary, therefore, requires more originality on the part of a writer than does a paraphrase. It requires discrimination, selection, judgment about what the original writer considered important, and a power to retain the original emphasis within a smaller compass. The writer who summarizes must discriminate between what is essential and what unessential; he must select from a number of subsidiary ideas and facts only those cardinal ones for which he has space; he must decide which ideas or facts were most important in the original authority's mind, and which render the most representative picture of that mind; and then he must express all this in a properly related and proportioned summary which may be a hundred times shorter than the original work.

To do all this, a writer should first read through the work to be summarized in order to find out and express in words its central thesis. He should then try to find out the half-a-dozen or so main divisions of the work, and express their significance in a sentence for each one. And finally he should supplement this bare outline with as many subsidiary ideas as he has room for. His summary, then, will be little more than an outline of arguments supporting a central idea.

d. *Interpretation* demands even more originality of a writer and involves a greater responsibility. The number of lawsuits brought to the courts annually, and the number of religious disputes among Christians for the last five centuries show how serious and vital the matter of interpretation may be. Yet despite all the money spent and all the lives lost in support of certain interpretations, few would-be interpreters really possess the interpreter's spirit. Too often they are concerned with twisting the meaning of their authority into something that will harmonize with their own desires. They do not try to enter sympathetically into the sense and spirit of an authority in order to find the absolute truth about that authority.

A truly honorable interpreter studies the personal conditions under which his authority wrote, finds out everything needful about the period and the place in which the authority worked, correlates different works by the same authority, and tries to discover what motives inspired him—what biases he had, what limitations of knowledge he possessed, what fundamental desires he worked to satisfy. Having done all this, and having resolved to keep an impartial point of view, the would-be interpreter may venture to undertake his task. He need not fear that his interpretation will lack originality. If it is the result of personal research and independent thinking, it cannot help being original—for the simple reason that no two human beings see and think alike. All he need fear is that the interpretation will not be fair to the original author.

We have now discussed four ways in which exposition by the presentation of authority may be written. Need we add that honesty and consideration for others require that all use of authorities be documented? Formal expositions require copious footnotes and complete bibliographies; less formal expositions require at least an acknowledgment in a foreword or in the text itself.

8. We may develop exposition by the *Method of Illustration*. Suppose a lecturer says, "The American dollar is worth less today than it was a year ago." His audience looks blank. And the lecturer adds, "Let me illustrate. A year ago you bought bread at five cents a loaf and milk at six cents a quart. Today you pay for these articles eight cents and eleven cents. That is what I mean when I say the dollar is worth less." The lecturer has used the method of illustration.

To employ this method is merely to take the advice already given for another purpose: "Convert the abstract into the concrete, and the general into the specific." An illustration makes clear a vague or complex idea; it shows how a theory works, or how a general law applies to specific facts. This *clarifying* function of illustration distinguishes it from the closely related method to be discussed next.

9. The *Use of Examples* is one of the most interesting, convincing, and informative of the methods of exposition. Sometimes it overlaps the method just discussed. That is, examples may be used to give clarity to general ideas; yet examples, properly speaking, are merely specific instances. They are subheads under a large division. But the distinction between illustration and example is largely academic; most writers use both terms almost interchangeably.

The following passage illustrates the method:

No general strike has ever been even partly successful in this country or in any other. In 1919 the Seattle general strike, the first experienced in the United States, officially collapsed on its fifth day under the weight of its own inefficiency. In the same year the Winnipeg general strike, which lasted six weeks, ended in riots, arrests, and trials for seditious conspiracy, with none of the aims of the strike accomplished. Great Britain's general strike of 1926 lasted thirteen days, and ended in failure because the general public co-operated against organized labor. The great general strike in Sweden in 1909 likewise failed because public sentiment and public co-operation aligned themselves against the strikers.

The writer here does not resort to examples to clarify a statement, for his original generalization is perfectly clear. Instead, he resorts to examples as a means of *amplifying* a statement which might otherwise have been unimpressively brief. Or perhaps he resorts to them as a means of *proving* his original statement, or as a means of *lending interest* to a generalized statement, or as a means of *conveying more specific knowledge.*

Examples may serve any of these four purposes of exposition. But to do so, they must necessarily be either (a) single examples thoroughly representative of many others like them, or else (b) numerous examples which are all relatively short.

The single example must contain within itself the plain and obvious proof that it is really representative. By way of illustration, a single beetle of a certain species is plainly and obviously representative of all beetles of that species; when we have found out about the structure of this one beetle, we have found out about the structure of its entire species.

Numerous examples ought to be individually short. A long illustration may be read patiently—but not a series of long examples. If they are individually long, they overshadow the main idea to which each should be subordinate.

As a rule, numerous short examples are preferable to a single long representative example. When their number is scanty, examples do not contribute to interest or variety, or prove much, or amplify greatly, or convey much knowledge.

10. Exposition by the *Use of Details* is allied to the preceding method; but it is more closely allied to definition by enumeration of qualities and to expository description. If I say that a bed has springs, mattress, a headpiece, a footpiece, linens, and a coverlet, I am defining it, describing it, and (at the same time) giving details about it. Or if I say that a man is handsome, and then go on to mention certain features (eyes, nose, mouth, and hair) which make him handsome, I am describing him, and yet at the same time I am giving details about him.

Often, however, details are neither definitive nor descriptive. They merely give more and more information. Mrs. Malaprop's famous speech on feminine education illustrates this use of detail.

We could find, perhaps, a more solemn illustrative passage, but never one more charming in diction:

> Observe me, Sir Anthony.—I would by no means wish a daughter of mine to be a progeny of learning; I don't think so much learning becomes a young woman; for instance—I would never let her meddle with Greek, or Hebrew, or Algebra, or Simony, or Fluxions, or Paradoxes, or such inflammatory branches of learning—neither would it be necessary for her to handle any of your mathematical, astronomical, diabolical instruments;—But, Sir Anthony, I would send her at nine years old to a boarding-school, in order to learn a little ingenuity and artifice.—Then, Sir, she should have a supercilious knowledge in accounts;—and as she grew up, I would have her instructed in geometry, that she might know something of the contagious countries;—but above all, Sir Anthony, she should be mistress of orthodoxy, that she might not mis-spell, and mis-pronounce words so shamefully as girls usually do; and likewise that she might reprehend the true meaning of what she is saying.—This, Sir Anthony, is what I would have a woman know;—and I don't think there is a superstitious article in it.

Much (one almost says *most*) exposition adopts the method of using details. A writer blocks off a certain area to be filled, and then, by means of detail, proceeds to fill it; he determines the general divisions of his composition, and then, by means of giving additional information about each, elaborates on his outline. This is the method of most textbooks, most newspaper stories, most encyclopedias, most histories—in fact, all types of exposition devoted to giving absolute factual information rather than arguments or inferences.

11. Every lecturer and every textbook writer ought to make liberal use of the *Method of Repetition* in exposition. Without being cynical, one may aver that a lecturer may depend upon having the attention of only about one-third of his audience at any time; and a textbook writer may depend upon having about the same proportion of attentive readers at any paragraph. (This esti-

mate takes no account, of course, of that ten per cent in any audience or any group of readers who never do listen and never are alert.) Accordingly, lecturers and writers should repeat at least their important ideas three times. Such repetition is a recognized method of exposition. It helps to inform, to clarify, and to convince—and that is all we can expect of any exposition.

As we have already seen in the chapters on style, repetition may involve words and phrases. Just now, however, we are concerned with the repetition of ideas as a means of developing exposition. As with repeated words, repeated ideas serve to *intensify* and to *clarify* writing. When, in the course of his funeral oration, Shakespeare's Mark Antony repeats six times in fifty lines the ironical phrase, "Brutus is an honourable man," he repeats in order to intensify. In the following passage from William Hazlitt's essay, "On Going a Journey," repetition serves to clarify. Each sentence repeats the idea expressed in the first sentence, and yet each sentence adds details which help the reader understand more clearly the basic idea in the passage:

It seems that we can think of but one place at a time. The canvas of the fancy is but of a certain extent, and if we paint one set of objects on it, they immediately efface every other. . . . The landscape bares its bosom to the enraptured eye, we take our fill of it, and seem as if we would form no other image of beauty or grandeur. We pass on, and think no more of it: the horizon that shuts it from our sight also blots it from our memory like a dream. In travelling through a wild barren country I can form no idea of a woody and cultivated one. It appears to me that all the world must be barren, like what I see of it. In the country we forget the town, and in town we despise the country. . . . All that part of the map that we do not see before us is blank.

Repetition of ideas may serve one purpose in addition to those served by the repetition of words. It may *amplify*. When a writer wishes to stress an idea, he cannot usually afford to state it in a short space. Taking advantage of the law of proportion, he will so enlarge upon his idea that the reader cannot avoid being impressed. In the following passage, H. G. Wells (having classified men into those who look toward the past and those who look toward the future) says that most people belong to neither of the types he has named. He repeats the idea three times in four sentences—all for the sake of giving it an amount of space proportional to its importance:

Now I do not wish to suggest that the great mass of people belong to either of these two types. Indeed, I speak of them as two distinct and distinguishable types mainly for convenience and in order to accentuate their distinction. There are probably very few people who brood constantly upon the past without any thought of the future at all, and there are probably scarcely any who live and think consistently in relation to the future. The great mass of people occupy an intermediate position between these extremes.

Naturally the method of repetition may be limited in its application: one cannot say something and then keep on repeating it throughout an entire composition. But it is a method too little used by inexperienced writers. As an old professor once remarked, "A thing worth saying once is worth saying twice." That is an aphorism which every young writer ought to remember.

12. We may write exposition by means of showing a *Cause-and-Effect* relationship between facts. We may begin with the fact as a cause, and proceed to show the effect it has or may have; or we may begin with a fact as an effect, and work backward to show its probable cause. In the first of the following passages, Alfred Russel Wallace uses the cause-to-effect method to explain why the sky is blue, and in the second he uses the effect-to-cause method to explain why certain parts of the sky are not blue.

We have seen that the air near the earth's surface is full of rather coarse particles which reflect all the rays, and which therefore produce no one color. But higher up the particles necessarily become smaller and smaller, since the comparatively rare atmosphere will only support the very smallest and lightest. These exist throughout a great thickness of air, perhaps from one mile to ten miles high or even more, and blue or violet rays being reflected from the innumerable particles in this great mass of air, which is nearly uniform in all parts of the world as regards the presence of minute dust particles, produces the constant and nearly uniform tint we call sky-blue.

If we look at the sky on a perfectly fine summer's day, we shall find that the blue color is the most pure and intense overhead, and when looking high up in a direction opposite to the sun. Near the horizon it is always less bright, while in the region immediately round the sun it is more or less yellow. The reason for this is that near the horizon we look through a very great thickness of the lower atmosphere, which is full of the larger dust particles reflecting white light, and this dilutes the pure blue of the higher atmosphere seen beyond. And in the vicinity of the sun a good deal of the blue light is reflected back into space by the finer dust, thus giving a yellowish tinge to that which reaches us reflected chiefly from the coarse dust of the lower atmosphere.

The logic of these two passages is unassailable (so far as one who is no physicist can tell) because each step of the reasoning is based firmly on demonstrable fact. Sometimes, however, the line between demonstrable fact and mere presumption is exceedingly hard to draw. Sir Oliver Lodge, a great physicist, believes that spirit-people are demonstrable facts; Professor Robert Andrews Millikan, an equally great physicist, believes that they are not. How, then, are we to use the idea of spirit-people to discover logical causes, or to argue toward logical effects? The answer is that we must rely on inferences. These we shall examine in another chapter.

EXERCISES

1. The Chronological Method.
   Tell how you could use the chronological method in expositions on the following subjects:
   The manufacture of brooms.
   The high school curriculum.
   Scenery along the Hudson.
   Social measures enacted by the present federal government.
   The British novel in the twentieth century.
   The natural history of the pelican.
   The exhibits in a certain museum.
   Living conditions on B Street.
   Bee-culture.

2. The Descriptive Method.
   In three expository paragraphs describe three of the following as individuals, and at the same time as representatives of types:
   One of your professors.
   A friend of foreign extraction.
   A railway conductor.
   A prominent building in your town.
   A small residence in your neighborhood.
   A street you know.
   A tree you know.
   A classroom.
   Your dog or cat.

3. The Method of Classification.
   Name several bases of classification which you could use in dividing each of the following into classes:

   College students.   Popular magazines.
   Preachers.   Sports in your college.
   Small cars.   Native trees.
   Dogs.   Dwelling houses.

4. The Method of Definition.
   Define each of the following in at least three of the ways mentioned in the text:

A dictator.	The one-hundred-per-cent American.
A lover.	The Democratic party.
Sentimentality.	The English long bow.
A Middle-Westerner.	A tabloid newspaper.
College spirit.	A good detective story.

5. The Method of Comparison and Contrast.

Suggest comparisons and contrasts that might be used in expositions on the following subjects:

Charity.	The ideal student.
Art.	Rembrandt's art.
Poetry.	Dickens's characters.
Communism.	Psychology as a science.
Fear.	Japanese imperialism.

6. The Method of Analogy.

See the Exercises for Chapter I, Section 10, i.

7. The Presentation of Authority.

   a. Paraphrase the following:

      Error of opinion may be tolerated where reason is left free to combat it.—Jefferson.

      Ill doings breed ill thinkings.—Roger Ascham.

      The Phylosopher teacheth a disputative vertue.—Sir Philip Sidney.

      A man that is young in years may be old in hours.—Sir Francis Bacon.

      Without an outlet for political initiative, men lose their social vigor and their interest in public affairs.—Bertrand Russell.

   b. Write summaries of the following:

      One of Bacon's essays.

      One of Lamb's essays.

      Gray's "Elegy."

      Keats's "Ode to a Nightingale."

      Arnold's "Literature and Science."

   c. Give your interpretation of the following:

      Answer not a fool according to his folly, lest thou also be like unto him.

Answer a fool according to his folly, lest he be wise in his own conceit.—*Proverbs* xxvi, 4-5.

But Nature, which is the Time-vesture of God, and reveals Him to the wise, hides Him from the foolish.—Carlyle.

Thanks to the human heart by which we live,
Thanks to its tenderness, its joys, and fears,
To me the meanest flower that blows can give
Thoughts that do often lie too deep for tears.
—Wordsworth.

"Love seeketh not itself to please,
    Nor for itself hath any care,
But for another gives its ease,
    And builds a heaven in hell's despair."

So sung a little clod of clay,
    Trodden with the cattle's feet,
But a pebble of the brook
    Warbled out these metres meet:

"Love seeketh only self to please,
    To bind another to its delight,
Joys in another's loss of ease,
    And builds a hell in heaven's despite."
—William Blake.

8. The Method of Illustration.

Explain each of the following topics by means of an illustration:

Why Germany cannot (will not) pay her war debts.

Why England retains a king.

What some policy of the federal government (NRA, AAA, RFC, HOLC) has meant to poor people; to rich people; to the middle class.

Why men have more (or less) artistic originality than women.

Why like seeks like.

9. The Use of Examples.

Develop the following ideas (or their negatives) by means of examples:

Our House of Representatives is unworthy of a great people.

The legislative and the executive branches of our government live lives antagonistic to each other.

American women are spoiled, and American men have spoiled them.

Interest in a subject is derived from knowledge of that subject.

Most salesmen are low in the scale of integrity.

Among the examples you have just mentioned, which seem to be representative enough to stand alone?

What are the functions of the other examples—to amplify, to prove, to lend interest, or to convey new knowledge?

10. The Use of Details.

Develop the following ideas by the use of details:

The first rule, then, for a good style is that the author have something to say.—Schopenhauer.

A sentence should read as if its author, had he held a plough instead of a pen, could have drawn a furrow deep and straight to the end.—Thoreau.

The first duty of the writer is to make the path easy for the reader.—Brander Matthews.

Logic compels us to throw our meaning into distinct propositions, and our reasonings into distinct steps.—John Stuart Mill.

If your language be jargon, your intellect, if not your whole character, will almost certainly correspond.—Quiller-Couch.

11. The Method of Repetition.

See the Exercises for Chapter I, Section 8.

By means of repetition, amplify each of the following statements into a single paragraph:

No law can be sacred to me but that of my own nature. —Emerson.

Either death is a state of nothingness and utter unconsciousness, or, as men say, there is a change and migration of the soul from this world to another.—Plato.

The more confidence a man has in himself, and the more

thoroughly he is fortified by virtue and wisdom, so that he is in need of no one . . . the more noteworthy is he for the friendships which he seeks.—Cicero.

Education is the instruction of the intellect in the laws of Nature, under which name I include not merely things and their forces, but men and their ways.—Huxley.

It is certain, to begin with, that the narrowest trade or professional training does something more for a man than to make him a skillful practical tool—it makes him also a judge of other men's skill.—William James.

12. The Method of Cause-and-Effect Relationships.

In the following pairs of phrases, the first member is a cause and the second an effect. Plan short expositions in which you move, first, from cause to effect, and then from effect back to cause.

Harsh parents—dishonest children.
Indulgent parents—selfish children.
Indifferent voters—corrupt officeholders.
Prosperous times—indifferent voters.
Prosperous times—religious indifference.
Religious indifference—corrupt officeholders.

Chapter X

THE METHODS OF EXPOSITION (*continued*)

THE methods of exposition considered in this chapter are really the methods of argument. They are methods by which the reader is instructed in the writer's beliefs, opinions, or point of view. In practice, this instruction usually becomes *persuasion*—that is, an attempt to influence others to have the same beliefs, opinions, and point of view. Persuasion, however, is not a method of exposition, not a method of instruction; it is merely a means of making the reader amenable to instruction. More will be said of it in another chapter of this book.

1. Inference.—We make inferences almost every moment of our waking lives. We speak to a person in the same room, and infer that he will hear; we write a sentence, and infer that other people will understand what we mean; we read in the newspaper that the Congress has passed a bill, and we infer that it is true. All these are simple, direct inferences. But sometimes we lengthen the step between demonstrable fact and conclusion. We **look** about our room for a book, do not find it, and infer that we **have** left it at the college; we see our friend dressing in his best clothes after dinner, and infer that he is going out for the evening; we notice that another friend is sneezing and sniffling, and infer that he has a cold.

Any inference may be wrong. That is why it is only an inference. The person in the same room with us may be so absorbed in reading that he will not hear us; the sentence we write may be unintelligible to others; and the newspaper account of the action of the Congress may be false. Likewise, we may have lost our book on the way over from the college; our friend may be dressing to receive a caller; and the other friend may be sneezing and sniffling because the pepper-shaker emptied itself in his plate at dinner. Any inference may be wrong—yet we spend our lives making inferences.

a. We make them on the strength of *evidence*. Now, evidence is of two sorts: evidence from *authority*, and evidence from *experience*. The first is what other people tell us, and the second is what we observe or experience for ourselves. Reading in the newspaper or listening to someone talk about a murder is obtaining evidence from authority; seeing the murder is obtaining evidence from experience.

If we merely present the evidence we have obtained, we are writing exposition according to the method of description or the method of presenting authority. But if, in addition to presenting the evidence, we try to decide for ourselves and others just who committed the murder, why he committed it, and whether or not he was justified in the deed, we are using the method of inference. We are making inferences, and we hope other people who read or listen to us will make the same inferences.

We move from evidence to inference along either of two roads. The first is called induction, the second deduction.

b. We use *inductive reasoning* when we collect a certain amount of evidence from authority or from experience, and then make an inference based on our evidence. This is the scientific method of reasoning.

Suppose the President of the nation is confronted with an undesirable economic situation in the country. Wishing to remedy it, he begins collecting evidence. He accumulates statistics, he makes comparisons, he learns what various authorities believe, he nvestigates what other nations have done to relieve similar situations, and he studies the effect certain remedies have had in the past. Then he makes an inference: he decides that a certain governmental policy will relieve the situation. He has worked inductively by making a generalization based on evidence. His generalization may be wrong, his inference false; but the error will be due to some fallacy in his judging the evidence. His method has been scientific.

Some inferences may be based on no such large amount of evidence, but on a single fact. If my newspaper tells me that the King of England is seriously ill, I accept that authority without demanding further evidence, and infer that he really is ill. If at night I hear what sounds like rain pattering on the roof, I accept that evidence, and infer that it really is raining. If I taste an olive on a dish and find it palatable, I infer that all the olives on the same dish are equally palatable—I need not taste them all. True, my single bit of evidence may be insufficient on each of these occasions, and my inference may be wrong. But the method is our main interest just now—it is inductive. We shall discuss the fallacies later.

A third kind of induction is inference from comparison or analogy. Suppose that we have two things which, evidence has shown, are alike in many ways. We often infer, therefore, that they are alike in a certain other way about which we do not have evidence. We have found, for example, that one of a pair of twins likes the color red; and we infer that the other one also will like it. Or we have found that a certain drug is fatal to monkeys, and we infer that it will be fatal to human beings as well. Or we have found that a horse works more efficiently if he is allowed to rest a few minutes every hour or so, and we infer that an automobile likewise will work more efficiently if it is allowed to rest occasionally. All of these inferences are based upon observed resemblances between two things: twins, monkeys and human beings, horses and automobiles. Some of these inferences may be right and some (like the last) altogether wrong. But the method is inductive. *It proceeds from particular instances by means of inference to a conclusion.*

   c. *Deductive reasoning,* on the other hand, shows how a general principle applies to a particular instance—or how a particular instance illustrates a general principle. A hoary example (put in the form of what is called a "syllogism") will illustrate:

   Major Premise: *All men are mortal.*
   Minor Premise: *Socrates is a man.*
   Conclusion: *Therefore Socrates is mortal.*

Here the reasoning works downward from the general principle to the particular instance (Socrates).

   Deductive reasoning, unlike inductive reasoning, always *begins* with an assumption. If the assumption has evolved from the inductive process, it may be justifiable. For example, the general principle that "All men are mortal" has been proved over and over again by inductive experience. But if the general principle were some such statement as this: "All millionaires are dishonest," the assumption that, since Mr. X. is a millionaire, Mr. X. is dishonest would not be justifiable. The major premise has not been proved inductively. But even if the major premise were true and yet the minor premise were untrue (if Mr. X. is really *not a* millionaire), the conclusion would still be unjustifiable.

   In any event, therefore, *deductive reasoning must depend ultimately on evidence derived from particular instances; that is, on inductive reasoning.*

   Inductive reasoning, in turn, always involves making inferences. In the next section we shall discover some of the most common reasons why some inferences are invalid and, by implication, why some are valid.

2. Exposing Fallacies.—Whether exposing fallacies is a method or a type of exposition is debatable. But since the process is closely connected with the method of making inferences, we shall discuss it as a method in this chapter.

a. *Fallacies of confusion* are those due to muddled method—to thinking that actually misunderstands or ignores the subject. These fallacies may be willfully perpetrated by dishonest people in order to cloud an issue, or they may be innocently deceitful.

(1) A common fallacy of confusion results from a writer's *ignoring the question*. Every teacher is familiar with this sort of thing. He puts the problem: "Compare Swift and Addison as satirists." Half the students taking the examination will at once begin writing down everything they know about Swift and Addison—life, character, works, style, and philosophy; they will ignore the real question. Or a politician, asked what course he intends to follow in dealing with the open-shop question, may answer by saying that he has always had a deep sympathy for the common man, and that, if elected, he will work hard for the best interests of his constituents. He simply ignores the question.

(2) *Begging the question* is very similar. A writer begs the question when he presents as arguments facts or inferences that actually have nothing to do with the question. A student fails to make a passing grade in a course. "But I was sick half the time," he says, "and could not attend the lectures or come to laboratory." That may be true, and the professor may feel very sorry; but the fact remains that the student did not know enough to pass his examinations. Or the politician asked to commit himself on the open-shop question may say that his attitude in the past has been well known: he has opposed the open shop. That may be true; but the fact remains that he has not committed himself to a policy for the future. He has begged the question.

(3) Much like begging the question is *argument beside the*

point; that is, argument which proves one thing, but not the point at issue. A writer trying to prove, for example, that canceling our foreign debts would improve the economic situation of the country may argue that America has already received ample repayment in its post-war prosperity. But does this argument have anything to do with his immediate contention that cancellation will improve present conditions? Take another example: A writer wishing to prove that Germany's safety requires her rearming may argue that the other major European powers are rearming, that Germany is as great a nation as the others, and that accordingly Germany deserves the same right to rearm. All this may be true; but does it prove that Germany's safety is menaced? Both of these writers are arguing beside the point. They have reached valid conclusions, perhaps; but these are not the conclusions the writers set out to reach.

(4) A subtle fallacy is that of *assuming a truth which involves the point at issue.* For example, a sincere and earnest old minister once advertised that, in his next sermon, he would prove from historical evidence that Jesus arose from the dead. But in the sermon the only evidence he educed was a series of references to passages in the New Testament. He assumed that the New Testament is historically sound, though that is exactly the point at which doubters would have taken issue with him. Another speaker, this time a politician, tried to prove that he was a fit person for office because his policies were in accord with those of Thomas Jefferson. He assumed that Jeffersonian policies were wise for all occasions, though that is exactly what doubters might not grant.

These two instances involve an inference which has not been justified inductively. Often the inference is made subtly in the use of vague or ambiguous words. "Why should a business man *waste his time* with literature?" "The President's *un-American* policies should be discouraged by the voters." "The *radical* notions of the Senator from Wisconsin will not mislead this august body." Each of these italicized words or phrases assumes as true that which, if it really were true, would necessitate no further argument. But the assumption has been made on insufficient evidence.

(5) A somewhat uncommon fallacy of confusion is that due to *argument in a circle*. Here the writer assumes something is true, reaches a conclusion on the basis of that assumption, and then doubles back to prove the original assumption on the strength of the conclusion just reached. An illustration will clarify. Lincoln once remarked, "God must have loved the common people, for He made so many of them." The implied assumption here is that whatever God has created in numbers, He loves. He has created a large number of common people. Therefore He must love the common people. And the fact that He loves them has made Him create them in large numbers. Another illustration: The Victorian Age, surveying its miserable and wicked industrial population, argued thus: God punishes the wicked by making them miserable. These people are miserable. Therefore God must have punished them. And the fact that God has punished them shows that they are wicked.

b. *Fallacies of evidence* are due to a writer's admitting as evidence that which is really inadequate or unreliable evidence. He states as true that which is not the truth, or else not the whole truth. "The utility interests have contributed ten thousand dollars to the campaign fund of my opponent," shouts a candidate. That sounds bad—but is it *true*? "The President has delivered the country into the hands of a visionary bureaucracy," shouts a Congressman. That is enough to condemn the President—but is it *true*? "Mr. X. is a very wealthy man," says the gossip. "To my certain knowledge, he has fifty thousand dollars in cash in the bank." This last may be true, but is it the *whole* truth? Perhaps

Mr. X. owes a hundred thousand dollars. Unsound reasoning is not nearly so common as the use of unsound evidence.

As we have seen, we may use two kinds of evidence: that from authority and that from experience.

(1) Before venturing to use *evidence from authority*, we should ask ourselves three questions:

Has the authority had the opportunity to know the truth?

Has he the desire to tell the truth?

Has he ability to tell the truth?

Suppose, for example, that we are trying to find out from a statesman something of the arms situation in Europe. We ask at once, Has he been to Europe recently? If so, did he stay long enough and travel widely enough to find out anything of importance? Did he talk to Europeans who really knew the situation? Has he had access to reliable documents? In other words, Has he had the opportunity to find out the truth? If not, we must not use him as an authority.

Even if he has had the opportunity, is he reliable? Is there some motive of self-interest, fear, patriotism, or prejudice which may make him desire to conceal some of the truth or distort it all? Perhaps the statesman is a Senator who desires re-election. Will he not be tempted to play up the arms situation in order to have a sensational campaign topic? Or perhaps he is writing a series of articles for a rabidly jingoistic chain of newspapers. Will he not be tempted to bow to the policy of the papers, and make European affairs look as dangerous as possible? Or perhaps he has a large interest in a munitions factory. Will he not be tempted to belittle the arms situation in order that his factory may continue selling arms uninterruptedly? Any number of such considerations may influence our authority to try to obscure the real truth, and so make his evidence invalid.

But even if he has had the opportunity to know the truth, and if he honestly desires to tell the truth, he may still be an untrustworthy authority. He may be incompetent. He may not understand national budgeting and international finance; he may not see through the evasions and subterfuges of European war parties; he may have no conception of the relative arms-value of light cruisers, say, as compared with destroyers, or of machine guns as compared with field artillery. In a word, he may have no ability to tell the truth. He is not a good authority.

(2) The other kind of evidence—that taken from our own *experience or observation*—involves a similar questioning of our own opportunity, desire, and ability to tell the truth. We say that seeing is believing. But we see smoke vanish into nothingness— and yet we do not actually believe that it has become nothing: we know that if we had the opportunity we could catch the smoke by means of certain apparatus, collect its particles, and even weigh it. We see a magician take money out of the air—and yet we do not believe that he does it: we know that we merely have not the ability to see through his trickery. And we see a close friend of ours do a questionable deed—and yet we do not believe he is wicked: we know that we "simply don't want to believe anything bad about him." Seeing, then, is not believing unless we, like the authority we have questioned, have the opportunity, the ability, and the desire to see straight.[1]

c. *Fallacies of the inductive method* may be due to generalization unjustified by the nature of the evidence educed (even though the evidence itself may be valid). It will be recalled that inductive generalization may evolve from one of three sources: many bits of evidence, one representative or conclusive bit of evidence, or comparison. Accordingly, inductive reasoning may break down along any of these three avenues to inference.

[1] To perceive how important is this "desire to see straight," the student should examine the implications of the verb "to rationalize" in its modern psychological sense. He is especially referred to Professor James Harvey Robinson's "Four Kinds of Thinking," in *The Mind in the Making*, 1921 (Harpers).

(1) The number of examples brought forward may be *too small* to justify generalization. Suppose my two cats like chocolate candy. From these two examples, would I be justified in saying, "All cats like chocolate candy"? By no means. The number of examples is too small to justify generalization. Or suppose ten people are in this room. I inquire how old each person is, but somehow manage to skip one of the ten. None of the nine people I have asked, however, is less than twenty years old. Would I, then, be justified in declaring absolutely, "Everybody in this room is over twenty years of age"? By no means. Anything less than the total number of examples here is insufficient to justify generalization.

All this does not mean, of course, that we must account for every single example in every group before we can safely generalize about it. We may safely generalize about thousands of individual birds or insects or flowers from examining a dozen specimens belonging to one species. Just why so minute a percentage is satisfactory here, whereas ninety per cent of the people in the room was not satisfactory, it is difficult for us to say. Experience alone (that is, inductive evidence) acquired almost unconsciously through a lifetime tells us when a number of examples is too small. That is a vague statement, but it is the only one possible.

(2) But what about generalization from a *single bit of evidence*? From eating one olive, are we justified in concluding that all the olives on a dish are good? Again the answer must be vague. Only experience we have had with other articles on other dishes will tell us whether we should trust the sample olive to be a representative example.

(3) The same thing is true when the basis of generalization is *an analogy or a comparison*. Experience has shown us that we cannot treat horses and automobiles alike, even though the function of each is the same. Experience has shown likewise that we

may treat one horse more or less as we treat another horse. A comparison is involved in each illustration; but only by experience can we know how far to carry the comparison.[2]

Experience, then, is the final authority, whether we argue from many examples, from one example, or from analogy or comparison. But experience itself (as the term is used here) is merely a rough generalization based on many years' accumulation of evidence. That is, experience is merely induction.

d. *Fallacies of the deductive method* usually spring from improper generalization in major or minor premise. This is equivalent to saying that most deductive fallacies are due to the inductive fallacies just discussed. For example: All Presidents of the United States are great men; Mr. X. is President of the United States; therefore Mr. X. is a great man. The major premise here is unsound; it has not grown out of a valid inductive process. Likewise, if the minor premise read: Al Smith is to be the next President of the United States—and if the conclusion were: Therefore Al Smith is a great man—we should have a fallacy due to an unsound minor premise. We do not know that Al Smith will be the next President.

The formula for the deductive process is this:

$$A = B \qquad\qquad A < B$$
$$C = A \qquad \text{or} \qquad C = A$$
$$\therefore C = B \qquad\qquad \therefore C < B$$

Any other arrangement of the elements in the syllogism creates a fallacy. The following syllogisms contain fallacies which the student may analyze for himself:

All horses are quadrupeds.
Fido (the dog) is a quadruped.
Therefore Fido is a horse.

[2] As a matter of fact, *all* analogies and almost all comparisons are false if they are carried to extremes. The proper use of analogy is for clarification, not proof.

All Frenchmen are Europeans.
Mussolini is a European.
Therefore Mussolini is a Frenchman.

e. *Fallacies of inclusion or exclusion* are those fallacies in which a writer has admitted into evidence or inference matter that is extraneous, or has excluded matter that is vital.

(1) One of the commonest sorts of these fallacies is due to the use of *words of double-meaning*.

Green-tinted finger-nails are common this year.
Mary has green-tinted finger-nails.
Therefore Mary is common.

Songs composed by a people as a whole are called popular songs.
"Old Black Joe" is a popular song.
Therefore "Old Black Joe" was composed by the people as a whole.

In each of these examples a word is used to mean two things. That is, each involves a fallacy of inclusion, for at the end of the syllogism the word is made to include more than it did at the beginning.

(2) A little different is the fallacy of *improper classification* (see Section 3 of the preceding chapter). The writer who says, "There are only two kinds of nations in Europe: those who pay their war debts, and those who don't," is forgetting to include in his classification several nations in Europe which have no war debts. And the writer who says, "There are only three kinds of Americans: those who are trying to get rich, those who are intellectual, and those who are in politics," may have created a smart epigram; but he has not produced a valid classification. His basis of classification changes from one thing to another throughout the sentence—from ambition, to intellect, to profession. Consequently, his terms are not mutually exclusive.

(3) Altogether different is the fallacy in which *appeals to humor,*

emotion, or prejudice are admitted as valid evidence or reasoning. Many a Nazi Storm Trooper has argued thus: "Everybody I don't like should be deprived of his civil rights; I don't like Jews; therefore Jews should be deprived of their civil rights." And many a staunch conservative in our own country has argued thus: "My ancestors for generations back believed that the government should not legislate about business; my ancestors were wise; therefore wise people believe that government should not legislate about business." In the first of these syllogisms, the major premise is based altogether on emotion; in the second, the minor premise is based on ancestral reverence. Emotion and reverence have their place in our lives—but not in logical exposition. They should be excluded as irrelevant.

(4) We often make fallacies when we infer that *a certain cause will produce only certain effects.* Exposing these fallacies is difficult, for no one can read the future. Any action of ours, however well considered, may produce tremendous effects for which we never bargained. Most writers, however, are guilty of excluding from consideration the possible effects which may result in addition to those desired. Yet every cause is like a two-edged sword; it works both ways. It has a certain effect, and also the opposite of that effect. Thus the hope of becoming a member of Phi Beta Kappa encourages students to work hard in their courses, and yet it also encourages them to take easy courses in order to make good grades. A writer interested in exposing fallacies in the cause-to-effect argument can usually do no better than to study other possible effects his opponent has failed to include in the argument.

(5) Fallacies in an argument from *effect back to cause* are easier to detect. Perhaps the most deceiving of them is the *post hoc, ergo propter hoc* (after this, and therefore because of this) fallacy. Since an effect usually follows a cause, many people are led to think that any fact that invariably follows another is an

effect of that other. For example, we have an ailment, are treated by a doctor, and get well. We think the doctor cured us. Yet the doctors themselves say that ninety per cent of their patients would recover successfully without medical attention of any kind. Or we elect a man to office; certain things happen in the country; and the man is defeated at his next candidacy on the strength of the things which have occurred—even though he is in no way responsible for them. *Post hoc, ergo propter hoc,* reason the voters. They forget that Monday always follows Sunday, but that Monday, nevertheless, is not an effect of Sunday. They forget to include in their reasoning other possible causes besides the immediately preceding event.

The opposite kind of fallacy is that in which *a cause is assigned for a condition, though the condition existed before the cause assigned.* People often say, for example, that the "modern" movement in American poetry was a result of the Great War. As a matter of fact, however, the movement began in 1912 and 1913, before the outbreak of war. The critics have failed to include that fact.

Sometimes *we mistake an effect for a cause.* We say that an instructor gives a bad grade because he dislikes a student; but perhaps the instructor dislikes the student because the latter has made a bad grade. Or we say that city politics are corrupt under a certain mayor; but perhaps that mayor obtained office because city politics are corrupt.

In much the same way, *two effects of the same cause, or different causes, may be taken for a cause and an effect.* I build a house on a vacant block, and immediately someone else builds a house on the same block. Is the first fact a cause, and the latter an effect? Perhaps not; perhaps we both build because times are prosperous. Or hot weather comes, and the wheat ripens. Is the former a cause, and the latter an effect? Perhaps not; perhaps

the first is due to the northward movement of the sun, and the
second to the age of the wheat. If we argue otherwise, we are
failing to include in our discussion two important causes.

The last fallacy we shall consider in studying arguments from
effect back to cause is the fallacy of *mistaking for a sole cause
that which is only an influence*. "President Roosevelt was elected
because I contributed one hundred dollars to his campaign fund."
The sum contributed was only an influence, not a sole cause. Fallacies in real argument are not often as simple as the one just
given. But existence is so complex that every effect usually has
more than one cause. Accordingly, a writer wishing to refute an
argument which tries to show the cause of a certain effect can
nearly always do so by finding another influence which operated
at the same time to help produce the effect.

EXERCISES

1. Inference.

a. Describe the kind of evidence you would use in expositions
on each of the following topics:

Chinese porcelains.

Tennyson's poetic art.

The honor system (or the proctor system) at your college.

Social philosophy in Galsworthy's plays.

What a man (or a woman) loses by going to college.

b. Which of the following generalizations would require many
bits of evidence for proof? A single bit of evidence? A comparison?

Crows are black.

Dogs naturally hate cats.

Shakespeare is more read in Europe than is Dante.

A newly discovered species of cedar will remain green all
winter.

Queen Mary probably likes to shop.

Calvin Coolidge is dead.

Small babies are not conscious.

Make a list of your opinions about certain individuals, people in general, politics, religion, etc. Discuss the evidence upon which you arrived at these opinions.

c. Invent syllogisms to fit the following conclusions:

Mary loves John.

Times will get better.

Times will get worse.

Women should take an interest in politics.

Public school teachers deserve higher salaries.

Professors should be more "human."

2. Exposing Fallacies.

a. Analyze and name the fallacies in the following statements:

He should be elected President, for he is a thoroughly honest man.

He would make a great President, for he was a great general.

I am sure he has no will power, for he is a confirmed drunkard.

Art should enter into the life of everyone, for it is beautiful and interesting.

I know he is intelligent, for I never saw a more intellectual forehead.

A radio is not worth having; it is merely an advertising mechanism.

Gentlemen of the Jury: How could anyone believe that this sweet and gentle little lady would murder her husband?

No one should obey prohibition laws; they are foolish restrictions on personal liberty.

As I thought—my job was too good to last.

You must know Greek and Latin in order to be cultured.

You are so much interested in writing that you should become an author.

He will continue on his course because he is too stupid to change.

He must love her; for if he didn't, he wouldn't send her flowers every week.

I can never win at cards, for I'm just not lucky.

This must be an oak tree; it has lobate leaves like an oak tree's.

b. Would the individuals in the following situations be trustworthy authorities? Why?

A man whose home was robbed while he was out of town.

A charwoman who felt sure the blood she mopped up was human blood.

A child of four telling what time of day an event occurred.

A private soldier telling the strategy of a great battle in which he participated.

A student giving a bad report of a course in which he had failed.

The same student giving a good report of the course.

A woman suing for divorce, and testifying about her husband's character.

A mother testifying in court about her son's character.

A district attorney trying to convict the son.

A defense attorney trying to have him acquitted.

An alienist telling about the mental condition of the son.

A scientist telling about a cure for cancer he thinks he has discovered.

Another scientist criticizing the first one's work.

Ourselves explaining how we made a large sum of money.

Ourselves explaining how a surgeon operated on us.

c, d, and e. Analyze and name these fallacies:

This book is certain to be clever; Bernard Shaw wrote it.

He must be a good man, for he is very kind to his mother.

My wife and my daughter are afraid of mice, and so I suppose all women are afraid of mice.

People never have flown at the rate of five hundred miles per hour, and they never will.

I had a bad accident once in driving a car, and so I suppose I am incapable of driving.

There's no use in your doing the outside reading; you can pass the course without it.

This bird is blue; it must be a bluebird.

Germany refused to pay her debts to France, and so France refused to pay her debts to America.

The veterinary said this medicine would cure horses of roundworms; so it will probably cure them of tapeworms as well.

I left my raincoat at home—and sure enough! it rained. I'll take my raincoat next time.

He is such a good scholar that I know he will make a good teacher.

He is a grouch; the only time I ever spoke to him he nearly bit my head off.

My friend Rip van Winkle over here in the corner hasn't yet got the birds' nests out of his hair; don't pay any attention to what he says.

There is gold in sea-water. It only waits for the enterprising chemist to extract it and grow rich.

One of the good things the Soviets have accomplished is the abolition of serfdom in Russia.

Ducks have acquired the habit of living on or near water because their webbed feet and squat bodies make them awkward on land.

My mother used to hang a little bag of asafœtida around my neck to protect me from diphtheria. And since I never took diphtheria, the old precaution was probably of some value, after all.

You should be ashamed of reading a book like that! What would your father say if he were alive?

Both the United States and Mexico would benefit materially if the United States would take over Mexico and give it a stable and honest government administered from Washington. Consequently, we ought to absorb Mexico.

President Wilson tried to negotiate the Versailles Treaty personally, and so the Treaty was a failure as far as America was concerned.

I argued with the professor too much, and so he failed me in the course.

Cats are so destructive of birds that it would pay us to do away with cats entirely.

Cats like to hunt at night because they can see in the dark.

People are hoarding their money, and that's why times are so hard.

He is taking almost every course I am taking in college. I think he is just imitating me.

SUGGESTED SUBJECTS FOR ARGUMENTS
(Choose either positive or negative side)

Economic:

America would profit if the war debts were canceled.

Renouncing the gold standard discourages speculation.

The people as a whole prosper when the government discourages speculation.

The government may prevent depressions by fixing wages, prices, and working hours in every industry.

Stabilization of wages, prices, and working hours harms small business.

Political:

The abolition of county governments would save the people's money by eliminating duplication of offices and taxes.

Crime could be lessened if all states would hand over their law-enforcing powers to the federal government.

A super-planning commission (something like the Supreme Court) with almost unlimited economic powers should be set up as a means of forestalling economic depressions.

Law enforcement would be more just and certain if twelve impartial federal judges, instead of twelve jurors, tried all cases.

All trial judges should be appointed by executive authority for life (unless impeached), instead of being elected by the people for short terms.

Social:

The federal government should grant old-age pensions, the money to be derived from taxation of all businesses employing more than five persons.

The federal government should operate an unemployment insurance system, the money to be derived from taxation of working people and their employers.

Divorce should be automatically granted at the request of either a husband or a wife.

Architectural plans for all proposed buildings should be passed on by a committee of artists who will study the plans not only for their individual artistic merit, but also for their fitness to the locality where the building is to be.

Children would be better educated if teachers were free of political and parental authority.

Historical:

King Arthur was a real person.

The Man in the Iron Mask was a brother of Louis XIV.

The Incas invaded America from Polynesia.

General Longstreet lost the Civil War for Lee.

Man originated in Africa.

Literary:

Chaucer's "Nun's Priest's Tale" is a political allegory.

The English popular ballad was of communal origin.

Elizabethan drama was derived from Greco-Roman classical rather than liturgical influences.

The Seventeenth Earl of Oxford (Edward DeVere) wrote the plays attributed to William Shakespeare.

Swinburne was really a Pre-Raphaelite poet.

Reflective:

Fixed moral standards result in unhealthy and unhappy mental states for all individuals.

The religion best suited for our times is a fixed system of morality.

Laughter arises from a feeling of triumph.

It is a crime to believe on insufficient evidence.

The state exists for the individuals within it.

Chapter XI

THE TYPES OF EXPOSITION

I. The Familiar Essay

INCLUDING the familiar essay in a discussion of exposition is almost an act of violence. Properly, the familiar essay is neither description, nor narration, nor exposition; it is a type unto itself. But because of the fact that it states ideas and does not much concern itself with the creation of images or the relation of actions, the familiar essay is closer kin to exposition than to description or narration.

The familiar essay states ideas; but these ideas are frequently trivial and always personal. They convey little objective instruction, and they constitute no philosophic systems. Usually, indeed, the ideas in a familiar essay are not expounded in sober earnestness and must not be taken seriously. Consequently, the familiar essay is a form of writing so fluid and imponderable as almost to defy analysis. Moreover, advice about how to write it is futile. An hour with Charles Lamb, Stephen Leacock, Max Beerbohm, or Christopher Morley will teach anyone more about the familiar essay than will a month with a textbook of composition.

In style this kind of essay is familiar, but not commonplace or vulgar; in structure it is formless, but not incoherent or chaotic; in method it may be illogical, but it is never clumsy or stupid. The familiar essayist writes about anything—silk stockings, German kings, or life in Alaska; but he is seldom in earnest about any of them. He is well bred, chatty, gossipy; sympathetic, but often satirical; good-humored, but sometimes cynical; he is never solemn. He is genuinely interested in everything, but he takes nothing seriously—himself least of all. He may write about serious subjects, but he will write in a whimsical style. Or he may write about trivial subjects, but he will write in a mock-serious style. He is informal and paradoxical—irresponsible and amused—urbane and playful—shrewd and irrepressible. And yet all the while he may be filled with quiet emotion and tender sentiment. He is the intelligent and cultured man off parade. He laughs good-naturedly at the world and at himself, and asks only that the world laugh with him. If, sometimes, a tear lurks behind the laugh, it is a hidden tear which finds no expression save in a little sigh.

In Edinburgh in 1863 Alexander Smith wrote about the familiar essayist in a style which may well be a model for the style of all familiar essays:

The essayist plays with his subject, now in whimsical, now in grave, now in melancholy mood. He lies upon the idle grassy bank, like Jacques, letting the world flow past him, and from this thing and the other he extracts his mirth and his moralities. His main gift is an eye to discover the suggestiveness of common things; to find a sermon in the most unpromising texts. Beyond the vital hint, the first step, his discourses are not beholden to their titles. Let him take up the most trivial subject, and it will lead him away to the great questions over which the serious imagination loves to brood—fortune, mutability, death—just as inevitably as the runnel, trickling among the summer hills, on which the sheep are bleating, leads you to the sea; or as, turning down the first street you come to in the city, you are led finally, albeit by many an intricacy, out into the open country, with its waste places and its woods, where you are lost in a sense of strangeness and solitariness. The world is to the meditative man what the mulberry plant is to the silkworm. The essay-writer has no lack of subject-matter. He has the day that is passing over his head; and, if unsatisfied with that, he has the world's six thousand years to depasture his gay or serious humour upon. I idle away my time here, and I am finding new subjects every hour. Everything I see or hear is an essay in bud. The world is everywhere whispering essays, and one need only be the world's amanuensis. The proverbial expression which last evening the clown dropped as he trudged homeward to supper, the light of the setting sun on his face, expands before me to a dozen pages. The coffin of the pauper, which today I saw carried carelessly along, is as good a subject as the funeral procession of an emperor. . . . Two rustic lovers, whispering between the darkening hedges, are as potent to project my mind into the tender passion as if I had seen Romeo touch the cheek of Juliet in the moonlight garden. Seeing a curly-headed child asleep in the sunshine before a cottage-door is sufficient excuse for a discourse on childhood; quite as good as if I had seen infant Cain asleep in the lap of Eve with Adam looking on. A lark cannot rise to heaven without raising as many thoughts as there are notes in its song. Dawn cannot pour its white light on my village without starting from their dim lair a hundred reminiscences; nor can sunset burn above yonder trees in the west without attracting to itself the melancholy of a lifetime.

II. Exposition of Events

History imaginatively re-created is not, properly speaking, genuine exposition, but is art. Yet custom makes us regard as expository any narrative which recounts, for purposes of instruction, events which have actually happened. It is with this understanding of expository narrative that the following paragraphs have been written.

1. *Institutional History* is the type which most of us first think of when someone mentions the word "history." It is expository writing which deals with the growth of some institution. This institution may be anything from the French Republic or the English Parliament down to the honor system in your college or the superstition about black cats.

An exposition recording the history of such institutions ought to be something more than a catalogue of events chronologically arranged. Our chief reason for studying the past is that we may better understand events that have come later. Consequently, an indiscriminate list of past facts narrated without regard to their proper value in the scheme of things may defeat the fundamental purpose of history. Incidents must be selected, facts arranged, and space allotted with due regard to the significance of things in the light of later developments. Institutional history not so focused is little better than a collection of images seen in a kaleidoscope. These may be charming to contemplate, but they have no meaning.

2. What we may call *Folk History* is altogether different. Its purpose is not to give readers a clearer understanding of large events or general conditions but, rather, to show readers how our ancestors lived, thought, worked, and died; to reveal potentialities of human nature that we moderns could never have dreamed of; to satisfy a normal human curiosity about other human beings who were once alive. Such history need be only true and interesting. Without attempting interpretation and evaluation, it may recount stirring events, or depict fascinating characters, or tell of curious or unusual customs or incidents. The more vividly all this is done, the better is the history. Factual truth alone may not always suffice. Imagination, understanding of human nature, story-telling power, an eye for effect, and a keen sensitivity to the strange or romantic —these the writer needs in addition to strict historical accuracy. Acquiring them is largely a matter of wide and tolerant reading. And what reading cannot supply, nature must.

3. *Biography* may be of either the institutional or the folk type. That is, it may tell the story of a man's life as it affected his times and the times which came after him; or it may tell the story of his life for its own sake—for the intrinsic interest of himself and of the things he did. Older biographies were, most commonly, of the former sort; but modern biographies, yielding to the contemporary interest in psychology (and, perhaps, making concessions to mod-

ern sensationalism), have drifted toward the folk type. This new desire to understand historical personages as *people*, men and women undergoing altogether human emotions and having altogether human weaknesses, is certainly praiseworthy. It has revitalized biography and brought about a new conception of history; moreover, it has raised the craft of biography into an art demanding the creative imagination of a novelist as well as the accuracy of the historian. As long as it retains this accuracy, the new art deserves all the popularity which it has attained; but when it becomes mere invention and imagination on the writer's part, the new biography is worse than useless. It not only fails to supply accurate information, but gives the appearance of authority to guesswork, apocryphal surmises, or absolute misinformation. Personal fancy, elaborate reconstructions of possible conversations, and bold imaging forth of personally invented scenes have no place in sound biography. An expert artist in words can bring a dead man back to live in print without resorting to such tricks.

No biography should be a mere running comment on events chronologically arranged. Instead, it should have a definite objective, a unifying idea, around which all the events arrange themselves according to a pattern. The pattern is the biographer's own contribution to the work. To one biographer, Napoleon was a selfish, cold-blooded egoist; to another, he was a dreamer who visioned for himself an Asiatic empire of which Europe was to be only a province; and to another, he was an unhappy man who found in activity a compensation for disappointed love. Each biographer uses the same facts; but because each has used a different pattern, each has created a different Napoleon.

Before setting pen to paper in writing a biography, the student should acquire by reading or by personal investigation as much information as possible about his subject. After this, the next step should be assimilation and meditation. For a time, the prospective writer should leave off research and devote himself to the task of expressing in words the dominant trait of his subject's character and the main pattern of his life. When this step has been taken, and not until then, comes the writing of the biography. This third step is now comparatively easy. All that the writer need do is to select from his previously gathered information facts and anecdotes which illustrate or prove the fundamental idea, and then present them in a more or less chronological order. A little additional investigation may be necessary, or a little explanation of seemingly contradictory facts; but the real work of writing a biography is done when the second step mentioned above is taken.

4. *Anecdote* is one of the chief instruments of biography. It may be a short account of some small incident, or it may be a bit of information about someone's personal habits. For example, the story of how Coleridge lectured an hour and a half on a subject he did not know until the man who introduced him announced the subject to the audience—this is an anecdote of a particular incident. And the information that Dr. Johnson used to touch every post as he walked down the street—this is an anecdote of personal habit.

But both sorts of anecdotes serve one purpose: They reveal character. They tell us something (not always to be expressed in words) about personalities; and they tell it more forcefully and memorably than could any amount of abstract analysis. Everyone who has read Macaulay or Boswell can recall a dozen anecdotes about Dr. Johnson; but who can recall many actual facts about him? When was he born; where was he born; when did he leave Oxford; when did he come to London; when did he die?

Not all anecdotes, however, are personal. Some reveal the characteristics of races, classes, or professions. The stories about the two Irishmen, about the Scotsman, about the traveling salesman, about the absent-minded professor are all anecdotes intended to depict the typical traits of certain groups. The scope of the anecdote may be even wider. It may reveal traits typical of a people, of an age in history, of human beings in general—or of dogs, or of parrots, or of ants. The anecdote about the medieval French bishop who tried in ecclesiastical court and burned for sorcery a rooster which had laid an egg reveals to us more about the medieval mind than could columns of statistics. And the stories telling how feminine mourners (some with onions in their handkerchiefs) filed past the bier of the dead actor Rudolph Valentino reveal to us as much about human sentimentality as does a tabloid.

The requirements of a good anecdote are these: that it reveal some characteristic of individuals, groups, or species; that it be short; and that, if possible, the incident told be curious, humorous, or emotional.

5. The *True-experience Narrative* is expository when its chief purpose is to give information. Yet this kind of narrative nearly always has the other purposes of being imaginative, of exciting the reader's emotions, and of pleasing by means of a skillful plot. Parkman's *The Oregon Trail*, Theodore Roosevelt's book on his African adventure, Tomlinson's *The Sea and the Jungle*, magazine accounts of explorations, hunting caribou in Alaska, catching trout in Colorado—these are narratives of true experience.

The first requisite for such narratives is that they be convincing. For no matter how interesting or exciting they are, they defeat their primary purpose if they do not sound true. To help him achieve this convincingness, a writer may use some of the following devices:

He will write in a direct, simple style instead of in a studied or elaborate style.

He will shun almost every temptation to be impressive by means of intensifying words or emotional details.

He will avoid trying to create artificial effects in climax, suspense, description, and alleged humor.

He will be wary of making statements hard to be believed; and when he does make them, he will explain them carefully.

If he is writing in the first person, he will minimize his own exploits and praise those of his companions.

He will give many specific (even though unnecessary) details about the weather, the route followed, the equipment taken, and so forth.

In addition to making his work convincing, the writer of true-experience narrative must make it interesting. His chief source of interest will be, of course, the inherent interest of his subject matter. Yet a few other sources of interest are worth mentioning.

Careful accounts of the emotional reactions people have under unusual strains are interesting. So are details of ingenious ways by which individuals circumvent difficulties; so are descriptions of unfamiliar ways of living or thinking among certain peoples; so are characterizations and descriptions of typical people. Judicious, non-spectacular use of suspense (see the last chapter of this book) will heighten the interest of a narrative. And organizing the narrative around a central figure will contribute a human interest to what might otherwise be too impersonal. This central figure need not be the most important person in the story, but some relatively insignificant individual such as the cook, the guide, a villainous native, or even a dog. Returning again and again to detail the actions and reactions of this individual creates a certain artistic unity which many narratives of true experience lack.

6. Closely related to the narrative of true experience is the *Narrative of Travel*. The writer of this latter sort of narrative tells not what has happened on one occasion (as does the writer of the true-experience narrative) but what exists permanently— that is, what other people would find if they went to the same places. Thus the narrative of travel borders on the true-experience

narrative at one side, and on description or factual exposition at the other.

Articles in the *National Geographic Magazine, Asia,* and *Travel,* the journals we keep when we go to Europe, the letters we write home when we are visiting in other places, the tales we tell when we come home from a journey—all these are travel narratives. They acquire interest through the writer's use of much the same devices as those mentioned in the previous section. And they lose interest when they become a mere list of dates and geographic names, or a mere collection of statistical facts about mileage, the height of buildings, the names of monuments seen, and the manufacturing resources of places visited.

The first rule for the travel writer is that he make his reader *see*. The reader must see landscapes, buildings, streets, crowds. But most especially, he must see people—their national physiognomy, their costume, their gestures, their daily familiar habits of life.

Not only must the reader see people; he must know about them as well. He must know their religions and superstitions, their customs and education, their hopes and desires. In a word, he must know how their thinking differs from his, how their understanding of the world differs from his, how their ways of getting a living differ from his, and how their attitude and actions toward other people differ from his.

And finally, giving the history of places visited makes travel narrative interesting. The most unspectacular hillside in Pennsylvania becomes an object of reverent emotion if it so happens that the Battle of Gettysburg was fought there; and the most commonplace rock on the Massachusetts coast becomes an object of veneration if it so happens that the Pilgrim Fathers first landed on it.

7. One final type of informational narrative we may discuss

very briefly. It is the *News Story*. Entire books have been written about this kind of narrative, but we must dismiss it briefly here. Different times, different places, and different editorial policies determine the length, the elaboration, the style, and the mood of every story. But once these forces have done their work, there remains a certain form which the news story usually assumes.

The story gives the gist of the whole narrative in the first two or three sentences of the first paragraph. These sentences are called the *lead*. The next group of sentences (usually three or four) restates the narrative in fuller detail. The next group (even longer than the second) amplifies the story still further. And still other groups continue the process still further.

The reasons for this structure of the news story are three: (a) so that the reader who is in a hurry, or who is not especially interested, can find out essentially what happened without having to read more than the first two or three sentences of the story; (b) so that the story can be logically cut off at almost any point if space requirements demand its abbreviation; and (c) so that the work of headline writers on the news staff may be facilitated.

III. Exposition of Facts

All narrative expositions are expositions of fact, but the reverse of this statement is not true. Many expositions convey information about things which do not change in time or place, and which, therefore, are not narratives. It is these non-narrative expositions of fact which we shall study here.

1. *Definition* is both a method and a type of exposition. As a type it is common and important. Indeed, it is actually the most important of all forms. If we can only get readers to accept our definitions, we can get them to believe and do almost anything. If we can get them to accept our definition of *right*, say, we can get them to risk their lives and do murder on bloody

battlefields. More arguments, disagreements, and misunderstandings in contemporary life result from confused definitions than from any other type of thought; and more philosophies, criticisms, creeds, and codes of action depend on certain definitions than on any amount of sound reasoning. Were the agricultural policies initiated by President Roosevelt in 1933 and 1934 *communistic?* Did the Republican party stand for pure *Americanism?* When is a person *immoral?* Is a certain novel *realistic?* Is it *sentimental?* —On the way we define any of these terms may depend results of large consequence.

2. *Descriptive Exposition* differs from imaginative description in not attempting to give the reader a unified image, to make him *see* the thing described. Imaginative description is synthetic: it builds up an image in the reader's mind. Descriptive exposition is analytic: it records the details which constitute the subject under inspection. Moreover, descriptive exposition need not concern merely concrete objects, but may involve abstract conditions. Indeed, descriptive exposition may be defined as *writing which gives informative details about any thing, fact, or condition which exists, has existed, or may exist.*

a. *Concrete expository description* gives concrete details about either specific things or typical things.

(1) The description of *specific things* may be some such piece of writing as a set of building specifications, notes on the identifying marks of a certain horse, an architect's description of the White House, a social worker's description of living conditions in a mining town, a surgeon's report on an autopsy, or any other collection of concrete details about specific things.

(2) The description of a *typical thing* may be a naturalist's description of a new species of bird, an architect's description of the Tudor manor-house, a psychologist's description of the physical characteristics which mark the criminal type, a doctor's de-

scription of the symptoms which characterize a certain disease, or any other collection of concrete details about typical things.

b. *Abstract expository description* likewise gives information about specific things or typical things.

(1) The *specific things* described may be either concrete or abstract; but the description itself deals with abstract traits of the subject. Thus it may be a character sketch of a certain individual (not a description of his physical appearance); or a set of statistics on living conditions in a mining town (not a physical description of those conditions). It may include descriptions of such things as specific organizations (like the United States government), economic surveys of agricultural conditions in Iowa, summaries of expository books and articles, outlines of a proposed policy or philosophy, and similar collections of abstract details about specific things.

(2) The *typical things* are described in abstract terms. A law describes a type of case which shall be considered an infraction, or describes typical actions that shall constitute legality. The abstract description of typical things may have such titles as these: "The Introvert," "The Criminal Mind," "The Music of the Future," "The Spirit of American Poetry," and "Democracy in the Twentieth Century"—all of them indicating that the exposition so entitled is a collection of abstract details about typical things.

c. *Classification* comes under the heading of expository description. But once a writer adopts the method of classification and divides his subject into its parts, he proceeds in one of the ways noted above—that is, with either concrete or abstract expository description.

3. *Exposition of a Process* is what we write when we give directions or tell how something acts or works. It is close kin to both narrative and descriptive exposition. But it differs from the former in concentrating on method rather than on actual events, and

from the latter in emphasizing the time element rather than static conditions. Thus an exposition on "How Dr. M. Performed a Cerebral Operation" will be a narrative; yet the chief interest will be in the methods Dr. M. employed. At the same time, the exposition will use descriptive details; but the chief interest will not be in one phase of the operation, but in all phases serially connected.

Expositions of a process may usually have titles beginning with "How." They may involve concrete processes like "How to Make Chicken Dumplings"; or abstract processes like "How We Think." They may involve future processes like "How the Next War Will Be Conducted"; or past or present processes like "How the RFC Operates" or "How Insulin Was Discovered." And they may involve specific processes like "How Joffre Won the First Battle of the Marne"; or typical processes like "How Cotton is Ginned."

Sometimes a typical process is made specific by the writer's choosing a single individual of the type, and following this individual through the entire process. For example, the last title given above could be made specific in some such way as this: "What Happens to a Boll of Cotton."

IV. Exposition of Opinion

Opinions may be about general laws of life or nature, or about specific things.

1. Expositions of *Opinions about General Laws* include reflective or meditative essays such as Emerson's; philosophical speculations such as Locke's; discourses on abstract principles of human nature and of human life such as Montaigne's; and essays giving advice about the conduct of life such as Bacon's. Representative titles by the writers mentioned are "Self-Reliance," "Poetry," "On the Nature of Human Understanding," "Friendship," "Love," and "Of Great Place." Columnists like Elsie Robinson, Mrs. Walter

Ferguson, and Arthur Brisbane often write expositions of this type; and magazines of the better sort frequently contain articles expressing opinions about general laws. Two or three old copies of *Harper's Magazine* and the *Atlantic Monthly* contain these articles: "Less Money and More Life," "The Tragic Fallacy," "Is America a Christian Country?" "The Creative Spirit and the Church," and "The American Way." But most magazine articles (and perhaps some of those just named) belong to the next group to be discussed.

2. *Expositions of Opinions About Specific Conditions, Facts, or Things.*—a. General *conditions* often elicit an expression of opinion. A lawyer has noted the cruelty and injustice of the "third degree" as practiced in America, and, writing in *Scribner's*, expresses his opinion about the condition in an article called "The American Inquisition." In the same magazine Howard Mumford Jones gives his opinion about life in the South in an essay called "On Leaving the South." Similar essays in other magazines are "Why Literature Declines," "The Curse of Leisure," "Probabilities of War in Europe," "Compulsory Chapel" (all in the *Atlantic*), "The Great God Football," "Our Passion for Lawmaking," "Is Sleep a Vicious Habit?" and "Is Japan Going Democratic?" (all in *Harper's*). These articles express their authors' opinions about certain conditions.

b. Sometimes an author expresses an opinion about *specific facts*. Scientific and scholarly articles are often of this sort. Some representative titles will illustrate what the group is like: "The Origin of the Longbow," "The Dating of Shenstone's Letters," "Thomas Mann's Indebtedness to Scandinavia," "The Relation Between the York and Townley Plays," and "Emerson's Theory and Practice of Poetry."

Many of these articles present new facts, and all express opinions about facts old and new. Their chief merit lies not in the interestingness, originality, and wisdom of their ideas, but in the amount and quality of evidence they can muster to support a certain opinion. Style, which counts for everything in the other exposions of opinion, counts for nothing here. All that matters is clarity, factual truth, and logical inference.

c. A not-quite-so-pedestrian sort of exposition giving opinions about *specific things* is criticism. We may criticize the opinions or criticize the works of other people. When we do the former, we use as measuring sticks those methods of detecting fallacies which were outlined in a previous chapter; when we do the latter, we use as measuring sticks certain standards peculiar to the type of work under inspection. Since we have already discussed the first kind of criticism, we shall proceed at once to the second kind— criticism of other people's works.

Other people's works may be classified into two sorts: artistic and non-artistic. Since non-artistic work (unless it be the pointless labor of an idiot) is always done for some use or purpose, we must criticize it according to the standards of its particular use or purpose. Accordingly, we cannot very well generalize about such criticism. Every use or purpose has its own standards, which often have no relation to the standards of other uses or purposes —as, for example, the use or purpose of a hairbrush has no relation to the use or purpose of a plow. We must confine our discussion, then, to the criticism which deals with works of art.

Just what art is may itself be a subject for exposition of opinion; and whether a certain piece of work is artistic or not may very well be a question for criticism. But we usually understand by the term art such things as sculpture, architecture, music, dancing, acting, painting, costumery; and style, structure, and imagination in writing. Generalizing about such diverse things in a short space is no easy task; but two or three generalizations we *can* make.

The first is that criticism should be *appreciation* in the literal sense of that word; that is, criticism should be a process of weighing, estimating, and setting a value on a piece of work. It should tell both the good and the bad; it should tell wherein the work succeeds and wherein it fails in its efforts to be good art; it should give credit where credit is due, and fix blame where blame is due. Criticism should never be mere fault-finding, and never mere extolling. Nothing is so bad that it has not in it some good, and nothing is so good that it has not in it some bad. It is the business of the critic to see impartially both the good and the bad.

The next generalization is that we must criticize the artist not on the basis of what he has tried to do, but on the basis of his success or lack of success in trying to do it. This means that we cannot justly criticize a writer, say, for writing novels instead of short stories, for being an essayist instead of a playwright, or for being a romanticist instead of a realist. To be sure, we may, as individuals, praise or deplore the writer's purpose; but as impartial critics, we have no business doing so. If a writer wishes to write a detective story, we must judge his work as a detective story, and not condemn it for failing to be a serious novel. Or if a musician wishes to compose an opera, we must judge his work as an opera, and not condemn it for failing to be a popular song.

The final generalization is that criticism is never mere arbitrary personal opinion. The fact that a critic likes or dislikes a piece of art has no more to do with criticism than the fact that he likes or dislikes strawberries. We may like to read the Tarzan stories and dislike to read Sir Walter Scott; but who would say that our like or dislike here has anything to do with the artistic merit of the two types of work? We know that Sir Walter Scott is a greater writer than Edgar Rice Burroughs, even though we never read the one, and read everything by the other. Criticism is based on certain standards. What these standards are may be difficult to say; but, in general, they are the characteristics possessed in common by works which have appealed to many people in many places over a great length of time.

Let us say that Chaucer's writing has characteristics A, B, and C.

Shakespeare's has A, D, and E.

Congreve's has A, F, and G.

Fielding's has A, H, and I.

Smollett's has A, J, and K.

These writers have had the universal appeal just mentioned—to many people in many places over a great length of time. They have many traits which differentiate them from one another, and yet all have one trait in common—A (perhaps it is the power to create convincing characters). We may presume, then, that A is a characteristic of all universally appealing literature (though, of course, such literature may have many other characteristics).

Turning to the new work which we are about to criticize, we ask, "Does it have characteristic A?" If it has, we may feel safe in saying that this piece of work promises to be universally appealing—that it is *great*. If it has not characteristic A, we may feel equally safe in saying that this particular work gives no promise of being universally appealing—of being *great*. In other words, we use the writers who have been universally appealing in the past as touchstones by which to estimate the work we are trying to criticize now.

All this means that the best critic of art must be widely read and experienced. He must know the art of the past, understand its characteristics, and be able to make comparisons. He cannot be merely an individual with a personal opinion.

This conception of criticism leaves room for originality at two points. First, the critic may have an original opinion as to what common trait the great art of the past possesses. He may think, for example, that Chaucer, Shakespeare, Congreve, Fielding, and Smollett possess in common not A (the ability to create convincing characters) but X (a certain shrewd way of looking at life). Second, the critic may have an original opinion as to whether or not this work he is criticizing really possesses A (or X). Some people may think it does; others may disagree.

But this conception of criticism has one weakness: It does not leave room for absolutely original genius. A new artist may appear with a work having some trait never before seen in works of that particular kind. The orthodox critic would be quite justified in condemning this new work; and yet it might happen that the new trait it possessed would turn out to be universally appealing ever afterward. The orthodox critic, therefore, would find himself altogether wrong in his judgment. But despite this weakness, criticism should remain what we have said—judgment based on a knowledge and an understanding of the past. Absolutely original artistic elements appear daily, but few of them have any but a daily appeal. The critic will be right ninety-nine times out of a hundred in refusing to recognize them as lasting. On the other hand, if he does have wisdom enough to recognize them, and time proves he is right, the critic takes his place among the highest critical geniuses. Which chance the young critic should take—being right ninety-nine per cent of the time, or perhaps being a critical genius, let his own self-esteem determine.

In writing a criticism (as of a book, a play, a motion picture, a painting, or a statue) the critic should let himself be governed by a few elemental principles.

(1) Remembering that he is writing to give information, he should tell something of the nature of the work—its length or size, its type (whether novel or drama, landscape painting or portrait, bronze or marble), its place of production or present location, its date, and any other such information as may be helpful.

(2) Next, he should give a few facts about the artist (or author), especially if the latter is relatively unknown, or if a knowledge of some details of his life and personality may help the reader to a better understanding of the work and the criticism. For instance, a review of a book by Helen Keller would be incomplete without some mention of her physical afflictions, and a criticism of a Gaugin painting would be unfair unless it revealed that Gaugin worked in the brilliant sunlight of the South Seas.

(3) The critic should tell what the work he is criticizing is about, that is, he should give its subject. *Ivanhoe* is about Richard I and England in the Norman-Saxon period; *Strange Interlude* is about a neurotic woman who required four men to make her life complete; Rembrandt's *The Nightwatch* portrays a party of soldiers issuing from a gateway; and Cellini's *Perseus* shows the hero just after he has slain Medusa. To say what a book is about does not mean that the critic should actually summarize it. And yet a summary may often be desirable. In a class report, a talk before a literary club, or a comprehensive lecture a summary is almost necessary. But in a book review intended for publication, and, in a way, intended as an advertisement for the book, a complete summary is hardly fair to the author. About all the reviewer should permit himself (unless the book is an unusually important work by an unusually important author) is a very brief sketch of plot and characters.

(4) After he has said what the work is about, the critic should probably tell its central theme (if it has one). That is, he should tell what philosophy, point of view, or criticism of life appears in the work. Thus the critic would say of most of Hardy's novels that the theme is the helplessness of human beings in the grip of an Immanent Will working by means of chance and coincidence to their destruction. Often a picture has such a theme, and most sculpture of the Rodin tradition has it. To take a single example,

the theme (shall we call it) of Rodin's "The Thinker" is, doubtless, that man, crude and earthy as he is, yet strives to think out the mystery of life, and because he is crude and earthy, never succeeds.

(5) When the theme of the work has been told, the method in which theme and subject are handled deserves attention. Here (if the work is a book) the style is analyzed, the characters are studied, the interestingness and the probability of the plot are criticized, the *genre* to which the book belongs is made evident, and any further opinions of the critic are enlarged upon. If the work belongs to another one of the arts (such as painting or sculpture), its composition, its technical method, and its "school" require comment. This part of the criticism is more fully and elaborately treated than any other. It is here that the writer applies those standards of criticism mentioned above, and exercises such judgment and originality as he possesses.

(6) Finally, the work is located in relation to other work by the same author; its importance as a contribution to its type is estimated; its place in the development of certain artistic movements is fixed; and, last of all, a brief summarizing evaluation is presented.

Probably not one criticism in fifty follows the procedure here outlined. The order of parts is changed; entire parts are omitted; certain parts are given preponderant amounts of space; and certain other parts are abbreviated almost to nothingness. Nevertheless, the elements of most good critical articles remain about as outlined. The following review (by Theodore Purdy, Jr.), which appeared in the *Saturday Review of Literature* some time ago is a good example of what the ideal review should be:

(1) Bibliographic facts: AXELLE. By Pierre Benoît. Dial. 1930, $2.50.

The stories of Pierre Benoît have been best-sellers in France for many years. No

(2) Information about the author:

(3) What the book is about, with summary:

(4) The theme of the book:

(5) The artistic method of the book:

(6) Orientation of the book:

railway book-stall is complete without "le nouveau Benoît," and his success has only been equalled by the rapidity of his production and the variety of his subjects. "Königsmark" and "L'Atlantide" have had their thousands of readers and their millions in the world's movie audiences,—the latter, in fact, had an almost unexcelled popularity as an adventure novel, reviving the Jules Verne tradition. "Axelle" is one of the Benoît's later and less popular books, the post-war history of a war-prisoner's romance with a fair enemy. In a prison camp near Königsberg the French sergeant Dumaine meets and falls in love (after appropriate ponderings and hesitations) with a local chatelaine, Fräulein Mirrbach. In the gloomy castle of Reichendorf in which she lives the Frenchman seems to enjoy unusual liberty of entry while against a background of warlike alarums the drama of these two pawns in an international struggle is played out to its obvious conclusion.

M. Benoît's book is more notable for its broad viewpoint and bold admission that in spite of propaganda to the contrary the German nation may have contained a few exceptional individuals worthy to rank as human beings, than for any great literary merit. It is written in a straightforward, serviceable style, and some of its descriptions of prison camp life seem authentic, though the melodramatic character of the Prussian general is in the old traditions. Not an important book, nor a particularly interesting one, it yet serves to class its author among the rapidly increasing party in France which tends to advocate a wary, but quite definite, *rapprochement* with Germany.[1]

EXERCISES

I. THE FAMILIAR ESSAY

Make a list of ten subjects suitable for familiar essays. How many subjects can you find by looking about you at this moment? Name the type of style which you think you might adopt for each essay (as jocose, mock-serious, whimsical, sad, exaggeratedly humorous, quietly genteel, simple and restrained, familiar and chatty, breezily frank, etc.).

Try to decide which expository *methods* would probably be most suitable for each expository *form* mentioned in the above chapter.

II. EXPOSITION OF EVENTS

1. Institutional History.
   Write a short history of one of the following:
   Some department in your college.
   Some campus periodical or organization.
   The last session of Congress.
   Your immediate family for three generations.
   The body of the automobile.
   Fashions in women's dress since 1910.
   Fashions in domestic architecture since 1900.
   English furniture in the eighteenth century.
   The game of bridge.
   The Boston Bull Terrier.
   Tell what might be the central thesis in a history of each item mentioned above.
2. Folk History.

---

[1] This review is reprinted here by permission of Miss Amy Loveman, Associate Editor of *The Saturday Review of Literature*.

Write a short history of one of the following:

A brief period in the early days of your native town; of your college; of your family; of your school career; of your first love affair.

Imagine you could translate yourself to any previous century. Write a rather long history on one of the following topics:

A year with Cæsar; Alfred the Great; William the Conqueror; Frederick Barbarossa; Edward III; Cromwell; Captain John Smith; William Bradford; General Sherman; General Lee.

3. Biography.

Write a "modern" biography of one of the following:

King John of England; Edmund Spenser; Chaucer; Sir Philip Sidney; Christopher Marlowe; Ben Jonson; James II; James Thomson; Horace Walpole; William Blake; Jane Austen; Patrick Henry; Poe; Ambrose Bierce.

4. Anecdote.

Find, and write down to hand in, two anecdotes about each of five men selected from those named in the two exercises above. Tell what characteristics of the men each anecdote illustrates.

5. The True-experience Narrative.

Write a rather long account of some true experience you have had, or some acquaintance has told you about. Be prepared to tell what devices you have employed to make the narrative convincing and interesting.

6. The Narrative of Travel.

If you have made any extensive journey, imagine yourself repeating it. Write a letter home (or an article for the home-town newspaper, or an entry in your journal) telling about the trip itself. Then write again, telling what you have done and found at the end of the trip.

7. The News Story.

Bring to class a copy of the local or campus newspaper. Analyze several of the news stories to discover whether they are constructed properly. If any seem faulty, try to find whether there is any justification for their being so.

III. EXPOSITION OF FACTS

1. Definition.

Write paragraphs defining five of these terms:

Americanism.	Progress.
Culture.	Tolerance.
A gentleman.	Morality.
Love.	Modernism (in art).
Religion.	Romanticism (in literature).
Socialism.	Victorianism.
Democracy.	Idealism.

2. Descriptive Exposition.

a. Write short concrete expository descriptions of three of the following pairs:

An oak tree you know—oak trees.

Your cat—cats.

The architecture of your home—the type of architecture to which your home belongs.

Your home town—the type of town to which it belongs.

A person you know—the physical type to which he belongs.

A picture by a certain artist—the type of picture usually painted by the same artist.

b. Write short abstract descriptions of three of the following:

The mentality of children about ten years of age.

A character sketch of an acquaintance.

Life in any small town (large town; the country).

Life in the dormitories of your college.

The administrative organization of your college.

The inferiority complex.

Hawthorne's philosophy.

The emotional effects produced by music.

The stock market situation this month.

c. Write an exposition in which you classify the members belonging to any of the groups mentioned in the exercises for Chapter IX, Section 3, above.

3. Exposition of a Process.

Write an exposition on one of the following subjects. Show how you might individualize the general processes suggested:

How the phonograph works.

How to study poetry.

How to study a picture.

How presidential candidates are nominated.

How the President is elected.

How a certain laboratory experiment is performed.

How the Atlantic was first spanned by air.

How Cornwallis was defeated at Yorktown.

How to plan and serve a dinner.

IV. EXPOSITION OF OPINION

1. Opinions about General Laws.

Write an exposition on one of the following topics:

What have we a right to believe?

Why men fight.

The art of living.

The new morality.

Living one's own life.

Fear.

How is freedom possible?

Prayer.

Love as a philosophy of life.

Can we afford to be rational?

2. Opinions about Conditions, Facts, or Things.

a. Write an exposition about one of the following topics, which refer to general conditions:

The causes of President Roosevelt's popularity in 1933 and 1934.

Organized labor thirty years ago and today.

Why home is no longer the center of young people's social life.

Good manners and the college student.

Tendencies in this year's fiction (drama, motion pictures, poetry).

b. Write an exposition about one of the following topics, which refer to specific facts:

Is pure mathematics a cultural subject?

Should college students be regular church members and attendants? (Movie-goers? Sports enthusiasts?)

Why do birds migrate?

Is smoking injurious to the health?

What was the nature of Cowper's mental derangement?

c. Write criticisms of some book, picture, example of architecture, and piece of sculpture with which you are acquainted.

Chapter XII

WRITING THE EXPOSITION

1. The Subject.—People often wonder why so many poor articles and bad books are published. Their number is due to the popularity and interestingness of their subjects. A bad exposition on a vital subject will find ten publishers willing to buy it before a good exposition on an uninteresting subject will find one. Young writers often fail to realize this fact. They write excellent essays on "The Mountains and the Sea as Vacation Resorts," "How I Spent My Vacation," "Types of Razors," "English Ceramics in the Eighteenth Century," "The Typical Landlady," "Why the Radio Has Developed so Rapidly," and similar subjects. But who wishes to read them? No one but some patient professor ever hopeful of discovering somewhere in the weekly wilderness of such subjects at least one paper which shows that its writer has been willing to attack a vital problem.

A man's reach should exceed his grasp—and a student's efforts should exceed his ability to achieve. Young people perceive the elemental issues of life far more vividly and feel them more keenly than do their elders. If the young people would only write sincerely about these issues, if they would only have the courage to grapple with the problems presented to them as growing men and women—problems of authority, religion, sex, immortality, marriage, family relations, fear of life, ambition, dreams, hopes, despairs, and all the rest of them—if students would only write about such problems instead of "How to Build a Boat" and "The

Typical Sophomore," they would produce something worth reading. But they won't. They will continue to attack small problems and decide unimportant issues until the boat is rotten and the sophomore has grandchildren.

2. Aims.—When a writer has chosen his subject, he should ask himself what his aims are in writing about it. First, he must decide what his expository *purpose* is—whether to give mere information, or to interpret facts, or to try to change the reader's point of view.

If, for example, the subject involved the conservation of wild life in America, the writer could merely catalogue facts about the steps being taken by the government to conserve wild life. Or he could go on to interpret: He could say that certain measures are unsatisfactory or insufficient, that the prospects of new and better measures are remote, and that though certain results have been achieved, much remains to be done. Or, finally, he could devote his work to attempting to influence his readers to take conservation more seriously and work for it more energetically. What his purpose is will determine what the exposition is to be.

Next, the writer should determine the *kind of readers* whom he wishes to reach.[1] The type of readers he expects will often determine the purpose of his work. Thus (in the example just given) a report of a government official to a superior interested in wild-life conservation would be purely factual and statistical. A report of the president of a conservation league to the members of the league would be interpretative. An article by the same president in a magazine of general circulation would endeavor to change the public's point of view toward conservation.

Even when the purpose of the exposition is fixed, a writer must know what type of readers he will have. For example, a

---

[1] Determining this often involves a consideration of the organ of publication. Practically all magazines, newspapers, and publishing houses have certain editorial policies which a writer must know and conform to if he expects publication.

surgeon trying to explain to a patient the nature of a prospective operation would use simple terms, comforting reassurances, and careful analysis of the results which might occur if the operation were not performed. But if the same surgeon were trying to explain the same operation to a group of other surgeons, he would use technical terms, would convert the personal reassurances into mortality statistics, and would probably omit as well known the analysis of what might happen if the operation were not performed. The type of readers addressed may determine, then, the purpose, the language, the persuasive elements (see Section 7 below), and the nature of the facts presented in the exposition.

Finally, the writer must decide *how long* his exposition will probably be. Only when he has done so can he select his material intelligently and organize his exposition with due regard for the laws of proportion. A newspaper paragraph, a magazine article, and a book on, say, wild-life conservation would require altogether different materials, different structures, and different methods of approach. Many a young author, inexperienced in handling papers of much length, writes the first half of his term-paper in great detail, and then, discovering that he will have neither time nor space to finish the paper in the same detail, will hurry to his conclusion in a manner quite inconsistent with his early leisureliness. And writers even less skillful will do the opposite—that is, hurry through the first half of the paper, discover that at such a rate they will finish the work before filling the required number of pages, and then conclude with a wealth of unnecessary detail and deliberate padding. A well-planned paper commits neither of these errors. It is consistent and well balanced throughout.

3. The Title.—Specialized exposition requires only a descriptive title in order to attract the readers for whom the exposition was written. Titles such as the following automatically select their own readers:

"The Physiology of Digestion"
"Mural Painting in America"
"Milton's Use of Du Bartas"
"Carlyle and German Thought"
"Color in Advertising"
"The Lewis and Clark Expedition"

But general exposition is different. In these days of intense competition when a thousand titles a week in newspapers, magazines, and bookstores clamor for the average reader's attention, every writer of general exposition must find attractive titles for his works if he expects to be read. Some articles and some books, indeed, sell and are read for no other reason than that they have irresistible titles. *Little Man, What Now?* is no better book than it should be, but with such a title its popularity was assured even before it was written. *Captain Jinks of the Horse Marines, Gentlemen Prefer Blondes,* and *The Hard-Boiled Virgin* are older novels with irresistible titles. Beer's *The Mauve Decade,* Bowers's *The Tragic Era,* and Allen's *Only Yesterday* are expository works with almost equally effective titles. Seeing them in a bookstore, almost any browsing reader would pick them up and look into them—which is the most important step in the sale of a book.

Just what makes a title attractive it is difficult to say. But a few general principles hold true:

a. The *subject* itself may be so interesting or unusual that the exposition requires no other advertisement in its title than a description of its contents. Such descriptive titles are these: "Probabilities of War in Europe" (*Atlantic*), "The Assassination of McKinley" (*American Mercury*), "Safer Childbirth with Less Pain" (*Parents' Magazine*), and "If Napoleon Had Fled to America" (*Scribner's*). A special form of such titles is that which proclaims superlatives, unusual magnitudes, or sensational ideas. Examples are: *20,000 Years in Sing Sing* (by Lewis E. Lawes), "$50,000,-

ooo Can't Be Wrong" (*Saturday Review of Literature*), "Money by the Ton" (*Asia*), and "In Search of the Smallest Feathered Creatures" (*National Geographic*).

b. Often the *diction* of a title may catch the reader's eye irrespective of the subject indicated. Devices which thus attract attention are the following:

(1) *Alliteration* is often effective in fixing the reader's wandering glance. Examples of alliterative titles are these: "Vice and the Volstead Act" (*Harper's*), "Hearst at Home" (*Fortune*), "Prospects for Peace" (*Harper's*), and "The Great Galilean" (*Atlantic*).

(2) *Antithetical ideas* expressed in titles attract attention. Examples are these: "Ladies and Lawlessness," "Less Money and More Life" (both from *Harper's*), "New Armies for Old" (*Current History*), "The Awful English of England," and "Insurance that Doesn't Insure" (both from *American Mercury*).

(3) *Incongruous words* have much the same rather startling effect that antithetical ideas have, and tempt the reader's curiosity to delve further into the exposition. "Fra Angelico and the Cabin Passenger" (*Harper's*), "Socrates Up to Date" (*Atlantic*), "Spinster Factories" (*Forum*), and "A Philosophy of Pith-Balls" (*Atlantic*) are good examples of such incongruousness.

(4) *Parodies* of well-known sayings attract attention, though often, it is true, the attention goes no further than the title. Examples are these: "The Trap that Jack Built" (*Collier's*), "Nature Says It with Flowers" (*American Forests*), "Burn Your Own Home" (*New Outlook*), "Why Poets Leave Home" (*Scribner's*), and "To the Brave Belongs the Fair" (*Vanity Fair*).

(5) *Made-up or unusual words,* such as those in the following titles, may pique the reader's curiosity and lure him to read the exposition: "Shirahama" (*Atlantic*), " 'Cheapies' Threaten Chain

Stores" (*Forbes*), "Capeadores of Wall Street" (*Atlantic*), and "Punnet sive Pundigrion" (*Atlantic*).

(6) *Single-noun titles* also excite curiosity. Yet unless the word used can touch a live spot in most readers, this sort of title is not satisfactory. In the following group, probably only the first and the last titles listed can meet the test: "Professor" (*Atlantic*), "Rio Grande" (*American Mercury*), "Conclusions" (*Atlantic*), "Paradise" (*American Mercury*), and "Earthquake" (*Scribner's*). Variations of this kind of title are single nouns preceded by an article (like *The Jungle* by Upton Sinclair), and single nouns followed by a noun in apposition (like "Lincoln the Lover" in the *Atlantic*).

(7) More common and, perhaps, less impressive is the *single-noun-and-single-adjective* title such as "The American Way," "The Larger Agnosticism," "Our Lawless Heritage" (all three in the *Atlantic*), "Hospital Night," "Burnt Offering," "Half-Told Tales," and "This Hard-Boiled Era" (all in *Harper's*). Titles like these have little to recommend them unless they include some unusual word or idea like the last one given, or excite curiosity like the two which precede the last.

c. Many titles draw attention by means of their *grammatical forms.*

(1) Titles beginning with *How, Why, Where, What, The Story of, The Future of,* etc., appeal to every reader's desire to enlarge his information: "How Not to Buy" (*Consumers' Research*), "Why the Business Man Fails in Politics" (*Nation's Business*), "Why Literature Declines" (*Atlantic*), "How Charles Dickens Wrote His Books" (*Harper's*), "Where France Hoards Gold" (*Living Age*), "The Story of Sutter's Gold" (*Golden Book*), "What a Man Loses by Going to College" (*Saturday Evening Post*), and "The Truth about Briand" (*Vanity Fair*).

(2) Very closely related is the title stated as a *question*. In

order that the question be effective, however, it must be pertinent to some universally interesting topic. In the following list of titles probably only the first and the two last meet this requirement: "Why Be Faithful in Marriage?" (*North American Review*), "Why Hold Back the Children?" (*Harper's*), "Are We Worthy of Our Destiny?" (*Forum*), "Will This Summer Be Hotter?" (*Scribner's*), and "Is Sleep a Vicious Habit?" (*Harper's*).

(3) Titles containing an *active verb* suggest a narrative, and are therefore more likely to encourage a reader than are mere static words. Note the hint of action or story in each of the following titles: "Emerging from One Other Depression" (*Catholic World*), "My Brother Commits Suicide" (*New Republic*), "Building a Futile Navy" (*Atlantic*), "Chemistry Makes History" (*Century*), and "America Discovers Itself" (*Vogue*).

(4) Of late years, what we may call *and-titles* have been popular. They are titles containing two words or phrases joined by *and*. They have no special virtue unless the two members so joined are alliterative, antithetical, paradoxical, or incongruous. Examples follow: "Sound and Sense" (*Vogue*), "America and the Russian Market" (*Current History*), "Juries and Justice" (*Atlantic*), "Logic and the Ladies" (*Harper's*), and "Prohibition and the Negro" (*Outlook and Independent*).

(5) The last sort of title we shall mention is that which contains a *prepositional phrase*. For some reason, such phrases run trippingly on the tongue and stick in the memory. Examples are these: "From Chicago to the Sea" (*Atlantic*), "Planks without Platforms" (*Atlantic*), "Miracles of Healing" (*Ladies Home Journal*), "Elected for Oblivion" (*Life*), "Czar of Song" (*New Yorker*), "Aristocrats of Publishing" (*Vanity Fair*), and "The End of an Era" (*Outlook and Independent*).

4. The Introduction.—Though short expositions seldom require formal introductions, long expositions would often lack clarity

without some preliminary explanations. The following scheme is customarily used in the introductions to formal debates and arguments. It is presented here as a suggestion of what may be done, rather than as a rule stating what must be done. The writer of an argument will probably follow the scheme rather closely; the writer of an informal exposition will use only such parts of it as seem to him suitable to the occasion. The latter writer, furthermore, may not use the parts in the order here given, and may place before any of them (at the very beginning of the exposition) some device for catching the reader's attention.

I. The immediate reason for the present discussion.

II. The origin and history of the question.

III. The definition of terms.

IV. The exclusion of

    A. Irrelevant matter

    B. Waived matter.

    C. Admitted matter.

V. The statement of the main contentions made by opponents.

VI. The statement of the actual issues to be discussed.

5. **The Arrangement of Ideas.**—The arrangement of ideas in an exposition practically always follows one of the methods named below. Since these methods are discussed in most freshman textbooks of composition, they will be only mentioned here:

a. The chronological order.

b. The order of procedure from simple to complex.

c. The order of procedure from known to unknown.

d. The order of procedure from particular to general (the inductive order).

e. The order of procedure from the general to the particular (the deductive order).

f. The order of climax.

g. The order of alternation when two things are being compared.

h. The order of simple enumeration.

The order to be adopted is often determined by the method and the type of the exposition. But not always. For example, suppose a student is trying to explain to his parents what his curriculum will be during his four years of college. The type of exposition will be "Abstract Description" and the method will be "Descriptive." But the student may arrange his details *chronologically* by telling what courses he will take in each year from the first to the last. He may arrange them by proceeding from the *simple to the complex*—that is, he may begin by explaining that his courses will all be either majors or minors, and then go on to explain more and more complicated details about these majors and minors. He may proceed from the *known to the unknown* by saying something like this: "As you know, I am specializing in Biology. You know, too, that Biology is based on Physics, Chemistry, and Geology. Consequently, I must take courses in those subjects. In addition, I must take French and German to help me read what foreign biologists have done. And finally, the administration requires me to take certain other subjects which I shall now tell you about"—and so on. He may proceed *from the particular to the general* by listing his courses, and then adding, "You see, I am specializing in science, and in Biology most of all." He may proceed *from the general to the particular* by saying the same thing, and then proceeding to list his courses. He may proceed in the *order of climax* by listing his courses in the order of their importance in relation to Biology. And he may content himself with a *simple enumeration* of the courses he will take in his four years at college.

The writer should decide on some arrangement he will give to his ideas, and then stick to that arrangement. Making this decision requires initiative and originality on his part; it does not come naturally as a result of the subject.

6. Division.—Division in exposition is of two types—logical and mechanical. Good exposition consists of a few major thought-groups, under each of which are collected subordinate thoughts. These groups are distinct from one another, and yet are linked together by means of transitional devices and logical relation. If they are too few in number (say two or three to every five thousand words), they require too long-continued concentration by the reader, and therefore weary him mentally. If they are too many (say ten or twelve to every five thousand words), they confuse him with their diversity and make him lose sight of the main objective of the exposition. Of these two sins of division, however, the latter is more forgivable. Indeed, it is a sin only in informal exposition where the writer attempts to secure an easy and flowing continuity. In more formal exposition, where ideas in a series may be plainly numbered or lettered (as in this book) the use of many thought-groups is quite permissible. The mechanical numbering or lettering makes for clarity even though it does detract from beauty of style.

This numbering or lettering of the different parts of an exposition is the other means of division mentioned above. If done with the slightest comprehension of the thought-groupings, mechanical division of this sort makes the exposition easy to follow and to understand. It appears commonly and elaborately in formal technical discussions, and it appears on a limited scale even in informal expositions. In the latter type of writing divisions are customarily indicated by Roman numerals. These have a double effect: They indicate a division of thought, and at the same time they break up the solid printed page in such a way as to rest the reader's eye and promise him relief from concentration too prolonged. The writer of exposition should nearly always avail himself of these devices for helping and encouraging the reader. They are tricks, but they are useful and legitimate.

7. Persuasion.—Writers seldom address sympathetic and enthusiastic readers. Usually they must overcome a dead inertia, and sometimes they must refute directly hostile opinions. For the accomplishment of either of these purposes clear logic is not always sufficient. It must be supplemented by persuasion.

Conviction involves intellectual approbation; persuasion involves emotional approbation. Most people will resist the former unless conquered by the latter, and many people do not require the former if they have been conquered by the latter. No writer can afford, therefore, to neglect the art of persuasion. It usually requires of him a double ability: to make the reader like him, and to make the reader like his arguments.

a. *Being likable* is an art that cannot be taught in textbooks; but perhaps a writer can be taught to make the best use of whatever likable traits he happens to possess. A few hints, stated as brief commandments, follow:

(1) Work toward persuasion in the first part of your exposition, and toward conviction in the latter part.

(2) Keep an air of sincerity and frankness throughout, but unless the occasion or the subject is unusually grave or sad, confine your most solemn earnestness to the latter part of the exposition.

(3) In the average exposition written for general reading, begin with some bit of humor, wit, whimsicality, or cleverness. Such a beginning need not, and usually should not, be a funny story. It may be only an idea expressed playfully, an amusing remark incident to the occasion, a witty paradox, or some other such bid for the reader's good humor. People are more tolerant when they are in a good humor than when they are solemn.

(4) Make some not-too-serious comment on your own lack of qualifications to write about the subject you are explaining. The

average reader does not like for the average writer to take himself too seriously.

(5) Flatter the reader by praising some custom, habit of thought, point of view, or opinion to which you know he holds. Appeal to his sense of local or racial pride. Pay tribute to his ancestors, to his individual enterprise, to his known efficiency and goodness of heart.

(6) Concede many virtues to those who believe differently from you, and even explain those virtues at some length if you intend to be particularly aggressive later on.

(7) Unless you know your readers will be unintelligent, never, never resort to vituperation, passion, and name-calling. Do not forget to be a gentleman. Nothing is quite so persuasive as a self-possessed, well-mannered gentleman. Remember Chesterfield's epigram: "A man's own good breeding is his best security against other people's ill manners."

(8) Do not write down to the reader. Act as if you were addressing a person of equal or superior intelligence. When technical details that the reader could not possibly know much about are to be explained, be modest and casual rather than ostentatious and painstaking. Act as if you thought that the reader might be as well off, after all, without knowing such details.

b. The writer's next problem is to *make the reader like the information given and the opinions expressed* in the exposition. Here are a few suggestions worth considering:

(1) Relate your information and opinions to the higher impulses and emotions of the reader. Nearly all people, though not very intelligent, are fundamentally good and well meaning. If you can show how your ideas may satisfy their higher impulses, or if you can use your ideas to stir their higher emotions, you can persuade your readers to believe almost anything.

(2) Try to show how your reader's acceptance of your ideas will

help him as an individual—physically, intellectually, or materially —or how it will help his children, his community, or his nation.

(3) As much as possible refer to authorities whom you know your reader views favorably. And when you must use authorities of whom you know the reader is suspicious, admit that he has some right to his suspicions, but that, for this once at least, you can show that the authorities used are reliable. If you must refute a well-liked authority, appear to do so with regret, and at the same time pay tribute to the authority in a way that will partly compensate for your showing that he has been wrong.

(4) Use a simple, direct style; have a clear and easily followed organization in the exposition; refer to familiar instances that "come home to men's bosoms" rather than to remote or specialized instances.

(5) Finally, if you know your readers are hostile, try to appeal to their sense of fairness. Try to show them that even people in the wrong (like you) deserve a hearing from fair-minded readers. But do not try to do so by pleading the justice of your cause. Instead, point out that you are depending on the reader's customary broad-mindedness, and are venturing to impose on his well-known charity and tolerance. It is not sufficient that the reader believe you have a right to be heard; he must be made to consider himself magnanimous for listening to you.

EXERCISES

1. The Subject.

Make a list of the personal problems (both specific and general) which have troubled you most during the last year. By making use of the "sources of exposition" mentioned in Chapter VIII above, develop at least one of these problems into an exposition of considerable length. Hand your list in to the instructor. When he has examined all lists, let him classify the problems of the class-members, and tell what kinds of problems are of most general interest.

2. Aims.

Turn back to the topics given under the exercises for "Definition" (Section 1, Division II) in the previous chapter. Show how three different purposes could lead to the development of three altogether different expositions from each topic.

Show how your method of developing each topic would be changed if you were writing to be read by (a) a radical labor agitator; (b) a conservative Vermont farmer; (c) a liberal-minded, thoughtful college professor.

Tell how your methods of exposition would differ if you developed each topic in (a) a paragraph, (b) two pages, and (c) ten pages.

3. The Title.

Try to find attractive titles for subjects mentioned in the exercises for the preceding chapter. Consider as many of the subjects as your instructor thinks necessary.

4. The Introduction.

Outline formal introductions for six of the expositions mentioned at the end of the exercises for Chapter X above.

5. The Arrangement of Ideas.

Set down more or less at random all the items of information you have about one of the following subjects:

Student self-government on your campus.

Student organizations on your campus.

The administration of your college.

Show how these items could be successively arranged in all orders (except the order of alternation) mentioned in Section 5 above.

6. Division.

Refer again to the topics mentioned in the exercises for "Definition" in the preceding chapter. Show how long, informal expositions (5000 words) on five of these topics might be divided.

7. Persuasion.

Refer again to the topics just mentioned. Suppose your exposition on each of the topics is addressed to readers whose ways of thought are completely hostile to the subject and what you believe about it. Outline methods of persuasion you would use in writing each exposition. Write a complete persuasive exposition on one of the topics.

What methods of persuasion would you use in the following expositions:

A plea for governmental control of railroads before a group of railroad owners; a group of railroad employees; a group of Congressmen; a group of average citizens.

A plea for reforestation before a group of farmers; a group of city-dwellers; a group of sportsmen; a group of lumbermen.

A plea before Southerners for social equality for the Negro.

A plea before Northerners for a strict application of the doctrine of States' Rights.

A plea for liberal education as opposed to professional education before a group of poor parents; before a group of engineering students; before a group of business men being asked to contribute sums to a liberal college; before a group of working men being asked to vote funds for a liberal college.

PART THREE

The Writing of Fiction

Chapter XIII

THE NATURE OF FICTION

ALL narratives relate an action. Before we can discover how to write narratives, therefore, we must learn something about this fundamental element of all narratives—action. In accordance with this necessity, the present chapter and the next one try to reveal a few truths about action in narratives, and leave to succeeding chapters the business of giving advice about how to construct effective narratives. Yet the student will do well to read over and work out the exercises at the end of this chapter while he is reading the chapter itself. He will find that the exercises help him understand the chapter better, and that they suggest ways in which the information in the chapter may be utilized in practice.

I. IMAGINATION AND FICTION

1. **What Is Fiction?**—Anything that changes over a period of time is an action. Consequently, both description and exposition often cross the line into the territory really belonging to narrative. An account of a football game, a description of the banks of a river as one drifts past them in a steamer, information about how Burmese hunters construct bird-traps—these are all narratives as well as descriptions or expositions.

Indeed, artistic narrative is inseparable from description. Mere narrative occurs in books of history:

The next morning, Morton, on visiting his concealed guest, John Balfour, found him asleep. But here was not the sleep of repose. Balfour's face and body moved restlessly, and he continually uttered words referring to the murder of the Archbishop.

Compare this with Sir Walter Scott's artistic and imaginative recounting of the same incident in *Old Mortality* (Chapter VI):

A ray of light gleamed on his uncurtained couch, and showed to Morton the working of his harsh features, which seemed agitated by some strong internal cause of disturbance. . . . Both his arms were above the bed-cover, the right strongly clenched and occasionally making that abortive attempt to strike which usually attends dreams of violence; the left was extended and agitated from time to time by a movement as if repulsing some one. The perspiration stood on his brow, "like bubbles in a late disturbed stream," and these marks of emotion were accompanied with broken words which escaped from him at intervals—"Thou art taken, Judas—thou art taken—Cling not to my knees—hew him down!—A priest? Ay, a priest of Baal, to be bound and slain even at the brook of Kishon."

This is art. The other is only clear writing. In this first essential of artistic narrative poor writers nearly always fail. They believe that merely *telling a story*, without troubling to make the reader *see* the action, constitutes good fiction. Pick up any of the magazines of confession, and notice what an overwhelming percentage of each of its stories consists of the simple recounting of incidents without a particle of imagination to enliven the account. Here is an example:

My friend went inside to phone a few more men in his effort to get an escort for me, and I waited outside with his "date." When he came out, I knew that he had failed. I figured there was no use in my spoiling his time for the evening; so I told the two to go ahead without me. I said that I wasn't feeling very well, and that I thought I would go home and get some rest. He was very gallant and polite, but finally I persuaded him to take me to my rooming-house, where he left me with a promise to call the next night.

Compare this bare account of happenings with a truly imaginative bit of writing from Stevenson:

All three peered covertly at the gamester. He did not seem to be enjoying his luck. His mouth was a little to a side; one nostril nearly shut, and the other much inflated. The black dog was on his back, as people say, in terrifying nursery metaphor; and he breathed hard under the gruesome burden.

"He looks as if he could knife him," whispered Tabary, with round eyes.

The monk shuddered, and turned his face and spread his open hands to the red embers. It was the cold that thus affected Dom Nicholas, and not any excess of moral sensibility.

"Come now," said Villon—"about this ballade. How does it run so far?" And beating time with his hand, he read it aloud to Tabary.[1]

Both of these passages narrate actions, and both are fiction. But the first differs from the historical narrative already quoted only in being untrue, whereas the second differs by being imaginative.

Fiction, then, is of two sorts: narrative which is untrue, and narrative which is both untrue and imaginative. In this book, we shall disregard the first sort completely, and shall concern ourselves with the second alone. For our purposes, fiction shall be *imaginative narrative*.

2. Imaginative Narrative.—Short stories, novels, and dramas are all alike in being scenic; that is, each of them is made up of a series of scenes imaginatively presented with short passages of necessary exposition sandwiched here and there between scenes. When the fiction writer has learned this elementary law, and has learned how to abide by it in his own work, half his task toward writing good fiction is done.

An example will illustrate. Stevenson's "A Lodging for the Night" (from which the passage quoted above is taken) is divided into the following scenes:

[1] From "A Lodging for the Night," in *New Arabian Nights*. Used by permission of Charles Scribner's Sons.

1. A description of Villon's company in a room on a cold winter night.
2. A murder.
3. The reactions of four people to the murder.
4. A description of Paris in the moonlight as Villon leaves the scene of the murder and goes out into the streets.
5. Villon's encounter with the watch and his discovery of the body of a dead woman in the street.
6. Villon's seeking refuge with his adopted father, and his being denied.
7. Denial at another door.
8. Admittance at another door.
9. Conversation between Villon and his host.

An examination of any well-written piece of fiction will reveal that it, too, is made up of scenes—sometimes one or two, as in some of Poe's stories; sometimes several, as in dramas; and sometimes a great many, as in novels and most short stories.

The intervals between scenes are passed over, as was suggested above, with the least possible ado—sometimes with the mere skipping of a line, sometimes with a row of asterisks, sometimes with a new chapter heading, sometimes with a few transitional phrases (such as, "On the following day . . ."; "It was three months later that . . ."; "He met her in the street a week later . . ."; and so on), and sometimes with a brief expository passage conveying necessary information.

3. **Drama.**—In this book we shall not consider drama separately from other fiction. Drama differs from other kinds of fiction only in the limitations imposed by the physical restrictions of the stage and the theater. The principal limitations are these:

a. Intervals between scenes are indicated in the program in the hands of the audience.

b. Necessary exposition must appear either in the program or in the dialogue of the actors on the stage.

c. The number of scenes must be limited so that scene-shifting will not be too frequent or too costly, and so that the total number of scenes will not hold audiences in their seats for more than two or three hours.

d. The nature of the scenes is determined by the physical restrictions of the stage; for example, an airplane battle could not be presented on the stage, nor could psychological changes which do not affect the actions of a character, nor could stories which hinge on meaningful looks passed between characters, nor could very short scenes which would not be worth the trouble of scene-shifting, nor could stories in which animals or very small children act or think, and so on.

Reason and experience assist a writer in determining whether a contemplated story may be good dramatic material; but once a writer satisfies the requirements of dramatic presentation, the methods of play-writing are the same as those of story-writing or novel-writing. All consist of a *series of scenes* imaginatively presented.

II. TRUTH IN FICTION

1. Definition.—Mark Twain congratulated himself on being able to write about Rome without once quoting, "The glory that was Greece and the grandeur that was Rome." But doubtless nobody has ever been able to write about narrative plots without quoting Aristotle's definition of plot as an action having a beginning, a middle, and an end. Artistic narratives are mere episodes in an endless succession of events. A young man meets a young woman, falls in love with her, has his suit rejected—beginning, middle, end. And then another episode commences: he meets another young woman, falls in love with her, and is accepted—beginning,

middle, end. The two marry, spend a few years adjusting themselves to each other and to marriage, and then begin to live as permanently and happily married people—beginning, middle, end. Or else they marry, do not succeed in adjusting themselves, and apply for a divorce—beginning, middle, end. In this way, story after story unwinds itself about the life of both the man and the woman until they die. And even then their deaths are starting-points for the stories of other people.

a. *A beginning,* according to Aristotle, is that which does not necessarily have anything preceding it, and which necessarily has something following. One automobile crashes into another at a street corner. That is a beginning. Who the drivers are, where they come from, and where they are bound is unessential. But something necessarily must follow the accident—high words, ambulance calls, lawsuits. All these make the story. A young man happens to meet a young woman at a summer resort, and becomes interested in her. That is a beginning. What comes afterward— whether he falls in love with her, whether he soon loses interest, whether he continues the acquaintanceship after they leave the summer resort, whether they marry—all this makes the story.

b. *A middle* is that which necessarily has something preceding it, and necessarily has something following. A car with a young man in it races down the street; just behind it races another car with a chauffeur at the wheel and an irate old gentleman standing up in the back seat shaking his fist at the young man and shouting imprecations after him. That is a middle. The next morning we search through the papers to find out what came before this scene, and what came after. Or as we walk down a country lane we come upon a large pool of blood surrounded by many footprints. That is a middle. We inquire of the next passer-by the source of the blood, why it was spilled, and what became of the victim.

c. *An end* is that which necessarily has something preceding it, and does not necessarily have anything following. We happen on a street fight just as one of the belligerents cries, "Enough!" That is an end: we are eager to know the cause of the fight and the details of the fight; but we have no interest in what happens to the two principals after they walk away. Or we see a dead buck lying along the fender of a car coming into town. That is an end: we are eager to know where, how, and by whom the buck was killed; but we never once think of its ultimate destiny.

The chief point, however, is that neither beginning, nor middle, nor end is complete in itself, but that it takes the three to make a story, and only the three.

Unskilled writers most frequently err in beginnings through the inclusion of material that does not *necessarily* call for something to follow. They give long explanations and histories; they mention pointless details of information and description. They do not *begin at the latest possible moment.* And unskilled writers err in endings through the failure actually to answer the question, solve the problem, of the beginning. Or else they continue to add details after the question is answered, the problem solved.

2. **Poetic Truth.**—Since beginning, middle, and end are linked together by the laws of necessity, it follows that the end is derived *inevitably* from the beginning. In a well-constructed plot there is little room for coincidence, chance, and accident. Even when Thomas Hardy brings ruin and destruction on his characters by making them victims of accident, or when Joseph Conrad writes a whole novel to prove that our lives are governed entirely by chance—even then the writer is only insisting that he considers the inevitable law of the universe to be accident and chance.

Aristotle himself uses an example curiously like an accident to illustrate his theory of the relationship of inevitability between beginning and end. If, says Aristotle, a murderer happens to be leaning against the statue of a man he has murdered, and if the statue suddenly tumbles down and crushes the murderer, we may justly regard the apparent accident as inevitable destiny. The belief in a destiny or fate existing superior to the gods themselves was a part of Greek religious faith. This belief, as much as anything else, is responsible for the grandeur of tragic conception, for the consistent and inevitable unity, for that perfection and simplicity of structure known as "classical" in Greek drama.

A similarly intense belief in destiny likewise forms the basis of that neat, almost tricky, unity of O. Henry's stories. The O. Henry ending is perfectly satisfying, not because it is a surprise, but because (when we take time to reflect) it is the only ending which, under the circumstances, could possibly have happened. His *Double-Dyed Deceiver* is of exactly the pattern of Aristotle's illustration mentioned above. A young man kills another young man; the murderer becomes a refugee from justice; through one chance after another he finally becomes the foster son of the parents of the young man he had slain. Here is destiny working itself out. The ending is a surprise; but under the circumstances (if we only believe in the inevitable rightness of things) it is the one ending possible.

The same thing is true of another story of O. Henry's, *Roads of Destiny*. A weak young man leaving home comes to a branching of the road. He takes one branch, has certain adventures, and comes by his death in a certain way. Then the story is recommenced: he takes the other branch, has certain other adventures, and comes by his death in the same way. And then the story is recommenced: he goes back home, has certain adventures, and comes by his death in the same way. The idea behind the story is that a man of a certain character will come eventually to an inevitable end, no matter what he does in the meantime—that a man's destiny lies within himself. This is an advancement over the old Greek idea of an external destiny, but the effect in fiction is the same.

Anything is possible; accidents do happen; rich uncles do die and leave a million; lightning does strike villains meditating the ruin of worthy folk. But as Aristotle avers, the business of the writer is not to record the merely possible but, rather, to record the probable. Historic truth is one thing; poetic truth another. Scott's famous example of killing off six villains (one of them by lightning) in a final chapter so that the hero may live happily ever afterward is not an example to be emulated. It *might* have happened, but it *probably* would not.

Critics have told many a young writer that a story written by the latter is improbable—only to be answered by the triumphant author, "But it really happened!" The fact that something really happened does not make it credible, probable, or suitable for good fiction. Indeed, just the opposite is almost always true: incidents or stories from real life usually make the poorest sort of art. The fact that a thing has really happened is almost proof positive that no writer should attempt to record it as fiction.

3. Coincidence.—The examples retold from Aristotle and from O. Henry sufficiently indicate that poetic truth and coincidence are not incompatible. Moreover, since coincidences occur in real life, since they are a part of the general law of life and of nature, they are justifiable in fiction. They are a part of normal probability.

Nevertheless, coincidence lavishly employed does not make for credibility or greatness. Most of the great novelists before the twentieth century made lavish use of coincidence; but one feels that they might have been greater had they been more sparing of accident. Coleridge called the plot of *Tom Jones* one of the few perfect plots in literature; but surely Tom's accidental discovery of the man who had been exiled twenty years before on the charge of having fathered Tom, Tom's affair the same week with the woman accused twenty years before of having been his mother, Sophia's arrival at the tavern the very night of that affair, Sophia's cousin's arrival the same night at the same tavern, Tom's finding the hundred-pound note dropped on the road by Sophia just when Tom was on the verge of starvation, Tom's happening to befriend a relative of the woman with whom Tom happened to take lodgings in London and who happened to be a friend of Tom's foster father—all this, with much besides, adds nothing to the greatness of *Tom Jones*. One may search the Greek tragedies, Shakespeare, and even Thomas Hardy and Joseph Conrad through without finding so prolonged a train of coincidences. Chance plays a large part in man's affairs, but cause and effect play a larger. An author who is unaware of this fact cannot construct a really great plot.

4. Surprise.—Despite popular opinion to the contrary, outright surprise in fiction is seldom used nowadays by great writers, and still more seldom does it contribute to their greatness. *Tom Jones* itself, with all its coincidences, has very few absolute surprises. We know very well that Tom's illicit love affairs are certain to bring him trouble eventually: if Sophia had not caught him in his infidelity at the inn, she would have caught him somewhere else; if Tom had not been restored to the good opinion of Allworthy through the agency of the landlady, he would have been restored by some other agency; if Blifil's duplicity had not been discovered through his attempted impressment of Tom, it would have been discovered through other devices. We may be surprised at the *means* by which all these things happen, but we are not surprised at the fact itself. This is just the declarative way of putting the old rule: "Give the reader the ending he wants in a way he does not expect."

A plot built up with any reasonable regard to probability, to natural law, to consistency of character, to philosophic necessity, to cause and effect, can surprise only in its externals, not in the plot itself. Real surprise is *prima facie* evidence of a poor plot. For this reason, the *deus ex machina*—the unforeseen and accidental force appearing at the critical moment to decide the issue of the action—the strawberry-mark on the left shoulder—the dying of a rich uncle—the appearance of the hero just in time to save the heroine from the clutches of the villain—this is bad art.

EXERCISES

I. IMAGINATION AND FICTION

1. What Is Fiction?

   Take a few sentences or a paragraph from some history or historical article, and convert it into imaginative writing. (For your present purposes, historical accuracy is unnecessary.)

2. Imaginative Narrative.

   Into what scenes would you crystallize the actions outlined in the three following paragraphs?

   A barber longs for the romance of faraway places and high romance; he joins the Marine Corps; and then he finds himself stationed permanently at a military post in Massachusetts as the company barber.

   An unsuccessful poet commits suicide because of his failure to find a publisher for his work. As a result of his suicide, public interest is aroused; and a book of the suicide's poetry is published and is successful.

   A young wife gradually loses faith in her husband's omniscience, but finds that she loves him just as well after she has lost her faith in him as she did before.

3. Drama.

   Could any of the stories you have just worked with be presented dramatically?

Read a few stories in current magazines such as *Harper's, Scribner's, American Mercury,* and *Atlantic*—or in one of the annual collections of the year's best short stories—or in the works of writers like Kipling, Maupassant, and O. Henry—and try to convert one or two of the stories into short dramas. Perhaps the campus dramatic organization will be interested in presenting your play.

II. TRUTH IN FICTION

1. Definition.

Which of the following situations are beginnings? which are middles? which are ends? and which are nothing in particular? Explain. Suggest possible complete stories for each of the beginnings, middles, or ends.

A man commits a crime.

A poor boy wants a violin.

A beggar goes to a cheap lodging house for the night.

A German family living next door have two interesting children.

A man runs past the house.

A lover gives a costly amber necklace to his sweetheart.

A dog bites a man.

A couple marry.

A ship's captain gets a new first officer.

A man wins a fortune in the stock market.

A man falls heir to a fortune.

A woman is deeply interested in national politics.

A child throws a cup at his mother.

A brutal army officer is shot in the back by some of his own men during a battle.

A child gets a long-desired toy for Christmas.

A man wounded in a brawl is brought to a hospital.

2. Poetic Truth.
3. Coincidence.

Make a list of all the coincidences which have happened to you or to acquaintances of yours. Suggest stories in which these coincidences will have the appearance of design. If you cannot recall any original coincidences, use the following:

A medical student finds that he is dissecting the body of a man whom he once knew.

A beggar on the verge of starvation finds a five-dollar bill.

A man misses a train, which is wrecked a few hours later.

The accidental appearance of a policeman prevents a highwayman from assaulting a certain pedestrian.

A rich uncle dies just when his only surviving relative, a young girl, needs money badly.

4. Surprise.

Think up surprising, yet probable, endings for stories about the following:

A man who, the doctors say, can live only two weeks.

A public official who is dishonest.

A pair of lovers who are angry with each other.

An escaped convict.

A student competing for a literary prize.

A woman on trial for shooting and wounding her husband.

A pair of lovers whose different religions seem to prevent their marriage.

An inquisitive person who reads, in the "personal" column of the paper, about arrangements for a meeting between a man and a woman, and who goes to their place of meeting.

Chapter XIV

THE ACTION

For convenience's sake the word *plot* has been used in discussion up to this point; yet all narratives do not have plot.

1. Straight Narrative.—Some narratives do no more than depict a continuous and simple series of events without much connection or relation among themselves. Stories of travel, accounts of picnics or hunts, narratives about curious or otherwise interesting events, newspaper stories, and the like are usually straight narratives in which different events are not mutually dependent. Other events could have been inserted or added, and some of those incidents narrated might have been omitted without the reader's knowing the difference. Narratives consisting thus of a mere sequence of events have no plot, nor do they have any place in fiction. In what follows, therefore, we shall ignore such narratives.

2. Obstructed Narrative.—A type of narrative not so elementary as the preceding is this next. It is the fundamental constituent of all artistic, non-chronicle narrative. Here, as in the preceding type, the story consists of a series of events. But each of these events consists of an interplay between what we shall call positive and negative forces. The positive forces have a common direction or movement toward one definite objective; the negative forces run counter to this general movement and tend to obstruct it.

For example, if I should tell how I left my home to go to the theater downtown at a certain hour, I should be constructing the elementary straight narrative mentioned in the previous section.

But suppose the story went like this: I leave home in my car, but halfway to the theater I discover that I have left my tickets at home and must return for them. Here we have a positive force making in one direction, and a negative force obstructing the positive. Suppose I go back and secure my tickets, and start out once more. Here is another positive force. But suppose I run out of gasoline on the way. Another negative force. Then I get gasoline and start out again—another positive force. But before I have gone far, I find one of the tires flat—another negative force.

All non-chronicle narrative of whatever length consists of interaction between positive and negative forces. The objective of the positive movement may change from time to time; but the negative forces always intervene, no matter what the objective may be. For example, the objective in *Roderick Random* shifts with the desires of the hero: First, Roderick desires to revenge himself on his teacher; later on, to find his uncle Tom Bowling; later, to become a surgeon's mate on shipboard; later, merely to come back alive from the expedition to Cartagena; later, to marry Narcissa; later, to marry anyone with money—and so forth. The events within each part of the story are concerned with the attainment of an objective. Some forces, some lucky accidents, some shrewd tricks, some honest efforts on the part of Roderick assist him toward his objective; other forces, other unlucky accidents, shrewd tricks by other people, dishonest schemes of others obstruct his progress.

This fundamental method of narrative may be worked into complex patterns. To give a few illustrations: The positive forces may overcome the negative; the negative may overcome the positive; the objective may be dual or triple; the objective attained may be different from that sought; several objectives may be grouped together as different stages in the attainment of a larger objective—these are examples of what may be done with the fundamental obstructed-narrative method.

3. The Narrative Graph.—The accompanying chart, applicable to all sorts of obstructed narratives, is conventionally employed to illustrate the structure of plot.

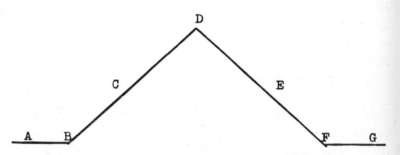

a. *Exposition.*—*A* on the graph represents the expository element necessary for the reader's understanding of the story—facts like dates, the place where the action happens, the social position of the characters, their relationship to one another, their past careers, the historical setting of the story, and the like.

The historical novelists of the last century—Scott, Cooper, Bulwer-Lytton, Reade, Kingsley—are noted for their interminable first chapters of description, history, and characterization; and even short story writers up to twenty or thirty years ago seldom penned a story without elaborate descriptive or expository paragraphs to start it off. Lately, however, the tendency has been all against the older technique. Get the story under way, is the precept of the modern writer. Begin with a sentence or so of description if you must; but limit it to a sentence or so. Better still, begin with a bit of action, with a scrap of dialogue, with a short characterization, with anything which will attract the interest at once and rivet the attention of the reader long enough to get him well started in the story. The student should examine the beginnings of stories in successive volumes by Kipling. In an early volume, like *Plain Tales from the Hills*, the beginnings are long, philosophical, expository, tiresome; in a later volume, like *Under the Deodars*, the beginnings are shorter, more pointed, more vividly interesting; and in some of the very latest volumes, like *Traffics and Discoveries*, the beginnings are positively abrupt.

But the exposition must be given somehow. If it is not huddled at the beginning of the narrative, as indicated in the graph, it must be inserted later in one of two ways. First, it may come all in a body after a more interesting beginning has caught the eye; or, second, it may be given piecemeal by hints dropped here and there in the course of the narrative—by bits of dialogue, by casual remarks, by chance references.

This last is the dramatic and natural method. Indeed (save for the meager information conveyed on programs) this is the only method available for the dramatist. Ibsen is a past-master of it. The first act of almost any of his later plays is a study in adroit characterization and veiled information about present conditions and past history. In a few pages of Act I of *An Enemy of the People*, for instance, we find, almost without our perception of it all, that the Burgomaster and Dr. Stockman are brothers; that the Doctor has been a frequent contributor to Hovstad's paper; that the life of the town centers about the Baths; that the town has enjoyed a period of prosperity on account of the Baths; that the Doctor has been "really indefatigable where the Baths are concerned"; that the original idea for the Baths came from the Doctor; that the Doctor and his family have only recently come from a small northern village where they had hardly the necessities of life; that the Doctor has "an ingrained propensity to taking his own course"; that the two brothers have a habit of disagreeing; that the Burgomaster and Hovstad usually disagree; that the Burgomaster is unmarried; that Petra is a school teacher—and much else besides. Yet none of this exposition is actually presented as exposition either by Ibsen or by any of his characters. It is the ideal method of conveying information to the reader or to the audience.

b. *Provocation.*—B, the next point on the graph, is the provocation of the story, the initial push which sets it going. It provokes a situation which cannot remain unchanged. Suppose two cats are sleeping peacefully in a room—a situation which may continue unchanged indefinitely. But now suppose someone opens the door and lets in a bulldog—immediately something begins to happen; the situation cannot remain unchanged. The opening of the door is provocation of the ensuing action.

This humble illustration may make clear to the student what happens when Dr. Stockman receives his long-expected letter, when Lord Windermere invites Mrs. Erlynne to the ball, when Captain Bluntschli climbs into Raina's bedroom to escape the soldiers, when the ghost demands that Hamlet seek revenge, when Nina learns that her husband has a taint of insanity in his family. All of these incidents provoke a situation which cannot remain unchanged.

The change may be due either to the desire of a character or to a necessity thrusting itself upon him. The necessity, in turn, may be due either to external circumstances or to an inward moral or spiritual necessity. The formula, then, for all beginnings is: (1) a new situation and a desire of a character; or (2) a new situation and a necessity forcing a character to act.

In *An Enemy of the People*, for example, the arrival of the letter is the new situation; and the desire is the Doctor's eagerness to help his town. In *Lady Windermere's Fan*, the new situation is Lord Windermere's insistence on inviting Mrs. Erlynne to the ball; and the necessity is Lady Windermere's feeling that she cannot honorably endure having Mrs. Erlynne at the ball. In *Arms and the Man*, the new situation is the Captain's climbing into the window; the desire is his desire to marry Raina. In *Hamlet*, the new situation is the appearance of the ghost; the necessity is Hamlet's sense of honor spurring him on to revenge. In *Strange Interlude*, the new situation is Nina's learning of the insanity in her husband's family; the necessity is Nina's feeling that, in spite of the hereditary taint, she must have a child to save herself and her husband.

A new situation without desire or necessity on the part of a character is not a provocation to a story; nor is a desire or a necessity without a new situation. On the other hand, a new situation may create a desire or a necessity (as in *Hamlet*); and a desire or a necessity may create a new situation (as in *Macbeth*, where Macbeth's desire to be king, together with the urging of his wife, leads to the murder of Duncan).

c. *Rising Action.*—*C* in the graph is ordinarily called the rising action, or the complication, of the narrative. It is the process of change which follows the situation that cannot remain unchanged. The change may be of various sorts:

(1) It may be a change in the relationship of characters to one another. A couple may be unmarried when the story opens, and married when it closes; the hero may be a victim of oppression at the beginning, and a victor at the end; he may be loved by others at the beginning, and hated at the end.

(2) The change may be in the relation between a character and his environment. Robinson Crusoe is apparently at the mercy of nature when he is shipwrecked, but as the story progresses he becomes master; in the old Alger books the poor boy would come to the city, where he would be duped and cheated on every hand until he at last became knowing in the ways of New York; in the old-fashioned picaresque novel, the hero would start life as a football of fortune, and would end as a successful and wealthy man.

(3) The change may be within a character himself—a change brought about by environment (as in Conrad's *Heart of Darkness*), by other characters (as in *Silas Marner*, where Silas's whole nature is softened by the presence of little Effie), or by deep physical or spiritual experience (as in *The Scarlet Letter* and *Macbeth*). This type of change has always appealed most strongly to critics, not only because it requires the most consummate skill on the writer's part, but also because it is creation in the process, human personality in the crucible, the actual labor throes by which all that is significant in character comes into being.

(4) The change may be in the reader's knowledge of characters; that is, it may be a gradual unfolding of the complexities of human characters. Meredith's *The Egoist* (where the reader gradually learns all the devious complexities of an egoistic character), James's *The American* (where the reader gradually learns all the hidden and abnormal possibilities within the characters of aristocratic Frenchmen), and *Vanity Fair* (where the reader gradually learns the full extent of Becky Sharp's selfishness and hypocrisy, and the amazing extent of human nature's stupidity and littleness)—all these are examples of fiction whose chief purpose is to tell the reader more about human characters.

(5) Finally, though this should probably be included under the change in the relationship of characters, the change may be in the knowledge which some characters in the story have about other characters. In *Tom Jones*, for example, most of the action centers about Tom's being misunderstood; and in many a nineteenth-century melodrama, it centers about a hero or heroine unjustly accused through five hundred pages, but vindicated in the end.

Whatever the change, however, it takes place or is brought about through a series of scenes linked together by short expository or descriptive passages. Each of these scenes, in turn, consists of an interaction of positive and negative forces—as was explained in connection with obstructed narrative above.

In the rising action, the general direction of all the scenes is the same; that is, either the positive forces always overcome, or else the negative forces always overcome. Thus, Macbeth at first succeeds in everything he undertakes, despite all the negative forces set in his path: he succeeds in his battle against the Norwegians, he succeeds in murdering the king, he succeeds in becoming king, he succeeds in disposing of Malcolm, Macduff, Banquo, and all his other important enemies. Now take an opposite sort of action: Tom Jones fails in making friends with his tutors, he fails in his first encounter with Squire Western, he fails in his love affair with Molly, he fails in his rivalry with Blifil, he fails in keeping Allworthy's favor, he fails in keeping Sophia's name secret—and he goes on failing until almost the end of the book. In each of these narratives, the course of the action is in a certain direction; and in each scene the action goes a little further in that direction. Whatever deviations occur are false leads and blind alleys going nowhere, and appearing in the story only to relieve monotony or to deceive the expectation of the reader.

It should be added that all these different scenes or episodes form separate little narratives in themselves. To indicate their entity and, at the same time, their place in the story as a whole, they appear in the story-graph as shown on the next page—*a, b,* and *c* being the separate scenes or episodes.

d. *Climax.*—In all stories of the types just discussed, there comes a decisive moment when the direction of the action turns about and goes in a different direction. This moment is called the climax of the story. It is indicated at *D* on the first graph. Macbeth prospers up to a certain moment; then one of his plans goes wrong. After that he begins to fail in undertaking after undertaking. Tom Jones is more and more unlucky up to a certain point; then he

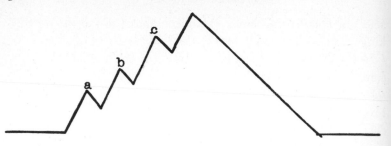

has the duel with the Irishman. After that his course is away from failure toward success. Each of these crucial moments forms the climax of a story.

The climax is not necessarily the most interesting point in the story. In *Macbeth*, for example, the action changes direction around the pivotal escape of Fleance, an altogether unimportant character; and in *Tom Jones* it changes direction around the pivotal wounding of an altogether unimportant Irishman.

A perfect climax follows *inevitably* from one of three things: (1) from a general philosophic law of nature in which the writer believes; (2) from a close-knit, logical series of actions; or (3) from some peculiarity of the character involved.

(1) In *Macbeth*, for example, the climax comes from Shakespeare's conviction that wrong cannot continue to triumph forever. And in *Tom Jones* it comes from Fielding's belief that virtue is not forever dogged by misfortune. If Shakespeare had been a cynic, or if Fielding had been a pessimist, the endings of the two stories would have been quite different.

(2) In *King Lear* the madness of Lear follows inevitably from the monstrousness of the previous action; and in nearly all detective stories the climax follows inevitably from the process of reasoning followed by the detective-hero.

(3) In *Antony and Cleopatra* the climax (Antony's return to Cleopatra) comes as a result of the weakness of Antony's char-

acter; in *Hamlet* the climax (Hamlet's refusal to kill the praying king) comes as a result of Hamlet's weakness of character; in *I Henry IV* the climax (Hal's promise to be loyal to the king) comes as a result of Hal's fundamental strength of character. This sort of climax, in which action is determined by character and reveals character, probably shows the ideal relationship between character and action.

At any rate, this method is superior to that in which the writer inserts the climax willy-nilly merely to bring a conclusion to the rising action. In *Much Ado about Nothing* the chance overhearing of Don John's plotting by people put into the play merely to overhear; in *Romeo and Juliet* and *Cymbeline* the absurd sleeping potions; in *The Ideal Husband* the lost bracelet; in *Ivanhoe* Athelstane's premature funeral—all these are unnatural and badly managed climaxes: they have no logical connection with the preceding scenes in the story; they grow out of no particular philosophy of the writer; and they have no relationship to character.

The climax usually comes late in artistic narrative; indeed, in many short stories (particularly those of the O. Henry and Maupassant types) the climax and the end of the story are simultaneous. The turning point in such stories is like a secret spring that opens the door to a treasure: the spring is touched, and lo! the door flies open and the treasure is revealed. In *The Pit and the Pendulum* a hand reaches out and catches the victim just as he is stumbling into the fatal pit; the clutch of the hand is a climax and, at the same time, the end of the story. Other narratives, particularly the formal tragedy, have the climax near the middle of the action: for example, it occurs in the third act of *Macbeth*, where Fleance escapes; and in the third act of *Antony and Cleopatra*, where Antony decides to return to Egypt in spite of all the good resolutions he has made. Still other narratives have a still earlier climax. In *An Enemy of the People*, for example, the visit of the Burgomaster to the newspaper office, where he turns all the Doctor's successes to failures, comes in the second act of the play. And finally, the climax may have happened before the beginning of the narrative. The turning point in the friendship of the maniac for Fortunato, in *The Cask of Amontillado*, has occurred before the story opens; we have in the story only the action subsequent to the climax.

As a final remark on climax, it should be said that every narrative has its grand climax—like that just discussed—and that most narratives have several sub-climaxes, one for each of the scenes which constitute the rising action. These sub-climaxes are exactly like the grand climax except that they are constructed on a smaller scale; that is, they are the turning points in minor rather than in major actions.

e. *Falling Action.*—On the first graph the portion (marked *E*) immediately following the climax is called the falling action. Here the main drift of the action is in a direction contrary to that of the rising action. After the escape of Fleance, Macbeth's fortunes become worse and worse; after the wounding of the Irishman, Tom Jones's fortunes become better and better; after the visit of the Burgomaster to the printing office, Dr. Stockman begins to fail in all his projects; after the decision to return to Egypt, Antony begins to lose the honor, power, and self-respect which he had been regaining during the first part of the play. In all four narratives, the action proceeds in a certain direction, pauses, and then reverses itself. The action which goes in this reverse direction is the falling action.

It has been indicated as a straight line on the graph. And sometimes, indeed, when the climax is near or identical with the end of the story, this falling action does appear as a straight narrative without episodes or sub-climaxes. But more frequently the falling action consists of a series of scenes, just as does the rising action, each with its own sub-climax. The only difference between what has happened before and what happens after the climax is that the main direction of the narrative has changed. Before the climax, Antony was succeeding in episode after episode; after the climax, he fails in two battles, Enobarbus deserts him, he quarrels with Cleopatra, he hears that Cleopatra has committed suicide, he falls on his sword—here are numerous eventful scenes following the climax. In each scene, moreover, the action progresses step by step down toward the destruction of both Antony and Cleopatra.

In tragedy, the falling action is quite as important as the rising action; accordingly, the falling action begins fairly early in the narrative and prolongs itself for some time. The chief reason for this characteristic of tragedy is that most authors believe that real character development can occur only through misfortune, and that they can reveal the protagonist's true character only by subjecting him to hardship. Comedy, on the other hand, usually has a late climax and a brief falling action; for the author has already shown the protagonist in the clutch of misfortune and has placed him in the revealing light of hardship. Nothing more could be gained by a prolonged falling action.

f. *Outcome.*—F on the graph is the outcome (or dénouement, or catastrophe) of the narrative. It is the real end of the story. Here the unrest subsequent to the initial unstable situation is made stable; the activity begun is finished; the goal sought is attained; the change initiated is accomplished. *Hamlet* begins with the necessity of revenge forced upon an unwilling heart; in the last scene the revenge is accomplished and the heart broken—the play is ended. *Macbeth* begins with an ambitious character encouraged by supernatural and conjugal powers to perpetrate great crimes; in the last scene the inevitable consequence of crime and overreaching ambition descends upon Macbeth—and the play is ended.

The outcome is the answer to the question asked, the problem stated in the initial situation. Will the misunderstanding between hero and heroine finally be cleared up, or will it endure always? Will Robinson Crusoe perish on his island, or will he survive? Will Tom Jones be forever estranged from Allworthy, or will he be reinstated in the latter's favor? Will the Percies succeed in their revolt, or will they be conquered? Will the little party conducted by Hawkeye finally reach safety, or will the Indians destroy them? The outcome of each narrative provides the answer to all these queries. And the answer being provided, the story as a unity consisting of beginning, middle, and end, is complete.

g. *Conclusion.*—The final portion of the graph is the conclusion. It forms no real part of the story, but consists, rather, of additional information appended to the story proper for the sake of satisfying the reader's curiosity. "And they lived happily ever afterward": this is conclusion. The final chapter in most nineteenth-century novels is even called "Conclusion." Here the author presents a brief history of what happened to the characters in the years of their life following the narrative just related—he tells how Richard the Lion-hearted was killed in attacking the fortress of a petty vassal; how Henry Esmond married and went to Virginia; how Roderick Random went back to his old home, bought property, settled down, and waited for his wife to have a child; how Mr. Micawber left London for Australia, and there became a successful sheep-rancher. In full-length novels such a concluding chapter, forming so small a percentage of the whole as it does, is probably no detriment to the structure as a whole. But in the more limited and concentrated short story, a conclusion of any length or importance is usually regarded as a fault. Not being a part of the story, it should be omitted.

4. **The Knotted Plot.**—The sort of plot heretofore discussed is simple; the knotted plot is considerably more complex. Yet the

elements of the knotted plot are simple, for they are merely two or more plots of the type just discussed, with each plot coinciding in some of its climaxes with climaxes in the companion plot. That is, a knotted plot consists of two or more simple plots running side by side but converging toward one another at various points, and uniting in incidents which are the turning points of both plots.

In *Hamlet* are two plots—one centering about Hamlet, the other about Laertes. The two plots converge and meet at the grave of Ophelia and in the last act before the king and the queen. In *Antony and Cleopatra* are two plots—one involving the love affair between Antony and Cleopatra, and the other involving the rivalry of Antony and Cæsar. The two plots converge at many places—in particular, at the point where Antony sends Octavia back to Cæsar, and at the point where Antony decides to fight by sea. In the first, the breaking with Octavia for Cleopatra's sake insures the enmity of Cæsar and the consequent destruction of Antony at Cæsar's hands; in the second, Antony's obeying Cleopatra's whim to fight by sea is a deciding event in the completion of his submission to Cleopatra and in his destruction by Cæsar.

In *I Henry IV*, there is the plot of which Hotspur is the hero, and the plot of which Falstaff is the hero; in *King Lear*, there is the plot of which Lear is the hero, and the plot of which Edgar is the hero; in the drama of the eighteenth century (of which Sheridan's *The Rivals* is an excellent example) a plot and a subplot become imperative; in all the eighteenth- and nineteenth-century novels appear one main plot and from one to half-a-dozen subplots; and in most modern drama and all modern motion pictures there is a comic subplot running beside the main plot.

Perhaps, indeed, the intricacy of the interplay of various plots in a narrative is one of the most important criteria for judging the plot of a narrative. A plot that keeps several issues before the reader at once, which weaves incidents and characters back and forth between plot and subplots, which gives the reader's intellect some such vigorous exercise as does a chess problem, and which displays ingenuity and technical skill on the part of the author— such a plot is worthy of tribute just as plot.

5. The Short-Story.—Perhaps this is as good a place as any to say something of the type of narrative known as the short-story (with a hyphen). Though the effect of making arbitrary rules about literature has been the killing off, at different times, of epic, of blank-verse drama, of ode, of pastoral, and of other sorts of literature, some people persist in laying down rules for the construction of the short-story.

The ideal short-story (according to the standards set by the originator of the type, Poe) is something more than a story which is short. Instead of attempting to create a multiplicity and variety of effects, instead of trying to analyze character, instead of presenting a theme, the short-story attempts to create a single emotional effect, a single mood in the mind of the reader—grief, fear, horror, pity, mirth, hate. Characters, setting, action—emotion displayed, places described, deeds told about—are selected and emphasized only as they contribute to the single emotional effect.

To accomplish its purpose, the short-story limits itself in every direction. It deals with moments or hours, not years: in *The Cask of Amontillado* an hour or two; in *The Pit and the Pendulum* an afternoon; in *The Masque of the Red Death* an evening. It begins at the latest possible moment, as close to the climax as possible, and with as little exposition as possible; and it ends as soon as the effect has been made on the reader. It has only one or two important characters. And the action occurs in the fewest possible places—usually in only one.

Nowadays one hears more about the short-story in critical works than one sees it in actuality. For though it is neat and effective, and though any writer may learn from it the value of compression, it is artificial in an age which has come to respect primitive naturalness rather than cultivated artistry. Paradoxically, however, the short-story's artificiality is its chief asset. Writing it, like writing a sonnet, is an æsthetic exercise in which many a word-artist has delighted to engage. Its limitations, its strict requirements, and its singleness of purpose tempt the writer's skill and offer a challenge to his literary power. At the same time, these definite standards make it possible for connoisseurs in literature to read the short-story with a keenly discriminating and appreciative taste. Accordingly, the form will doubtless persist, much as the sonnet has persisted, despite all primitivistic and naturalistic tendencies of contemporary fiction. Yet it will probably never again have the universal popularity that it enjoyed in the nineteenth century. Its appeal will be to artistic and critical minds rather than to the general public.

EXERCISES

1. Straight Narrative.
2. Obstructed Narrative.
   Make a list of the imagined obstructions which might delay the smooth progress of the straight narratives suggested below:
   A love affair between college students.
   A six-day voyage.
   A one-day train trip.
   A new job.
   An interview with a celebrity.
   Finding a boarding place.
   A girl trying to marry a man for his money.
   A man trying to escape the unwelcome attentions of a young woman who has taken a fancy to him.

The problems of a young man who has just been elected to office on the reform ticket.

The problems of a young man who has graduated from an agricultural school and gone back to his native county to start farming.

3. The Narrative Graph.

a. See whether the exposition at the beginnings of Kipling's *Plain Tales from the Hills* and of the stories in almost any volume of Maupassant might be scattered along the course of the narrative instead of being bunched at the beginning.

Write an expository paragraph about the life and character of some person you know. Then try to present this information dramatically in the course of a short narrative about an incident in which the character figures.

b. Below is a list of situations new to characters. Make them into provocations for stories by having the characters feel a desire or a necessity in connection with the new situations:

A young husband gets a new son.

A family with a grown daughter moves next door to you.

You find that you love a person your good friend loves.

You fall in love with someone beneath you.

You get a new job.

A young man goes to live with a rich aunt.

You notice that for several days a man has been following you wherever you go.

c. Plan five different stories showing five different kinds of change which may grow out of each of the following situations:

A sixteen-year-old city boy who has been left an orphan goes to live with his uncle in the country.

An idealistic, pure-minded young man gets a job as a common sailor in order that he may work his way to Europe.

d. Plan a climax for each of the actions suggested in the exercises for Sections 1 and 2 above.

For at least two of the situations, work out three different climaxes: one depending on some philosophy of yours; another depending on a logical series of events; and a third depending on some peculiarity of the character involved.

e. As an experiment, make some of the situations just mentioned end tragically, and then revise them so as to make them end happily. How does the position of the climax change with the alteration of the stories?

f. Plan an outcome for each of the actions suggested in *b* above.

4. The Knotted Plot.

Try to link together in plans for at least five stories some of the actions suggested anywhere in the exercises for this chapter and others in this book.

Try to imagine subplots which will contain characters, actions, and ideas contrasting with characters, actions and ideas in the main plots of the actions just suggested.

5. The Short-Story.

Could any of the stories you have planned above, or any part of these stories, be made into a short-story? Explain.

Chapter XV

THE CHARACTERS

WE MAY say at once without reservation that the most important element in fiction is character. If a writer of fiction can portray character well, he will be remembered; if he cannot, he will be forgotten. The plot may be stolen (as it nearly always is in Shakespeare and in Chaucer), the social purpose may be forgotten today (as it is with Dickens), and the satire may now be useless (as it often is with Thackeray); but if the characters are well-rounded, convincing, true-to-life human beings, we remember the author who created them. Excellent characters make excellent fiction—this is a rule-of-thumb to which there are few exceptions.

1. The Elements of Character.—Every character in life and every well-imagined character in books is a product of several major forces, the interaction and interrelation of which are reflected in the personality of the character. Every true character, then, is made up of several major elements created in him by the major forces at work upon him. The first of these elements is a compound of emotional, mental, and spiritual traits such as are common to all humanity; the second element is a compound of traits normal in a race, a trade, a profession, a cultural group of any sort; and the third is a compound of traits peculiar to the individual.

For example, the impulses to love, to hate, to lust, to seek gain, and to fear death are so universal that we expect to find them in every character. Sometimes, indeed, the vague, unimportant characters on the outskirts of the main action of a story have no other traits than these.

Other sorts of characters may have a distinctness a little more pronounced in that they possess not only universally human traits, but also the traits of a social group. One meets the typical Negro, the typical American, the typical Indian, the typical Jew; and one meets the typical sailor with all the characteristics of his profession, the typical statesman, the typical doctor, the typical preacher —Uncle Remus, Reuben Biglow, Chingachgook, Shylock; Tom Bowling, Throttlebottom, Arrowsmith, Gantry. Sometimes such individuals represent not a race or a profession, but a way of thinking and acting. Habitual malcontents appear in Shakespeare as Don John, Jaques, and Malvolio; and in our own day, most of Shaw's and Galsworthy's characters represent specific levels of society, or class divisions, or mental attitudes toward social problems.

The last of the constituents of character are those individualizing traits which distinguish one person from other members of the same race, profession, or way of thinking. These traits may be no more than peculiarities of physical appearance (like a bald head, a greasy beard, a stubby hand, a patch over one eye, or a wooden leg); they may be tricks of action (like a leer, or a graceful waving of the hands, or Uriah Heep's "writhing," or Jeremy Cruncher's picking at his hands); or they may be tricks of speech (like "Barkis is willing"; or "Something will turn up"; or "I can never be persuaded to desert Mr. Micawber"). Such traits make a character stand out vividly from his background, a sharp-limned product of an accurate imagination.

But even more important than these traits are certain deeper characteristics which set an individual off as more than just another person. These consist, on the one hand, of exaggerations of racial, professional, or mental traits; and, on the other, of an incongruity between what one might expect of certain races, professions, or ways of thought.

As for the first of these—an American who is too American, a Jew who is too Jewish, a sailor who is all sailor, a farmer who is nothing but farmer, a lover who is all lover, a socialist who is nothing but socialist—these make convincing characters. On the other hand, an American who detests America, a Jew who is not industrious and saving, a sailor who is interested in horses, a farmer who likes airplanes, a lover who subordinates his sweetheart to his business or his hobby, a socialist who hobnobs with capitalists—these, too, make individualized characters.

2. Static Characters.—Sometimes we are interested in characters for their own sake—as in the Prologue of Chaucer's *Canterbury Tales*; in the complexities within characters—as in Meredith's *The Egoist*; in the reaction of characters to one another—as in almost any of the lesser novels; in the reaction of characters to environment—as in almost any tale of adventure; and simply in what happens to characters in whom we have become interested. In none of these situations is it necessary that the characters themselves change. They may serve their purpose, or their creator's purpose, and yet remain static.

3. Developing Characters.—But probably more interesting characters are those who undergo a change. They are more interesting because they indicate more skill and understanding on the part of the author, and because they are more true to life than are static characters. In the real world, our mannerisms vary from year to year; our opinions, our habits of action, our customary reactions change as we change places of residence, grow older, and learn more from experience. When a teacher is young, he wants to fail all his students; as he grows older, he wants to pass them all. When he is young, he believes he knows a good deal; as he grows older, he doubts whether he knows anything. When

he is young, he tries to help people with good advice; as he grows older, he knows that nobody ever takes advice.

A writer who can trace the growth of such differences in character, can account for them by the experiences he allows his character to undergo, and can present them convincingly, always has a higher place among the critics than does a writer who portrays merely static characters. Nearly all the greatest works of fiction show the development of characters: *Macbeth* shows it; *Hamlet* shows it; *Julius Cæsar* shows it; *Antony and Cleopatra* shows it; *Les Miserables* shows it; *Crime and Punishment* shows it; *The Doll's House* shows it.

The words "development" and "change" as used here are meant to signify *growth*. The mere changing of a character's nature from good to evil or from evil to good, or from wisdom to folly or from folly to wisdom, and so on, is easily portrayed. Moreover, such out-and-out transformations may, at first glance, seem quite plausible. A man's son dies—and the father, grief-stricken, resolves to be sober thereafter. Or a respectable woman cannot retain her lover, and so, in vexation, resolves to be bad. Or a man who has intervened to help settle a family quarrel gets into difficulties with the entire family—and so resolves never again to be so foolish as to interfere in a family quarrel.

It is easy to project such changes, mere transformations as they are, into fiction. But if we regard character development not as mere change, but as growth, we must ask ourselves, "What did this new phase of character grow from? What was the seed within the character which was only waiting the proper encouragement to unfold?" Before a writer can venture to attempt the portrayal of character growth, he must ask himself, Have I planted the seed for such growth? If Macbeth had not had the seed of ambition within him, the witches could never have egged him on into crime; if Hamlet had not had the seed of strength in him, he could never have grown into the resolute courage which was his after his return from England; if Brutus had not had the seed of personal honor and affection in him, he could never have become the sad and remorseful man he was on the eve of Philippi. Sudden conversions do not indicate character growth: they are always unwarranted in a well-constructed plot, and they are not true to life.

Moreover, it is not character growth when, under the pressure of extraordinary circumstances, some hitherto reliable bulkhead of character gives way. For example, when, in the almost notorious play *Rain*, the woman's wickedness at first gave way, and then the preacher's virtue, there was no real change in either the woman or the preacher. Neither had before been subjected to such a strain as both encountered on the island; if they had been, they would have given way before. On the island they underwent new experiences; but after those experiences the woman was actually no better and the man actually no worse than they had been before. Their true characters were merely exposed by the new incidents. But character exposure and character development are not the same thing.

4. The Tragic Character.—When misfortune befalls a bad man, we consider it a just punishment for his misdeeds; when misfortune befalls a good man, we consider it merely a shocking occurrence. Misfortune befalling a man good in most ways, but weak in one way, is the true substance of tragedy. The weakness is called a "tragic flaw," after the terminology of Aristotle, who first tried to define tragedy. The tragic flaw in Antony is his love for Cleopatra; the tragic flaw in Hamlet is his tendency to think too much and act too slowly; the tragic flaw in Brutus is his mistaken patriotism; the tragic flaw in Macbeth is his overweening ambition. All these characters come to tragic ends because of the one flaw in their character. They are not crushed by

fate, they are not destroyed by accident or chance. They have only their own weakness to blame. Perhaps the most tragic thought in the world is the thought of what might have been—and all these characters might have been heroic figures if only they could have overcome the tragic flaw.

Utter destruction or utter degradation, whether it be physical, mental, or moral, does not make a figure tragic. But rather, as Joseph Wood Krutch has pointed out, the genuinely tragic figure retains even in his destruction some element of nobility which makes him triumph over physical defeat and even over death. Antony and Cleopatra dying are finer, nobler figures than they have ever been before; Hamlet dying redeems his honor in his own eyes; Brutus dying perceives, as never before, the true nature of personal nobility; Lear dying understands, as never before, the reality and the beauty of love. The tendency of modern tragedy (that of O'Neill, for example) has been away from this conception of the tragic figure, and toward the conception of complete spiritual disintegration of the principal character in fiction. Which conception the student adopts for himself will depend on his private philosophy of life; yet it is probable that Shakespeare is more nearly right, and certainly more perfectly artistic, than is Eugene O'Neill.

5. The Comic Character.—To understand the comic character, we must understand comedy—which nobody has ever been able to do to the satisfaction of others. Yet a few statements about comedy most people will accept. Laughter and comedy assert or imply a superiority of the laugher over the comic figure, the thing laughed at. We never laugh at what we feel to be superior to us. We do not laugh at God, we do not laugh at our parents when we are small, we do not laugh at great spectacles of nature, we do not laugh at beauty, we do not laugh at our heartfelt ideals and hopes. But if laughter puts the laugher in a place of superior-

ity, it also puts the thing laughed at in a place of inferiority. It is cruel.

This is the key to comic characters. They are inferior. But this statement immediately brings forth a question: How are they inferior? George Meredith and Henri Bergson have answered the question by saying that comic characters are inferior by being foolish—in particular, by being foolishly non-social. That is to say, in Bergson's words, the comic character has a "growing callousness toward social life." He pegs along in his own path, oblivious of his obligations to society, of what society thinks of him, of society itself. He has a rigidity of character, a single-mindedness, an absent-mindedness which makes him overlook elements in his own nature.

Shylock, Don Quixote, Mr. Pickwick, Jeremy Cruncher, Sir Willoughby Patterne, the fools and clowns in Shakespeare, most of the "humorous" characters in Ben Jonson, Lydia Languish, Thorvald in *The Doll's House*, Sergis in *Arms and the Man*— all these are comic characters because they are victims of a foolish absent-mindedness about themselves. We laugh at them; but even our laughter cannot stir them into a realization of their folly. They continue on their way as members of types which are unconventional and non-social without being aware of it.

6. The Relation of Character to Action.—In the ideal narrative, the relation of character to action is simple. In brief, (a) the nature of a character should determine the course of action; and (b) the course of the action should reveal the nature of the character. The critical points at which these relationships become most necessary and obvious are the beginning and the climax—whether it be the beginning and the climax of a single episode, a single scene, a single chapter, or the entire narrative.

We may illustrate the relationships from the action of *Antony and Cleopatra*. At the beginning of the play Antony receives a message requiring his immediate desertion of Cleopatra and his return to Rome. That he has sufficient strength of character to break with the imperious queen not only determines the course of the succeeding action, but more especially reveals that Antony is no spineless weakling who has no thought, ambition, or sense of responsibility, and has become subservient in body and soul to Cleopatra. Without that sort of character-revealing beginning, Antony could not have appeared as the colossal figure which he really is in the play—an unquestionably great man with a great weakness.

The climax of the play still more aptly illustrates the perfection of the plot-character relationship. Satisfying a whim of Cleopatra's, Antony resolves, against all the advice of seasoned military men, to meet Octavius on the sea. Nothing reveals the tragic weakness of his character so much as this decision; and at the same time, no one peculiarity of character could have had more momentous effects on subsequent action. This is perfect plot construction, and perfect character revelation.

If this explanation of the proper relationship between plot and character is accepted, it is plain that a fiction writer may fall short of the ideal relationship by committing one of two errors both in beginnings and in climaxes.

a. The action may proceed quite independently of character-attributes—as it proceeds, for example, in most of *Roderick Random*, where Roderick, thrown into the slimy current of eighteenth-century worldliness, is swept on from adventure to adventure with no power either to alter or to halt the action. Practically all picaresque stories, and many stories of adventure depicting man in conflict with nature or with comprehensive social movements such as wars and famines, are stories of this type. In these, character has no influence on action.

b. More commonly, characters appear at the beginning of a

narrative and in a few pages reveal to the reader everything worth knowing about themselves. Thereafter they play their parts in the action, giving it one direction or another perhaps, checking it, swaying it, changing it this way or that, but never revealing more about themselves than the reader knows at the beginning of the story. At every turn in the plot, the reader knows exactly what the reaction of each character will be: the villain will be villainous—the hero, heroic—the comic character, comic; and knowing so much, the reader feels that the characters are almost mechanical.

Someone says that the best test of an author's characters is to inquire whether they can surprise convincingly. Whoever said that had in mind the power of an author to reveal convincingly unexpected attributes in his characters. If I kick a stone, I know beforehand almost exactly how the stone will react. But if I kick a dog, I do not know what to expect: he may howl or remain silent, run away or stay where he is, cringe or bite me. Whatever he does will not *surprise* me, perhaps; but, nevertheless, it will show me or prove to me something about his character which I did not know about before I kicked him. Hamlet's failure to stab the king does not surprise us, perhaps; but it reveals to us that Hamlet is not a man of action.

Scott is an old offender at this game in all his Waverley Novels: once we have been introduced to his characters, we know all that is to be known about them—during all the subsequent action we can predict with absolute certainty the reaction of any character to any given circumstance. It is no slight condemnation of Ibsen to say that the same thing is, in some measure, true of him; it is true of Stevenson; it is true of Wilde; it is true of Galsworthy; it is true of Shaw. To the fact that it is not true of Jane Austen, that every new reaction of her characters to circumstances reveals new angles, new facets, new attributes, all of

them as mutually consistent as they are fresh and unexpected—
to this fact Jane Austen owes most of that bright and perpetual
charm in which her novels so abound. Dickens, too, has this
power to reveal character by action throughout a novel; Thackeray
has it; Henry James, George Meredith, Arnold Bennett, and
Joseph Conrad have it *par excellence*.

EXERCISES

1. The Elements of Character.

   Write thumb-nail character sketches of twenty people you know.
   First, give the subject's racial, social, or (and) mental type; and
   then give some individualizing trait. Here are examples:

   The intruder turned out to be a slow-witted Swedish plumber
   who smiled broadly and acquiescingly at every remark made to
   him.

   The French professor was a conceited little man whose most
   notable characteristic was a perpetual graceful waving of his
   fingers.

2. Static Characters.

   Write longer sketches of five of the above. Include something
   about their parentage and education if these factors might have
   influenced the characteristics of the five.

3. Developing Characters.

   How might the personal traits of the people mentioned below
   grow into quite different (not necessarily opposite) traits under
   the circumstances mentioned?

   A rebellious girl is forced to suffer hardships.
   The same girl falls into a life of wealth and luxury.

   A gay but foolish man marries a phlegmatic woman.
   The same man marries a serious, ambitious woman.
   The same man marries a foolish, vain woman.

Any of the women just mentioned marries the same man.

A wise and thoughtful author becomes a popular success.
The same man is never able to become a popular success.

A somewhat stupid girl goes to college.
The same girl stays at home on the farm.

A very kind man goes to war.
The same man becomes a social service worker.

4. The Tragic Character.

Name the chief fault in the characters of ten people you know. Imagine situations in which these faults would lead to misfortune or disaster for the people.

5. The Comic Character.

Write down the names of five people who amuse you.

Next, try to discover exactly what it is about them that amuses you.

Third, try to imagine characters in which these amusing elements are considerably exaggerated.

Fourth, imagine situations in which custom or convention would demand that these characters be exactly opposite to the way you have imagined them.

Finally, place your characters in these situations, and write out what happens.

6. The Relation of Character to Action.

Outline fully one of the stories suggested by the developments in character you have traced in doing the exercises under Section 3 above. Show how the action in your story may reveal a stage in the character development, and how the character development may influence the action.

Carefully read some story of Maupassant. Now imagine the chief character (or characters) to be just the opposite of what Maupassant has imagined. Rewrite the story as it would happen to these reconstructed characters.

Chapter XVI

PURPOSE, SUBJECT, THEME, AND SETTING

1. Purpose.—Before he writes any piece of fiction, an author should decide and state to himself his purpose or purposes in writing it. If he fails to do so, his reader may be tempted to say at the end of the piece, "Well, what of it?" Some of the purposes a writer may have in mind are suggested in the following list:

a. As worthy a purpose as any is that of mere *entertainment*. And indeed, if a fiction writer ignores this purpose, no one will read him—and he had as well not write. The *Arabian Nights*, most of the great eighteenth-century novels and tales, much of Stevenson, ninety-eight per cent of the magazine fiction today, ninety-nine per cent of the movies, and all the musical comedies have no other purpose in view except entertainment.

b. The fiction may be intended to *excite an emotion or create a mood*—as in Poe's tales of horror, Lord Dunsany's tales of fantasy, and Synge's Irish plays.

c. It may be intended to *exercise the intellect*—as in Poe's tales of "ratiocination" and in the best of the modern detective stories.

d. It may be intended to *reveal a condition*, as Upton Sinclair's novel *The Jungle* was intended to reveal working conditions in the Chicago packing houses, and as *Uncle Tom's Cabin* was intended to reveal undesirable conditions of slavery.

e. It may be intended to *reveal and analyze an interesting character*, sometimes simply for the sake of the character—as in *The Egoist* and *The Old Wives' Tale*; sometimes for the sake of showing the growth or development of the character—as in *Macbeth, Julius Cæsar, Strange Interlude* (in parts), and the book about Sophia in *The Old Wives' Tale*; and sometimes for the sake of showing an interesting character in his reactions to certain situations—as in *Hamlet, Weir of Hermiston, Youth,* and *Typhoon.*

f. It may be intended to *reveal some law of life*—as *The Second Mrs. Tanqueray* is intended to reveal that society will not allow a woman who has gone wrong to go right again; as Shaw's *Candida* is intended to reveal that sometimes the men who seem strongest are really weakest, and that women love weak men; and as James Branch Cabell's novels about Poictesme are intended to reveal certain truths about the spiritual relations of husbands and wives.

g. Not very different from the sort of fiction just mentioned, and, as a matter of fact, overlapping it so thoroughly that the line between the two sorts is indistinguishable, is the kind of fiction whose purpose is to *promulgate some belief or doctrine* of the author. Shaw's *Arms and the Man*, for example, is intended to show that sentimentality is foolish; his *The Doctor's Dilemma* is intended to show that genius is more valuable than morality; his *Joan of Arc* is intended to show that Joan was not foully or illegally treated by the English or by the French; Galsworthy's *Strife* is intended to show that strife between capital and labor ends in disaster for both; his *The Pigeon* is intended to show that private almsgiving is frequently worse than useless.

h. The purpose of some fiction is merely to *present a place, a people, a time, or a social group* to the imagination of the reader. Kipling's stories imaginatively re-create India for the reader; Roark Bradford's stories present a race of people; Scott's *Ivanhoe* resurrects a period in the development of the English nation; and Dickens's and Thackeray's novels show us the ways of certain social groups.

i. The purpose may be to *re-create imaginatively some action or incident of history*—as most historical novels from Scott to Sabatini have done.

j. And finally, as a kind of over-purpose which may accompany any of the others, the purpose of a piece of fiction may be *to satirize or to vindicate* a condition, a character, a doctrine, a place, a people, a time, a social group, or an incident of history.

2. Subject.—It needs no discerning textbook to point out that the subject of a piece of fiction is what (or who) it is about. A book about a young married couple, for instance, might have any of the purposes mentioned above—but it would still be about the young married couple. *Uncle Tom's Cabin* may have been intended to reveal a condition and make propaganda for the betterment of that condition—but it is still about Uncle Tom, Little Eva, and plantation life before the Civil War. *Arms and the Man* may have been intended to satirize sentimentality—but it is still about Captain Bluntschli, Raina, and life in the Balkans.

In general, the subject of a narrative is always the three elements, *action, character,* and *setting.* Sometimes one of these dominates, sometimes another—and sometimes all are of about equal importance. But they are all present in any narrative.

3. Theme.—We can understand what is meant by the *theme* of a story if we relate narrative to the inductive method of reasoning. The inductive method consists of the accumulation of particular facts and the formulation of a generalization to cover those facts. Suppose that a biologist discovers an albino sparrow, and studies it in nature. He will see that hawks single out the albino from the rest of the flock and chase it; he will see that cats are attracted to the albino before being attracted to normally colored birds; and he will see that little boys shoot at the albino at every opportunity. The scientist will make the generalization, therefore, that an albino sparrow has a smaller chance to survive

in nature than has a brown sparrow. Here we have scientific observation and a subsequent formulation of a generalization. Later on, the scientist may reverse the procedure: he may say that sparrows not protectively colored have small chance to survive, and he may illustrate his generalization by reference to the albino sparrow.

The fiction writer is somewhat like such a scientist. He observes life long enough to come to certain conclusions, to make certain generalizations, about it. Starting with this generalization, he then proceeds to illustrate it by reference to certain particular cases.

Thus, Hawthorne had observed life enough to know that people who must seek perfection in everything, who are not content to let well enough alone, nearly always bring grief to themselves. To illustrate this generalization, Hawthorne tells the story of a young surgeon who attempted to remove the birthmark which marred the otherwise perfect beauty of his wife, and who succeeded only in killing her. The generalization here is the *theme* of the story.

The theme is not always so obvious as it is in this story of Hawthorne's, and, indeed, the writer of a story may not be aware of and may not care about the theme in his story. But a reader can always formulate some sort of theme out of every piece of fiction or, for that matter, every happening in real life. The theme of *Don Quixote* is that the customs of chivalry were foolish; of *Main Street,* that life in small towns is debasing; of *Strange Interlude,* that woman needs, even demands, at least five kinds of love; of *Lord Jim,* that a weak man will always be weak; of any Hardy novel, that our lives are governed by the Immanent Will rather than by our own desires and efforts. All fiction has some sort of theme—from the parables of Christ, the fables of Æsop, and the allegories of the Middle Ages right down to the contemporary detective story and the musical comedy. But only since Ibsen showed us the way, in the middle of the last century, has fiction become self-consciously, almost aggressively, thematic. The problem-play and the problem-novel appear on every hand. Life has become a laboratory for fiction writers, and fiction has become a demonstration room. The worst of the problem-literature has gone, it is true; but it has left its mark on the taste of this generation. People have grown tired of problems in fiction; but they still want their theme, even as their ancestors of a hundred and a thousand years ago wanted their moral, in a story.

4. Setting.— A complete setting for a piece of fiction would involve time, place, and social rank; but now that the days of the local-color story and the historical novel have largely passed, the first two elements of setting are not so important in the eyes of fiction writers as they once were. And now that the days of social problems are upon us, the last-mentioned element exercises many a writer—Dreiser, Anderson, Lewis, Galsworthy. A generation which believes that an individual is what his environment has made him will always be more concerned with society than with picturesque places and romantic ages.

But whatever element in the setting a writer wishes to emphasize, he will find that he can convey a sense of the setting to his reader only by doing one or several of the following things:

a. He may *describe the physical setting* of his story—as Kipling describes the Himalayas in "The Miracle of Purun Baghat," or as George W. Cable describes New Orleans in *Old Creole Days*.

b. He may *present typical characters* of a region, a time, or a social rank—as Sarah Orne Jewett presents typical characters of New England, as Scott in *Ivanhoe* presents typical characters of England in the twelfth century, and as O. Henry presents typical characters of the lower working classes of New York.

c. He may *introduce typical dialect*—as does Charles Egbert Craddock in her stories of the Tennessee mountaineers, and Joel Chandler Harris in his stories of the Southern Negro before the Civil War. This typical dialect (as well as the other typical details to be mentioned immediately) may be typical, of course, of a place, a time, or a social rank.

d. The writer may *describe typical costumes*—as does Scott in all his historical novels (Carlyle says that he "describes his characters from the skin outwards").

e. He may *describe typical customs*—as Synge does in *Riders to the Sea* and as Flaubert does in *Salammbo*.

f. He may *describe typical mental attitudes*—as Maupassant describes the cold and selfish cruelty of the typical Norman mind, as Hawthorne describes the narrow and austere Puritanism of the typical New England mind, as Oscar Wilde describes the impudent and cynical sophistication of the typical aristocratic mind in London of the nineteenth century, and as Bret Harte describes the generous, rough, and impulsive sentimentality of the typical California mind in the gold-rush days.

EXERCISES

1. Purpose.

    Refer back to the narratives suggested in Section 3, *c,* of Chapter XIV. Tell how different purposes could make different kinds of narratives out of the two situations given.

2. Subject.

3. Theme.

    Find subjects for the following themes (all taken from the *Maxims* of La Rochefoucauld):

    Passion often makes able men foolish, and foolish men able.

The constancy of wise men is only the art of suppressing the agitation of their hearts.

In order to establish oneself in the world, one must do all one can to seem established.

In the business of life we please more often by our faults than by our virtues.

Great names lower instead of elevating people who do not know how to support them.

People often do good in order to be able to do evil with impunity.

We are so accustomed to disguising ourselves from others that at last we disguise ourselves from ourselves.

There are people who would never have loved if they had never heard of love.

It is not enough for one to have good qualities; one must make use of them.

Weak persons cannot be sincere.

4. Setting.

How would you reconstruct the following settings imaginatively:

Your school.

Your social class.

The part of town in which you live.

Your mother's girlhood.

Chapter XVII

CREATING A STORY

1. **Where to Find Materials.**—Once in a great while something happens in reality that may be transcribed into the form of fiction with practically no change; but such occasions are extremely rare. Few fiction writers, therefore, can depend on unadulterated reality for ready-made plots. Indeed, it is *almost* a rule that unadulterated reality is no fit subject for the fiction writer; it practically always requires addition, subtraction, or alteration before it can be suitable for presentation.

Yet reality (or the writer's own experience) is the best source of material for fiction. Reality presents the germ; the invention of the writer stimulates the germ into flourishing growth. Reality gives the suggestion; the invention of the writer carries the suggestion to a triumphant conclusion. Reality gives the clue; the invention of the writer follows the clue into the creation of a fully developed story. In a word, a story is built up on the writer's conception of what might have been.

The neighbor woman has gone to town and left her child in charge of the grandmother; the child has disappeared (it is probably around the corner playing with other children), and the grandmother is calling it. Presently the child answers, and the grandmother goes into the house again. There is the reality. But let the invention enlarge upon it: suppose the child does not answer; suppose it has run away, or has been run over by a passing automobile. What a finely tragic figure we could make

338

of the grandmother now, who, loving the child and feeling that her carelessness caused its death, would have to face the child's parents! And what a complex of human relationships could we evolve by picturing the way in which the parents condemned the grandmother in their hearts, and yet tried to continue loving her—we might go on, indeed, to picture how the daughter-in-law or the son-in-law of the old lady grew more and more hostile toward her, while the other member of the young couple defended her, until a separation came about between the married couple; or until the grandmother was cast out of the home; or until the grandmother committed suicide to remove the source of irritation and unhappiness between husband and wife; or until the grandmother recompensed the young couple by doing them some great favor—and so on almost *ad infinitum*. All this from a grandmother's calling a child playing around the corner! It is the building up of what might have been out of a trivial experience in real life.

Or suppose you are a young man. You make a purchase in the ten-cent store, and as the salesgirl hands you the package, she touches your hand as if by accident and looks into your eyes invitingly. In real life you pretend not to notice. But suppose you *did* notice—what then? On the strength of what might have been, you can build up an affair that will wreck some fictional young man's life. Or suppose you are a young woman. Someone offers you a stenographer's job in a large corporation. Suppose the offer has come from a young man engaged to be married to another woman. He hires you, and before long is attracted by your beauty and intelligence. He feels that he is being attracted, and resists temptation. You, too, feel that you must not come between him and his fiancée. But a business depression is on; you know you cannot get another job if you quit this one; the young man knows it too, and so hesitates to discharge you.

What would you do? What would the young man do? What would his fiancée do? What might happen to straighten out the difficulties? Would the fiancée die? or would she decide to marry another man after all? or would you try to become as disagreeable and unattractive as possible? or would you pretend to be in love with another man who might not even exist? However you finish the story, you will be building up on a simple everyday incident a vast structure of what might have been.

In such a fashion you may construct a thousand stories based on trivial occurrences or commonplace realities. You read one of Hardy's novels in which tremendous consequences follow as a result of some accident. Why cannot you write a similar story in which the all-important accident does not occur? You remark, "What on earth she can see in him to make her want to marry him is more than I can understand." Why not write a story in which you explain what she sees in him and why she wants to marry him? You remark, "I'd like to show that person how unimportant he is." Why not invent incidents in which others will show him? You remark, "I'd like to be in charge of this affair about five minutes." Why not write a story in which a person symbolizing you is put in charge? No incident is so trivial that it cannot be transfigured (through the magic of what might have been) into a story. The breaking of a shoestring, the missing of a street car, the drinking of a glass of water, the acceptance of a ride in a stranger's automobile, the mispronunciation of a person's name, the losing of a necklace, the finding of a piece of string, the dropping of a handkerchief—all of these may form the germ of a two-volume novel or a five-act tragedy.

2. **Building on an Event.**—Sometimes a writer may happen upon an incident or event in his daily life which, he thinks, has in it the elements or the possibilities of a story. It may be an item in the paper, a chance remark heard on a street corner, a significant

look passed between a man and a woman, a "personal" in the
advertising column of a journal, or some other such contribution
to the writer's store of observations and experiences. As he waits
on the corner, he may see a little girl come up to the old woman
selling papers nearby, and tell her something, whereupon the old
woman begins to weep softly. Sitting in the subway, he may see
a burly gentleman slowly lift a long blonde hair from his coat-
sleeve, deposit the hair in the aisle of the car, and smile. Walking
along the street, he may see an urchin suddenly assume a pitiful
expression, sidle up to a well-dressed gentleman, beg for money
and, on being refused, run back and start laughing and romping
with other urchins on the street corner. Every person with eyes
in his head and senses alert notices a dozen such incidents every
day.

But how to make them into a story? The student may reach
a satisfactory answer to this problem by following the suggestions below, and following them in the order in which they are
listed.

a. Try to *imagine what might have come before and what may
come after the event you have observed.* Sometimes, of course, an
event may obviously be at the beginning of a story or at the
end of a story, and consequently may demand either nothing before it or nothing after it. The incident of the gentleman in the
subway at night is obviously the end of a story; the incident of
the urchin asking for money may be the beginning. And the
incident of the woman who sells papers may be the middle.

The purpose the writer has in mind will largely determine the
position of the event in the story. For example, if his purpose in
the story about the old woman is merely to excite an emotion,
he may well end with her weeping; and if it is to reveal a condition or to present the life of her social group, the story may
go on to describe her life when she is not selling papers. Accord-

ingly, the writer should consider together this step in creation and the step which immediately follows. He should jot down all the possibilities which his imagination suggests to him as antecedents and as sequels to the event he has observed, and then he should determine which of the possibilities will best serve the purpose he has in mind. Thus he will be able to locate his observed incident at the beginning, in the middle, or at the end of the contemplated story. Locating it properly, he will know where to begin his story in relation to the observed event, and where to end it.

b. *Find a purpose for your writing the story.* Look back over the list of possible purposes given in the previous chapter, and decide which purpose the incident you have observed seems to fit best. For example, the incident about the little girl and the woman who sells papers would probably harmonize with only a very few possible purposes: to excite an emotion, to reveal a condition, or to present the life of some social group. The incident about the man on the subway might harmonize with the following: to entertain, to reveal or analyze some interesting character, or to reveal some law of life. And the incident about the urchin begging for money might harmonize with the following: to entertain, to reveal a condition, to satirize, or to reveal a law of life. Of the possible purposes which each event may serve, the writer must make a choice of one or two, and ignore the others. What his choices will be will depend on his temperament, his previous successes in writing, his knowledge of his own abilities, his willingness to experiment with new sorts of writing, the market for which he is writing (if he is a professional), and so on. But before he takes the next step, he should settle on a purpose of some sort.

c. Next, *decide what the theme of the story is to be.* The purpose of the writer will, of course, largely determine his theme. If it is to reveal a condition (such as the fact that boys begging on the street are often not nearly so miserable as people believe), the theme is already made. Or if the purpose is to promulgate a doctrine (such as the desirability of not giving casual charity to beggars), the theme is already made. Or if the purpose is to satirize a social group (such as beggars who prey on kind-hearted people), the theme is already made.

But when the purpose of the story is to entertain, to excite an emotion, to exercise the intellect, to present a character, and so on, the writer must think up some theme to incorporate into his story. If he is writing about the man on the subway at midnight, he may take as his theme various truisms: that it requires very little to make some people happy; that lovers are usually happy no matter what befalls them; that a woman may mean no more than a hair on the coat-sleeve to some men; that everybody falls in love at some time or another; and anything else which the experience of the writer has shown to be true.

d. Fourth, *decide what change is to occur in the story.* The change, it will be remembered from the discussion, in a previous chapter, of the rising action of a plot, may involve (1) a change in the relationship of characters to one another; (2) a change in the relation between a character and his environment; (3) a change within the character himself; (4) a change in the reader's knowledge of characters; or (5) a change in the knowledge which some characters have about others.

To decide what the change shall be is easy after the theme has once been chosen. The writer has merely to state the opposite of his theme, and then picture the change from the negative to the positive. For example, if the theme is that beggars are not nearly so miserable as people believe, the opposite will be that people believe beggars are as miserable as they pretend. The change, then, will be from some individual's good opinion of beggars to his acquiring a bad opinion.

If the theme is that it requires very little to make some people happy, the opposite will be that somebody thinks it requires very much to make him happy. The change, then, will be from a person's despair and skepticism about being happy to his being made completely happy by getting a blonde hair on his coat-sleeve.

e. Fifth, *decide what the provocation of the story is to be.* As already explained, the provocation is the first hint that a change is to take place, the beginning of a development, the situation that cannot remain unchanged. About the best rule a writer can follow is this: Present the provocation at the latest possible moment. If he is intending to have the urchin ask the gentleman for money, the writer should not tell all that has happened to the urchin before, or who the gentleman is, or where he is going; but he should begin with the urchin's stopping the gentleman. If he is intending to show that love can make a despairing and skeptical man happy, the writer should present no more of the reasons why the man is despairing and skeptical than is absolutely necessary for the proper characterization of the man. The story should begin with his meeting the blonde who is destined to make him happy.

f. *Invent a rough sketch of the method by which the change is to occur.* Doing this will involve creating a setting of some sort, describing or characterizing several people, bringing several people together either by accident or by the design of one or both, and (above all) inventing a climactic scene in which the action takes a definite turn in the direction of the contemplated change. Much of this step in planning the story will be included, however, in the next stage.

g. *Invent obstructing events which will tend to halt the progress of the change.* These obstructing events may be due to accidents, to the selfish designs of other persons, to misunderstandings, to caution and hesitancy on the part of at least one character, to disagreeable necessity, to misjudgment, and to other forces which the circumstances of the story will suggest. For instance, the gentleman's giving the money to the boy may be obstructed by his wondering whether he can spare the money, whether the boy is honest, what the boy will do with the money, whether the boy looks hungry, and whether he had better give the boy a comparatively large sum and tell him to take it home. All these doubts and questions are obstructions lying across the path of the boy's getting the money successfully. The climax will come, perhaps, when the gentleman notices a cigarette package in the boy's shirt-pocket; this will make him decide to refuse the boy money. The more such obstructions a writer can find to lay across the positive course of his story, the longer and more complex will the story become, and (in general) the more suspense will it have.

h. *Add a subplot.* The people in this subplot may be instrumental in putting the obstructions just mentioned across the course of the story, or they may be instrumental in helping the main characters overcome the obstructions. The writer should decide which of these two functions the subplot is to have, and should work out the rest of the plot in relation to this function. For example, the gentleman who is accosted by the beggar-boy may be accompanied by a lady. The gentleman may hate to refuse the boy in the presence of the lady whom he wishes to impress; and yet he may think the lady will consider him weak if he gives to the boy. On the other hand, the lady may even urge the man to give, or not to give; and he may resist her entreaty, or comply. The possibilities are varied.

Moreover, the story may possess more than one subplot. The boy may bring up a small dirty child, obviously in need of better care, and present him as a brother. Thus he may work on the sympathies of the gentleman and his companion. The smaller child may then make a plea of his own, so that he instead of the larger boy receives the money; or the smaller boy may inadvertently (as children will) let escape some bit of information which will be disastrous to the larger boy's scheme of begging money.

i. *Divide the plot, with its subplot, into scenes.* Exposition should be eliminated, and imaginative writing substituted in its place wherever a due regard for proportion will permit. The action itself should be *presented* to the reader—not *told* to him; he should *see* it happening—not merely *know* that it has happened. The writer, therefore, must decide how much description of character and of setting he will use; how much action he will describe; how much conversation he will quote. He must try to conceive of his story as a series of episodes—not a continuous, unbroken surface of narrative; he must picture it to himself as a string of beads—not a ribbon. Each episode, each bead on the string is itself a story-in-little, and should be treated as such: it should have a provocation, a climax, and a dénouement; and it should be worked out in the writer's mind before he sets pen to paper.

j. Finally, the writer should *examine the sections on suspense, character portrayal, and point of view* given in the next chapter, and should try to apply to his story the information there presented.

3. **Building on a Situation.**—Sometimes a writer comes across, in real life, a situation which strikes him as having possibilities; or he invents such a situation from a suggestion. The situation differs from the event already discussed in being a static condition rather than a happening or an action. Thus, any of the following may be regarded as a true situation: A man knows he has only two months to live; a woman has married a man she doesn't love; a man is in love with a woman of another race; an old lady who has been wealthy all her life suddenly finds her-

self penniless; a girl is in love with a man to whom all her family objects.

To make a story out of this sort of material, the writer will follow several of the steps already mentioned, and now repeated in the new relationship.

a. *Find a purpose for your writing the story.* (See *b* of Section 2 above.)

b. *Decide what the theme of the story is to be.* (See *c* of Section 2 above.)

c. *Determine whether the situation is a provocation or a dénouement.* Some of the examples of situations mentioned above may obviously be either the beginning or the end of some story; other examples (especially the last) can probably be nothing but the beginning.

If it seems best suited to be a provocation, the writer should decide what change is to occur in the story consistently with his theme and purpose (see *d* in Section 2 above), and then should proceed from here as is advised in the portion of Section 2 following *d*.

If the situation seems best suited to be a dénouement, the writer should work backward through a series of imagined events by means of which the change he observes might have come about. This series must be consistent with his theme, of course, and must end (in its backward movement) with a provocation. The provocation is the first change in a former static condition. The provocation may be due to a necessity forcing itself on the principal character, or it may be due to a desire of his to change his condition.

d. From this point on, the writer may proceed as is advised in the portion of Section 2 following *f*.

4. Building on a Plot.—Sometimes a plot comes to a writer almost full blown. For example: Parents work, slave, and deprive

themselves of necessities in order to send their son to college; then he dies a month after he graduates. Or the Prodigal Son returns home, but soon leaves on account of his father's too officious welcome. Or a politician has a mistress who, on the eve of an election, threatens to denounce him; he has her killed.

These are true plots: they have (or imply) beginning, middle, and end. To make them into stories, the writer should:

a. *Find a purpose for his writing the story.* (See *b* in Section 2 above.)

b. *Find a theme for the story.* (See *c* in Section 2 above.)

c. *Begin with* g *in Section 2, and proceed as is advised in the remainder of that section.*

5. Building on Character.—Some people a writer meets in real life seem designed purposely to go into stories. But the trouble with many would-be writers is that they are unable to invent adequate action for the display of the character. A writer faced with such a problem may help himself out of his difficulties by building up a story in the following steps:

a. *Determine the chief characteristic or the main interest of the character.* Sometimes, of course, the chief characteristic may be a conflict of desires or interests or capacities within the character. This conflict, then, will be the writer's chief concern. But in general, the writer will try to find out what the guiding motive of the character's life may be—whether it is to get rich, to have lovers, to succeed in a profession, to act with utter disregard of others, to be always tender toward others, or anything else.

b. *Present an issue to the character.* That is, present the character with a necessity or a desirability of acting. If the chief characteristic of the character is an inner conflict, present the character with the necessity or the desirability of resolving the conflict. Thus, if the conflict consists of love of someone and a desire to advance in the world, the writer will present the character with the necessity of coming to some decision, of making some definite choice.

The word "necessity" is used; but, it should be added, it may not be actually necessary for the character to reach some decision: he may crawl out of the dilemma in some unexpected way, or he may flatly refuse to make a decision. Whether there shall be a decision and, if so, what it shall be, will depend on the writer's purpose.

If there is no conflict in the character, if he is dominated by one major trait, interest, or motive, the writer must present the character with such an issue that, in deciding it, the character will (1) display his dominant trait, interest, or motive; or (2) be forced to alter or abandon this dominant trait, interest, or motive. Again the writer's purpose will determine which kind of issue shall be used. If it is to reveal character, for instance, he will choose the first; if it is to reveal some law of life, he will choose the second. Consequently, the writer's next step is to

c. *Find a purpose for the writing of the story.* (See *b* in Section 2 above.)

d. *Next, beginning with* c *in Section 2, the writer should proceed according to the directions given in the remainder of that section.*

6. Building on a Theme.—Probably the easiest and, at the same time, the most effective kind of story is that which is built upon a theme. Here the purpose is always to reveal some law of life or some condition, to promulgate some doctrine, or to satirize or to vindicate something. All these purposes being so nearly identical with the first one named, the writer need not trouble himself much about distinguishing between purposes, but may proceed directly from his theme to the construction of the story.

a. First, let the writer *express the general theme in terms of individual characters.* If, for example, the theme is "Women love weak men," let the writer express it thus: "Mary Jones loves John Smith because he is weak." If the theme is "Sentimental people are foolish," let the writer express it thus: "Tom Brown's senti-

mentality makes him foolish." If the theme is "People may re-
pent, but they never change," let the writer express it thus: "Sam
Johnson repented, but did not change his fundamental nature."

b. Next, let the writer *express the negative of the theme, and
then translate this generalized negative into terms of the same
particular characters as were used in the individualizing of the
theme itself.* Thus, the writer would say: "Mary Jones detests
John Smith because he is weak"; or "Tom Brown's tender emo-
tionalism makes him an admirable man"; or "Sam Johnson has
repented, and is a changed man."

c. Third, let the writer determine that *the change in the story
shall be from the reader's believing the negative of the theme at
the beginning to his believing the positive at the end.*

d. Fourth, let the writer *determine on a setting for the story*
(that is, the time, the place, the race of people, and the social
group involved), *and particularize his characters with reference
to this setting.* The writer's experience, his knowledge, and his
interests alone will determine what the setting is to be, unless,
of course, his theme is so narrow as to fit only one special setting.
But if he does not have such a narrow theme limiting his selection of a setting, the writer may put his theme in any setting he
chooses—Africa, Alaska, the Middle Ages, the future, or fairy-
land. His private taste will govern him.

e. Next, let the writer *create a provocation which will make
the reader believe the negative of the theme.*

f. Next, let him *work out a situation which will serve as a
climax to the story,* that is, a point at which the reader will begin
to disbelieve the negative and begin to believe the positive of the
theme.

g. From this point on, the writer may *begin with g in Section
2 of this chapter, and proceed according to the directions given in
the remainder of that section.*

7. **Building on Setting.**—Some places or social groups cry aloud for stories to be written about them. The plains of North Dakota, the Mexican border country, the people who live in the beggar-colonies near the city dump, gangsters, people who follow the races, farmers in the desolate parts of New England—all these demand stories for themselves, and may become stories if the writer follows a certain procedure:

a. First, he should *create a character or characters representative of the setting or in contrast to it.*

b. Next, if he wishes (although this step is unnecessary), the writer may *decide that the change is to involve the relationship between character and environment.* That is, he may decide to let the environment influence the character or decide an issue presented to him; or he may decide to let the character alter the environment or successfully resist its influence.

For example, a girl may be born in one of the squalid river-towns along the Mississippi. Is she representative of her surroundings, or is she superior to them? The writer must decide.

Will her surroundings gradually absorb her until she becomes a part of them, or will she resist their influence? The writer must decide.

Will the girl's surroundings frustrate some plan or desire of hers, or will she alter her surroundings or get free of them? The writer must decide.

c. From this point on, the writer may *proceed according to the directions given under Section 5* ("Building on Character").

EXERCISES

1. Where to Find Materials.
   During the next two or three days jot down notes on everything

that happens to you outside your regular routine of eating, sleeping, and going to classes. Include talks with people, casual glances on public conveyances, missing a streetcar, letters, getting home late at night, seeing a show, and other such incidents. At the end of two days, look over the list, let your imagination play with what might have been, and see how many ideas for stories you can produce.

2. Building on an Event.

Following the plan outlined in the text, construct a story from one of the following events:

You go out at night to put your car in the garage, and find a strange woman sitting in the car.

You go out on your front porch at night, hear a scuffling on the doorstep, and see a man coming up the steps on all-fours.

At the Public Library you notice across the table from you a young woman with the most beautiful hands you have ever seen.

In a restaurant a person who has been eating at another table and staring at you while you eat gets up when you get up, and follows you (or seems to follow you) out.

Someone gives you a strange red-eyed tree-frog which has been taken from a bunch of bananas just shipped in.

3. Building on a Situation.

Following the plan outlined in the text, construct a story from one of the following situations:

A young farmer must always leave his sweetheart just at nightfall in order to go home and attend to his cow.

Of twin sisters, one goes through college successfully, and the other has refused to go to college.

A brilliant and forceful young wife adores her husband without realizing that he is shallow and weak.

A wife thinks constantly of the man she *could* have married.

One of your classmates, who has seemed to be perfectly normal, has stopped school suddenly and entered a convent.

4. Building on a Plot.

Following the plan outlined in the text, construct a story from one of the plots suggested below:

A rich man who has been poor, and who knows the hardships of poverty, has a daughter (or a son) who is thoughtless and inconsiderate of the poor. The father influences the younger person to be more sympathetic.

A preacher who entered the ministry as a youth fired with zeal finds in his mature age that he no longer has his early enthusiasm and belief.

A farm woman engaged to be married to a farmer is called away to live in the city for a year. When she returns to the farm, her sense of values is so changed that she cannot bring herself to marry the farmer.

Or the farmer may not be able to care for her as she now is.

Or she may hate the farm which she loved before going to the city.

As a child, a man sees (or thinks he sees) a ghost with a horrible face. Years later he sees the same face on a ship in which he has planned to sail. He refuses to make the voyage on that ship. A week later he learns that the ship sank on the voyage he had intended to make.

5. Building on Character.

The instructor may have each member of the class write on three slips of paper short character sketches of three different people. All the slips from the entire class may then be jumbled together, and afterward redistributed to the class so that every student gets three character sketches different from the ones he wrote. These three should then be worked into a story.

6. Building on a Theme.

Following the plan outlined in the text, construct a story from one of the themes suggested in the exercises for Section 3 of the previous chapter, or from some theme of your own.

7. Building on Setting.

Following the plan outlined in the text, construct a story from one of the settings mentioned at the end of the exercises for the preceding chapter.

Chapter XVIII

WRITING THE STORY

IN THIS chapter we shall discuss a few principles which the writer should keep in mind during the actual composition of the story and the putting of it on paper. These principles do not involve a high amount of creative ability, but only a certain careful ingenuity.

1. Suspense.—The plot of a story may answer all the requirements of plot construction which we have already discussed; it may have a carefully built plot revolving around a significant climax; it may demonstrate poetic truth; it may interweave plot and subplot. But if it does not have suspense, it will not be interesting, and nobody will read the story.

Suspense (it will be remembered) is built up of three elements: first, a hint that something is going to happen; second, a period of waiting for the thing to happen; and third, the happening. An author skillful in plot construction will, like the press agent of a circus or a theater, tell us beforehand what we are to expect. The press agent prepares the public during several weeks for the giraffe-necked women, the man shot from a cannon, the sea-elephant, and the rest of it; and even the motion pictures give us pre-views and scenes from coming shows, and try to build up an eager expectation, an impatient waiting for heralded attractions. Press agents and authors alike tempt us with the promise of our seeing remarkable events. It is an old saying that "Promising opens the eyes of expectation."

To create suspense, the author must make the reader wait and know that he is waiting for something. Suspense is not a matter of sentences or of paragraphs, but of pages. Perhaps the commonest fault of plot construction in amateur writers is the swiftness with which the climax appears. People appreciate a thing only when they have waited and longed for it. If they have not waited and longed, the thing comes to them "stale, flat, and unprofitable." If the ghost in *Hamlet* is so effective, it is due to our having been forced to wait so long for him; and if Banquo's ghost in *Macbeth* is ineffective, it is due to our not having been required to wait for him.

Mere waiting may be, of course, mere boredom. To prevent its being that, the skillful author makes the reader feel that there is really something to wait for—that something is bound to happen. Making him feel this eager anticipation is a matter of a few tricks, some of which may be applied to almost any story.

a. First, *each scene of a well-constructed plot ends with a question,* an issue, a problem, a difficulty to be faced in the next scene. The reader is thus led on, step by step, scene by scene, because he always expects a solution of a problem which has caught his attention. In Hugo's *Ninety-three*, for example, we come upon the scene of a ship waiting in the darkness of an English port for a mysterious passenger who is to be transported on a dangerous voyage. At once we are eager to know more about this mysterious individual. He arrives and the ship sets sail. At once we desire to find whether the voyage will be successfully completed —and we read on. A cannon breaks loose on the vessel, and endangers the whole voyage. Will it be made fast, or will it break the ship to pieces? We read on to find out. It is chained up; but hardly has this been done before a hostile fleet appears. Will the ship and its precious passenger escape? We read on to find out. The fleet begins to pursue the vessel. Will the fleet overtake it?

We read on to find out. The fleet does overtake it, and begins a battle with the lone ship. Will the fleet or the ship conquer? We read on to find out. And so on. The story for a hundred pages consists of scene after scene linked together in the manner just mentioned—with the result that, once the reader commits himself to the first scene, he can hardly bring himself to put the book down.

b. We have seen that a good narrative must consist of positive and negative forces working against each other toward a certain end. To keep the reader in suspense about this conflict between positive and negative forces, the author must *make the issue at stake seem important*. Poker is a dull game without betting, but with betting it is fascinating. Stories are like that. Adult minds cannot become very interested in a narrative where the issue at stake is only the winning of a race or the success of a business. Accordingly, writers make larger issues (frequently the success of a love affair or the vindication of someone's honor) depend on the outcome of these minor issues. Readers will then grow as interested in the game or the business as the writer wishes. Through mutual consent, practically all readers will take as vital issues honor, life, and love. Other issues are of less importance. Dryden wrote the story of Antony and Cleopatra and called it *The World Well Lost*; he did not see, as Shakespeare did, that Antony lost something more than the world—his honor. Consequently, Shakespeare's is the deeper tragedy.

c. But even though the issues at stake are made to seem important, *the narrative has little suspense unless the conflicting elements are pretty evenly matched*. When the score is forty to nothing, half the spectators leave at the end of the third quarter; and if they feel certain before the game that the score will be something like that, they will not even buy tickets.

From the knowledge we have of Antony's character, we may

know that he will return to Cleopatra. But to keep the play from being merely a chronicle of the obvious, Shakespeare introduces the more evenly matched conflict between Cæsar and Antony. Hamlet's character, on the other hand, is more nicely balanced; the need of other sources of suspense, therefore, is not so great here as in the other play. For the very reason that creating a consistent character whose reactions may be relied upon would be inconsistent with suspense, Shakespeare usually presents, as a subsidiary to his character-plot, a pure action-plot upon which he relies for suspense. *Macbeth, Julius Cæsar, Coriolanus, King Lear, Othello*—all are studies in character conflict; but because the protagonist in each play is a consistent character, the outcome of whose inner conflict is seldom in grave doubt, Shakespeare deliberately adds to each play an external conflict of more evenly matched forces whose actions create suspense. Hamlet is the single one of his great characters whose actions one cannot foresee; for this reason, *Hamlet* is the single one of the great plays without an elaborate external structure of the unpredictable.

d. Other devices which authors use for creating suspense are more mechanical. One of the oldest and most important is the use of *temporary distractions*.

Just as the harrowing moment arrives when we are breathless to know whether the upraised knife of the villain is to penetrate the viscera of the hero, the screen flashes blank and we read the words, "The next episode of this picture will be shown here one week from today." Or just as we are on fire to learn the fate of the abducted Rowena and Rebecca, we are gently but firmly led off to find out what became of the Black Knight. Such distractions serve a double purpose: they make the reader peruse chapters in which he is only secondarily interested but which may be important for the development of the story, and they prolong the waiting period which must be present if there is to be any suspense.

The distractions may take the form of incidents in the sub-plot, descriptive passages, philosophical comments, exposition, or anything else that will halt the main action for a period.

e. *Foreshadowing* is a vague hinting at what is to come. It fills the reader with uneasiness and a repressed eagerness to go on and find out whether the obscure suggestions he has noticed will materialize into actualities. Hawthorne's "The Ambitious Guest" is a model of a story gaining suspense by means of fore-shadowing. The student should read it, noting carefully how the inevitable disaster is suggested so skillfully in the midst of some-what tiresome characterizations that the reader finds himself tense with excitement even though practically nothing happens in the main body of the story.

The foreshadowing in a story may take a variety of forms; but the most common are premonitions on the part of characters, an uneasiness or a suspicion expressed by characters, a casual adjec-tive like "sinister" or "kindly" or the like thrown in by the author in describing a character, and minor incidents which, like straws in the wind, show the general direction the action is to take.

f. Sometimes an author *anticipates* a scene by actually telling us what is to happen before it happens. This is the exact device used by the circus press agent who tells us weeks in advance that the man will be shot from a cannon or that the animal trainer will enter the arena with forty lions and tigers. The reader is interested in *seeing*, not in merely *knowing*. Accordingly, if he is assured that something is going to happen, he will read on to *see* it happen. Having heard Lady Windermere declare that she will strike Mrs. Erlynne with the fan, who could possibly leave the play without staying to see Lady Windemere keep her promise? Having heard Polonius and the King plotting to have Ophelia approach Hamlet, who could possibly leave the play without stay-ing to see the working out of the plot? Having heard Hamlet tell the players to perform the damning action before the King, who could possibly leave the play without staying to see the players perform?

g. Similar to anticipation by brief summary is extensive *preparation* for action which the reader knows will follow. This method for the attainment of suspense can be better explained by examples than by definition.

The old balladists of three hundred years ago, realizing the value of such preparation, resorted to the device of incremental repetition to lead up to a climax. A portion of the ballad "Edward" is quoted in the first chapter of the present book. By referring to it, the reader may see how the tremendous fact of Edward's having murdered his father is prepared for in preceding stanzas by his explaining the blood on his sword with the statement that he has killed his hawk—then his horse—and finally, his father.

In *An Enemy of the People* Dr. Stockmann's eagerness to know whether a certain letter has arrived, the impatience with which he awaits the postman, the vexation with which he hears that his daughter has had the letter all morning—so much talk about it makes us almost as eager to know what is in the letter as is the Doctor himself. Without all this preparation, the letter's coming or its failure to come would have been matters of no moment to us. All the talk about the ghost in the first scene of *Hamlet*; the praising of Macbeth in the first scene of the play; the description of the bizarre apartments in "The Masque of the Red Death"; the many evidences of Kurtz's work, remarked on before Kurtz himself appears in person, in "Heart of Darkness"; the elaborate geographical information in O. Henry's "A Municipal Report"— all such preparation keys the reader up to a high state of expectancy and suspense.

One of the commonest and most effective kinds of preparation is that which informs the reader of an impending encounter between important characters, and then makes him wait for the encounter. Practically all of Tom Jones is preparation leading up to the meeting of Tom and Sophia and, after that, the meeting between Tom and Allworthy. In *The Light that Failed* it is the meeting between Dick and Maisie; in Conrad's *Victory*, the meeting between the set of desperadoes and Heyst; in *The Last of the Mohicans*, the meeting of the girls and their father at first, and, after that, various encounters between friends and enemies; in *Antony and Cleopatra*, the first meeting with Cæsar in Rome, the meeting between the triumvirate and Pompey, and finally the meeting between the forces of Antony and the forces of Cæsar; in *Macbeth*, the murderous encounter of Macbeth and the King in Glamis Castle, and, after that, the engagement between Macbeth and Macduff.

h. The last of the devices to be mentioned here as useful in helping a writer achieve suspense is *concealed identity*. Whether we are much interested in a character or not, we will not leave him until we find out who he is. Scott perpetually uses this curiosity of ours for his own purposes. Indeed, it is difficult for one to think of a single novel or a single long narrative poem of his in which he does not employ this trick of concealed identity at least once, and often five or six times. In so far as suspense is concerned, it makes little difference whether the reader knows the true identity of the masquerader. If the reader knows, he reads on to see the other characters in the book find out about it; and if he does not know, he reads on to find out about it for himself. In general, however, for the sake of plausibility if for no other reason, a writer would do better to let his reader in on the secret.

2. Plausibility.—Some of the devices mentioned above may serve to give a narrative plausibility as well as suspense. The fact that they hint at a thing long before it happens, or suggest a con-

clusion of a certain sort early in the narrative, makes the event
or the conclusion seem natural and plausible when it does come.
Without the early hint, the reader might be surprised by the
course of happenings, and would declare them unnatural. Foreshadowing is particularly useful to a writer desiring to overcome
the reader's possible incredulity or surprise. This foreshadowing
may be of the delicate sort already mentioned as occurring in
"The Ambitious Guest"; or it may be more crude and obvious,
like dreams, horoscopes, omens, and auguries foretelling events.
It may be an actual incident like Macduff's knocking at the gate
right on the heels of the murder of Duncan; or it may be some
obsession in the mind of one of the characters, like the thought
of madness which constantly recurs in Lear's mind and crops
out in his speech long before he becomes mad. It may be a secret
kept from the reader, like the identity of the Black Knight and
the Disinherited Knight in *Ivanhoe*; or it may be a secret revealed to the reader but not to the other characters of the narrative,
like the identity of Captain Absolute in *The Rivals*. It may be a
series of events tending in the same general direction, like the
failure of several of Hotspur's allies to come up in time for the
battle in *I Henry IV*; or it may be a deliberate and expressed purpose of one of the characters, like Hal's "I will redeem all this on
Percy's head" in the play just mentioned.

Another method of giving plausibility to a narrative is the use
of the first-person point of view in the story. The reader is naturally more inclined to believe the story of a supposed eye-witness
than the story of someone talking about other people. The reader
will remember that nearly all, if not all, of Poe's stories of the
supernatural are told in the first person—a fact which adds im-
measurably to their credibility and therefore to the tremendous
emotional effect they have on the reader.

Still another way in which tall stories may be made more credible is by the writer's use of a simple, plain, unaffected style, and by his careful description of many unimportant details of the scene or of the event. Exact details about dates, about the kind of clothes people were wearing, about the direction of the wind, about what someone ate for dinner, about some inconsequential remark by some inconsequential person—all this lends a great appearance of veracity to any story. Yet a caution should be voiced. Unless the writer thinks there is some reason why his story will be disbelieved, these unimportant details should never be included in a story. A plain narrative in which no laws of nature or of probability are violated requires no unusual precautions against its being disbelieved.

3. Point of View.—The following paragraphs give most of the facts worth knowing about the advantages and the disadvantages of the different points of view, and suggest all possible points of view except the freakish.

a. The *personal point of view* is that in which the narrator is a character in the tale he tells. The advantage of this point of view is that it always gives a look of veracity to any story in which it is used. The disadvantage is that the adoption of this point of view prevents the author's showing events occurring in different places at the same time, or events kept secret from the supposed teller of the tale, or the thoughts and intentions of anybody in the story except the teller.

(1) The *principal character* point of view intensifies the chief advantage of all personal points of view, that is, it makes the narrative seem altogether credible unless the narrator obviously has some axe to grind, some benefit to be gained by lying. But it prevents the narrator from making himself out a hero or a witty person; for obviously he could not, in good taste, tell the fine things he did or the clever things he said. Moreover, if the principal character happens to be an illiterate person, a spirit, or an

108

animal, he could not plausibly be pictured as writing down his experiences.

(2) The *minor character* point of view is that in which the action is performed in the presence and with the knowledge of the narrator, who himself participates in the action but plays an inconspicuous part in the events he narrates. This is one of the most effective, but one of the least used, of the personal points of view. It has the advantage of plausibility, as does the principal character point of view, and, in addition, it has the advantage of impartiality, since the narrator here is telling what he saw happen to other people, rather than what happened to him. Moreover, the minor character here is a kind of emotional intermediary through whose personality we ourselves experience emotions about the action narrated—the fact that he feels the emotions makes us feel them. The minor character point of view does not have the disadvantages peculiar to the principal character point of view. But one serious disadvantage that it does have is the fact that the character may seem to the reader an undignified and ridiculous tagalong (as Mackellar seems, for example, in *The Master of Ballantrae*). And another is that he cannot very well appear in love scenes, or know anything about love scenes which involve the principal character. The latter would not make love in the presence of the minor character; and if the minor character overheard the other making love, he would appear to the reader as nothing better than a gossiping eavesdropper.

(3) The *reportorial* point of view is that in which the author reports (as does Kipling in *Soldiers Three*) stories told to him by other people in the language of the other people. We may say at once that this point of view is usually to be avoided. From a dramatic point of view it is bad, for it first interests the reader in one series of actions (the reporter's meeting one set of characters and getting them started on a story), and then it starts all over

again and begins interesting the reader in another set of characters; and finally, it must end with a flat, expository conclusion in which the reporter brings the reader back to the first scene once more. It is bad from the standpoint of plausibility, for the reader wonders how the reporter could remember all the words, expressions, and accents of the teller of the story, and then write them down accurately. And it is bad from the standpoint of psychology, for it keeps a third party constantly between the reader and the teller of the story. Yet the point of view of the reporter has one advantage: it permits the reader to get a story in the colorful and amusing language of people who are witty or picturesque, but who are too illiterate to write their own stories.

(4) The point of view of a *non-participant* is that in which the narrator tells a story as he saw it, though he himself did not participate in it. It is the point of view of Conrad's Marlowe. The advantages and the disadvantages which accompany its use are very much the same as those which accompany the point of view of the minor character already discussed. But the non-participating point of view does not endanger the dignity of the narrator as does the minor character point of view. On the other hand, to have a non-participant tell a long story does not make for plausibility: the reader asks how the narrator knows so much without being a prying individual. Furthermore, the introduction of the non-participant is sometimes as awkward as is the introduction of the narrator in stories having the reportorial point of view; and the quoting of what the non-participant said is sometimes as unreal as quoting from the reportorial point of view. In general, therefore, this point of view is dangerous. It has its uses, and it has very real advantages; but when it is misused, it is chaotic and unreal. Even Conrad would have done well to avoid it more often than he did.

b. The *impersonal point of view* is that in which the narrator of the tale never enters into the action, or names himself, or uses the first personal pronoun.

(1) The *omniscient* point of view is that in which the writer knows everything that happens to all his characters at any time in any place; he knows their thoughts, their hearts, their purposes; he may skip from England to the Holy Land in an instant; he may overhear all secrets; he may pry behind all doors; he may look in at all windows. He knows the characters better than they know one another, and better than they know themselves. The advantages of this point of view are too obvious to deserve comment. The chief disadvantage is that it loses a certain flavor of veracity which the personal points of view have. Yet this disadvantage may be ignored because of the fact that long traditions of tales told from the omniscient point of view have made it acceptable to readers. They are willing to bow to convention and not ask the author, How do you know?

(2) The *dramatic* point of view (such as is used in all plays) is certainly the most natural and convincing point of view. The spectator of a play does not have to take anybody's word for anything; he himself sees the action progressing under his eyes. He sees the villainy of the villain and the heroism of the hero; he interprets character, reads his own meaning into speeches and actions, and works out the implication and involvement of events. Obviously, this is the perfect point of view. Yet it is not always practicable. For reasons stated in the first chapter of this study of fiction (reasons which need not be repeated here), authors can profitably avail themselves of the dramatic point of view only occasionally. Generally they must make a choice from the other five points of view.

In addition to the point of view of the writer as a writer, there is the point of view of the writer as a vicarious character in the story he is writing. That is, every story (or part of a story) should be written from the mental, emotional, and physical point of view of some one character in the story. The action should usually be told, the characters portrayed, and the setting constructed as they appear to one character. If thoughts or feelings are analyzed, they should be the thoughts or feelings of that one character. If opinions are expressed, they should seem to be the opinions of that one character. In other words, the writer should endeavor (as a general rule) to tell his story as it appears to one of his characters, not to the author himself. If the story is short, deviation from this one character's point of view should occur only when it is absolutely necessary; if the story is long, each scene of it should be told from one character's point of view, though different scenes may have different dominant characters.

4. Convincingness of Character.—What constitutes a living, breathing, convincing character? How does he differ from the flat and lifeless automata so frequently met with in fiction? If there is an accurate answer to these questions, no one has ever found it. Yet there is an approximate answer. It is this: A character seems to have the breath of reality in him when the reader has several different emotions about the character. A character who is all good is not convincing, and neither is one who is all bad. A character whom we merely admire is not convincing, and neither is one whom we merely despise. To be convincing, he must make us pity him and hate him; like him and be angry with him; despise him and admire him; think him false and yet true; regard him as bad and yet good. This joining of contraries in a character is not a universal recipe for character-making; but without such a joining, no character can be convincing in the slightest.

Both the goodness and the evil in a character must be presented frankly and unapologetically; neither of them is to be ignored or glossed over by too casual treatment. Bret Harte's miners, gamblers, and strumpets are false characters because their creator, though admitting their immorality, minimizes it by neglecting it; at the same time, he magnifies their goodness by insisting on it to the exclusion of all their other traits. On the contrary, the villain of the contemporary motion picture, of the melodramas and melodramatic novels of the last century, of the average boys' book, of the mystery and detective story now so popular, is a creature of unmitigated depravity. If he does occasionally redeem himself by an act of generosity in the last chapter, still he has been painted so thoroughly black in all preceding chapters that his conversion is actually the climax of his implausibility, not of his convincingness.

Tom Jones is an excellent character from a literary standpoint. He is a well-meaning, well-behaved soul, and yet he gets Molly Segrum with child; he is deeply in love with Sophia, and yet he returns to Molly and, later on, has an affair or two with other women. Fielding, quite different from Bret Harte, hides nothing, shuns nothing, mitigates nothing—and he makes a convincing character. Who are the convincing characters in *Ivanhoe*? Not John, the unrelieved villain; not Richard, the ideal knight; certainly not Ivanhoe and Rowena, the pure and guileless hero and heroine. But Bois Guilbert, a mixture of passion, villainy, courage, self-hatred, and love; and Cedric, a mixture of patriotism, faithfulness, courage, narrowness, and meanness; and Front de Bœuf, a mixture of frankness, honesty, self-knowledge, fortitude, and brutality. Hamlet is a compound of strength and weakness; Macbeth, of fidelity and treachery; Lear, of ability and senile conceit; Hotspur, of honor and folly; Cleopatra, of an infinite variety of contraries. The real man or real woman is "half dust, half deity."

5. **Character Portrayal.**—The actual method of character portrayal in any narrative is either direct or indirect. An author who uses the first method may tell his reader, either by blunt character analysis or by interpretative description, exactly what sort of person a certain individual is—as Sir Walter Scott and James Fenimore

Cooper have a habit of doing at the first introduction of any principal character. A variant of this method, though actually identical with the device just mentioned, is the portrayal of character by means of reports of other characters about him. Cæsar characterizes Antony several times in Shakespeare's play; King Henry characterizes Hotspur early in *I Henry IV*; and Hotspur's ambassador returns to his chief with glowing tributes characterizing Hal. Such direct character portrayals have the virtue of informing the reader, from the very first, about some person who is to figure in the story. Yet this virtue can hardly compensate for the fact that this direct method halts the action and is unnatural. People in real life do not bear labels, nor do they subject themselves to immediate and full analysis when we first encounter them.

Much more natural is the indirect method of character portrayal. A writer using such a method introduces his characters by name or business, and then allows them to reveal themselves just as new acquaintances reveal themselves to us in real life.

a. Sometimes a man's *conversation* exposes his nature to the listener much better than could any studied analysis of his character. Coleridge tells of a banquet at which a mysterious and interesting-looking guest ate and said nothing during a large part of the meal. Coleridge conceived that the man must be a man of genuine importance. But at length, when the potatoes were passed, the stranger reached for them and cried out, "Them's the bullies for me!" That one remark characterizes the man completely.

b. Sometimes the *actions*, impulsive, deliberate, or habitual, of a person will reveal his character:

At the height of that fearful tempest, with Mrs. Johnson hysterical and the children dumb with fright, Mr. Johnson stood by the door methodically tamping down the tobacco in his pipe, and trying to strike one wet match after another on the door-facing.

We need no more analysis of Mr. Johnson: we know him already. This next shows habitual actions which thoroughly characterize a man:

He had worked as a section-hand on a railroad for fifteen years; he had never married; he had denied himself all luxuries and many comforts, even necessities; and he had done all this in order to send back to his home in Greece a yearly sum to support a disabled father and an aged mother.

What else need be told of this man?

c. *Habitual environment* is a third means of portraying character. We understand Don Quixote much better when we see his untended and dilapidated paternal estate; we understand Gerald (in *The Old Wives' Tale*) better when we see the expensiveness of his surroundings in Paris; and we understand Miss Prittle when we read the following description of her surroundings:

Miss Prittle's gate clicked behind him. A clean-swept, glistening brick walk, red with white mortar, led straight to a clean-swept front step between two rows of straight zinnias. The door-knob gleamed in the sun, and the bell buzzed sharply when he touched it.

d. Finally, a description of *the effect one character has on others* is an excellent means of depicting character. For example, we might be tempted to take Glendower's sentimentality seriously if we did not see the skeptical Hotspur ridiculing the Welshman. Or we should miss half the humor of Don Quixote's folly if we did not see the effect of it on the unimaginative Sancho.

The child had been playing with her dolls on the sofa; but as soon as her father entered the room, she collected her toys and disappeared.

We know now both the father and the daughter.

6. Dialogue.—Dialogue is not absolutely necessary in fiction; yet most writers of fiction use dialogue because it helps creates an illusion of reality, because it is more vivid and direct than a mere

roundabout summary of what people in the story say, because it helps in characterization, because it may sometimes advance the action swiftly, and because it affords variety. Though dramatic writers must necessarily give information through dialogue, writers of other sorts of fiction ought to be a little wary of purely expository dialogue. They ought to take it as a rough rule-of-thumb that dialogue has no place in a story unless it serves one of two purposes—to illustrate character, or to advance action. If it serves neither purpose, or some other purpose, it should give place to another sort of writing.

The chief problem of most writers is to make dialogue sound natural. As a matter of fact, however, readers will readily accept even very unnatural dialogue provided it is consistent. That is, readers will accept stilted and artificial dialogue if this sort of dialogue is consistent with the tone of the work as a whole, and if it is consistent within itself. For example, if a writer pictures a character as using modern slang, he could not have him talking in well-rounded Johnsonian periods; or if he pictures the character working in a realistically conceived contemporary setting, the writer could not have the character talking in the more elaborate fashion of our grandfathers. The point is that readers will accept dialogue just as the writer wishes to present it if only he remains consistent in his own presentation. Nobody objects to the poetic speeches of Lord Dunsany's characters; nobody objects to the inhuman wit and glitter of the speeches of Oscar Wilde's characters; nobody objects to the impossible distortions of grammar, pronunciation, and logic in the speeches of Dickens's characters; and nobody objects to the oracular and philosophic disquisitions in the speeches of Bernard Shaw's characters. All these speeches are consistent within themselves and within the author's work as a whole; and accordingly, all are acceptable to the reader.

But though naturalness of dialogue is not all-important, it is often desirable and necessary. Naturalness will come if the writer has conceived his characters perfectly, and has entered completely into their imagined existence. Nevertheless, a few suggestions about writing dialogue cannot come amiss; they are short cuts to the knowledge which the writer would eventually come to through experience even if he had never read a textbook on writing.

The first of these suggestions is that long passages of uninterrupted dialogue do not make good writing. This is a general rule to which almost anyone can find many notable exceptions in literature. But it is a good rule, nevertheless. If the young writer finds himself reporting over a page of uninterrupted dialogue, he should catch himself up and ask himself if a paragraph or so of description, comment, exposition, or straight narrative should not be inserted in order to break up the dialogue.

The next suggestion is that dialogue should usually be mixed with a good measure of detail from the author's own imagination. In the following passage from Arnold Bennett, for example, notice how large a proportion of the words are Bennett's, and not Constance's, Sophia's, or Mr. Povey's:

The tension was snapped by Mr. Povey. "My God!" he muttered, moved by a startling discovery to this impious and disgraceful oath (he, the pattern and exemplar—and in the presence of innocent girlhood too!). "I've swallowed it!"

"Swallowed what, Mr. Povey?" Constance inquired.

The tip of Mr. Povey's tongue made a careful voyage of inspection all round the right side of his mouth.

"Oh yes!" he said, as if solemnly accepting the inevitable. "I've swallowed it!"

Sophia's face was now scarlet; she seemed to be looking for some place to hide it. Constance could not think of anything to say.

"That tooth has been loose for two years," said Mr. Povey, "and now I've swallowed it with a mussel."

"Oh, Mr. Povey!" Constance cried in confusion, and added, "There's one good thing, it can't hurt you any more now."

"Oh," said Mr. Povey. "It wasn't *that* tooth that was hurting me. It's an old stump at the back that's upset me so this last day or two. I wish it had been."

Sophia had her teacup close to her red face. At these words of Mr. Povey her cheeks seemed to fill out like ripe apples. She dashed the cup into its saucer, spilling tea recklessly, and then ran from the room with stifled snorts.

"Sophia!" Constance protested.

"I must just—" Sophia incoherently spluttered in the doorway. "I shall be all right. Don't ——"

Constance, who had risen, sat down again.[1]

These two suggestions about dialogue are of prime importance; those which follow are only suggestions about minor devices which make for naturalness.

Dialect should not be reproduced accurately, but should be merely suggested. The distortions of spelling necessary for the accurate transcription of Negro dialect, Irish brogue, broken English spoken by foreigners, and so forth, are confusing to the reader. A few words or constructions written in the manner of the dialect are enough to suggest the entire dialect to the reader's imagination.

Speeches by individual characters ought to be fairly short—seldom over fifty or a hundred words in length. Sentences in dialogue ought not to be always grammatically complete; there should be elliptical constructions, self-interruptions, exclamations, phrases suggesting whole sentences (like "You don't say!" "What for?" "Why not?" "And me not there!" etc.).

Above all, dialogue should not consist of mere questions and answers. If one character asks a question, the other character may ignore it (as Mr. Povey ignores Constance's question in the passage quoted above), or answer an anticipated or implied question, or ask another in return. For instance:

[1] From *The Old Wives' Tale*, by Arnold Bennett, reprinted by permission of Doubleday, Doran and Company, Inc.

"Are you going to town?"
"I must finish this book before I go anywhere."

Here the question asked is not answered, but a question anticipated ("Why aren't you going to town?") is answered.

"What are you doing?"
"We are to have an examination tomorrow, and so I have to finish this book."

Here the question "What?" is answered as if it had been "Why?"

"What are you doing?"
"Why do you ask?"

Here one question is answered by another.

By such slight devices as these an author can often give the breath of life to his speaking characters.

EXERCISES

1. Suspense.

    Invent as many devices as you can for getting suspense in a narrative (fictitious or true) about

        A journey by train, auto, or ship.

        A young man who has arrived penniless in a large city.

        A battle or an episode in a battle.

        A girl who wants a certain young man to propose to her.

        Any of the stories suggested in any of the exercises of this book.

2. Plausibility.

    Re-examine the stories you have worked on in the exercises for Chapter XIII, and see where you can use devices for making the surprise endings of the stories more plausible.

    What devices would you use to secure plausibility in stories about the following:

An individual with a certain weakness of character.

A catastrophe of nature.

A supernatural incident.

The apprehending of a criminal.

The faithlessness of a loved one.

3. Point of View.

Study the narratives suggested in different exercises of this book to determine the point of view which would be most suitable for each narrative.

Suppose you are writing some such story as this:

A young man graduates from college, goes into business, and finds himself in charge of a group of working girls. He allows himself to fall in love with one of the girls, though she has no education, no culture, and no worthwhile background. Eventually, however, the young man realizes that he and the girl are utterly unsuited to each other. The theme is, of course, that oil and water will not mix.

What point of view would you take if you were trying to show the folly of the young man?

If you were trying to show the folly of the girl in thinking she might permanently hold the affection of the young man?

If you were trying to show the different stages in the development of the young man's feeling about the girl?

If you were trying to show the effect the whole affair might have on the young man's character?

If you were chiefly interested in emphasizing the theme?

4. Convincingness of Character.

In the story just mentioned, what traits of character could you combine to make the girl seem convincing? To make the young man seem convincing?

Write short accounts of incidents in which the following characters figure; or write short character sketches of these persons. Let your principal aim here be convincingness of character.

An old man.

An old woman.

A Negro porter.

A boy about ten years old.

A university professor.

A sophisticated society girl.

An effeminate young artist.

5. Character Portrayal.

In each of the ways mentioned in the text, characterize three of the individuals listed above, or three characters of your own acquaintance or invention.

6. Dialogue.

Pretend that you are the doorman of a large hotel. Write a story made up of bits of dialogue which you overhear and piece together. Remember that you know nothing about the characters in the story except what you learn from overhearing them or from seeing what goes on right before you; yet you must make the characters vivid and convincing to the reader.

INDEX OF PROPER NAMES

377

SUBJECT INDEX